AF321803

THE MINIATURE PAINTER REVEALED

THE MINIATURE PAINTER REVEALED

AMALIA KUSSNER'S GILDED AGE PURSUIT OF FAME AND FORTUNE

KATHLEEN LANGONE

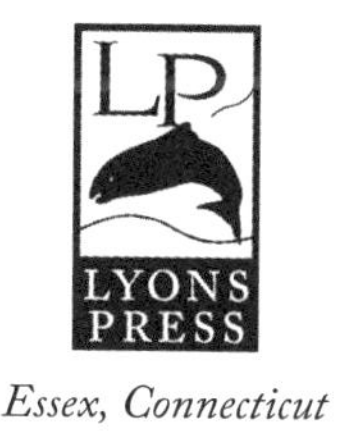

Essex, Connecticut

An imprint of The Globe Pequot Publishing Group, Inc.
64 South Main Street
Essex, CT 06426
www.globepequot.com

Distributed by NATIONAL BOOK NETWORK

British Library Cataloguing in Publication Information Available

Library of Congress Cataloging-in-Publication Data

Names: Langone, Kathleen, 1955– author.
Title: The miniature painter revealed : Amalia Kussner's Gilded Age pursuit of fame and fortune / Kathleen Langone.
Description: Essex, Connecticut : Lyons Press, [2025] | Includes bibliographical references and index.
Identifiers: LCCN 2024042665 (print) | LCCN 2024042666 (ebook) | ISBN 9781493087099 (cloth) | ISBN 9781493087105 (epub)
Subjects: LCSH: Kussner, Amalia, 1863-1932. | Miniature painters—United States—Biography. | Portrait painters—United States—Biography. | Women painters—United States—Biography.
Classification: LCC ND1329.K88 L36 2025 (print) | LCC ND1329.K88 (ebook) | DDC 759.13—dc23/eng/20241230
LC record available at https://lccn.loc.gov/2024042665
LC ebook record available at https://lccn.loc.gov/2024042666

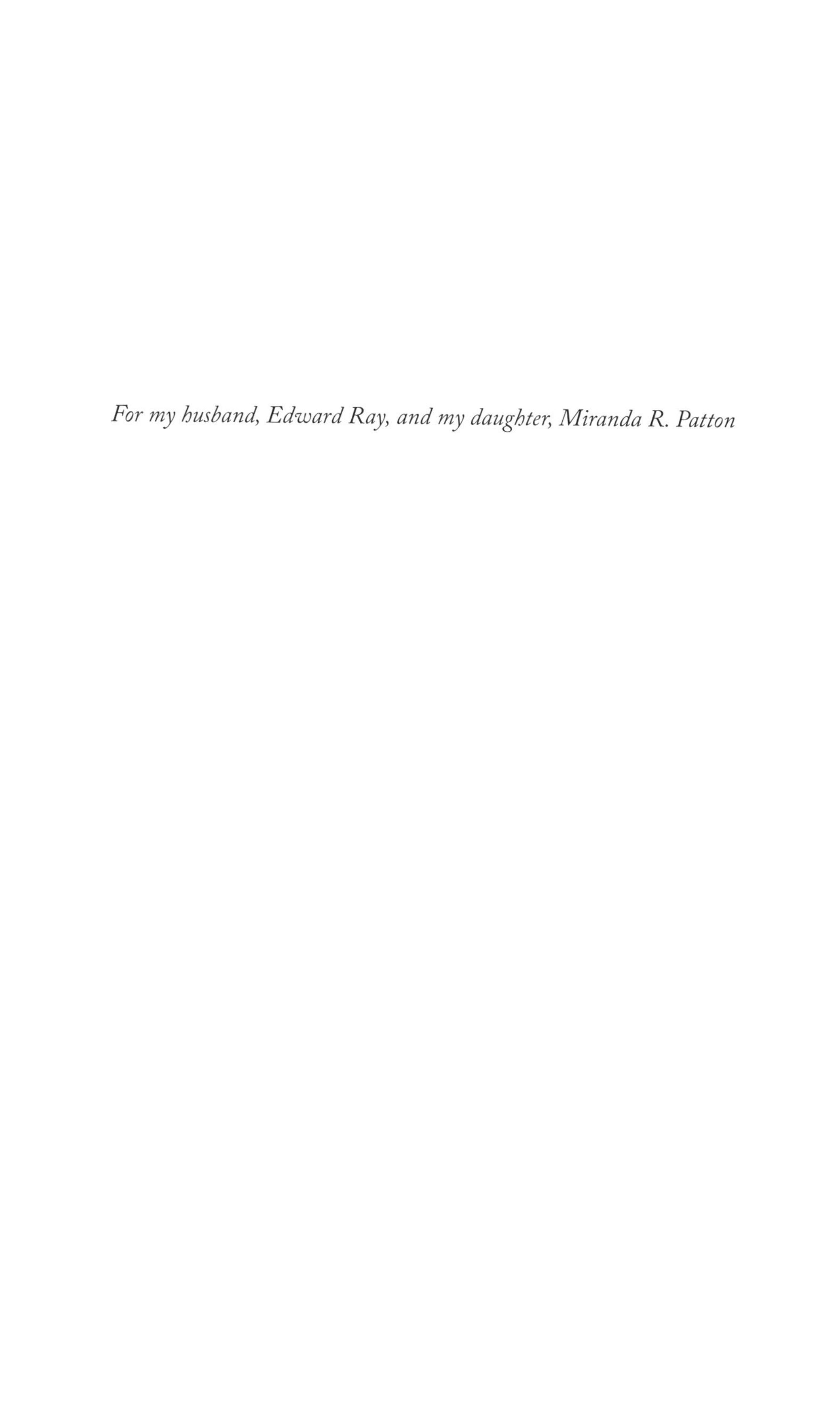

For my husband, Edward Ray, and my daughter, Miranda R. Patton

Contents

Foreword

The Gilded Age conjures up images of ostentatious, elegant mansions embellished with plush furniture and exquisite artwork, fancy balls and dinner parties, and stylish, expensive clothing. In short, anything that flaunted significant monetary wealth. This excessive opulence was a direct result of the technology, inventions, and fresh ideals that proliferated during the era.

Since innovation was the foundation for this extreme wealth, it also spawned new opportunities, particularly for women. Prior to the Gilded Age, sharing intelligent, inspiring thoughts or creativity through writing, lectures, or artistry was an achievement only a few lucky women ever managed. It was tough to be taken seriously. But then women's organizations such as New York's Sorosis Club and Philadelphia's New Century Club came on the scene. These clubs encouraged free thinking, creativity, and charitable work among women and the promotion of science, literature, and art within a comfortable and convenient meeting place. The Women's Suffrage movement also helped push the needle for women, enabling them to air and share their thoughts more freely, exchange ideas, and rally together.

These factors likely helped propel Amalia Kussner's success as a miniature painter. Artistic, adventurous, and independent, she was "a 'self-made' woman ahead of her time, with a passion and a personality that made her one of the most sought-after artists of the elite women" of the Gilded Age, notes *The Miniature Painter Revealed* author Kathleen Langone. Exposed to art and music at a young age, Amalia displayed painting and creative talents early on and had the support of family members, allowing her to pursue her interests. And she, in turn, appreciated this same sense of independence in the women she painted and befriended.

Although she enjoyed being a financially independent woman, her lifestyle and philosophies mirrored other women of means at the time. She admired and emulated the high society women who were her subjects, considering herself on the same playing level rather than a member of the working class. As Langone speculates, "her approach might have further put her subjects at ease and encouraged conversation while she worked." This ability to engage in conversation with her clients was a skill both affable and practical, helping grow her list of patrons and name recognition within the field.

Art exists in many forms—not just in paintings and music but also in the culinary world. I have written quite a bit about the cooking school instructors and chefs who were so popular during the Gilded Age, and I see similarities with Amalia—she too was sought after for her craft. Just as wealthy Gilded Age women needed their portraits painted in the latest style, they also needed their cooks and servants to prepare the intricate foods required for their receptions, balls, and banquets. Cooking instructors trained in French culinary techniques saw this as an opportunity and began to hold classes for the young ladies who worked in these mansions as domestic help. Society women would also pay French chefs to work as their personal chefs in order to pull off extravagant dinner parties successfully. These chefs soon became an upper-class fixture, with society women such as Marietta Stevens (the wife of hotelier Paran Stevens and one of Amalia's sitters) paying reputable French chefs upwards of forty-five dollars a week (equal to about twelve hundred dollars today) to do their personal cooking. Some ladies would even try to steal away a particularly exceptional chef from another wealthy household by offering more money. For those who did not employ a chef, Gilded Age society authority Ward McAllister recommended knowing an "artist" that could be hired for special occasions.

Just as Amalia spent time making a "wish list" of the elites she wanted to paint and cultivating her connections to them, these culinary experts often worked for months planning and preparing food for high society events. These occasions included extremely detailed dishes, such as decorative molds made from cold cooked foods set in aspic (a savory, transparent gelatin) and embellished with fashionable garnishes. Lavish centerpieces, ranging from floral arrangements to ornate sugar molds to plaster-cast animals, were front and center on banquet tables. A famous ball given by Mrs. Cornelius (Alice) Vanderbilt in 1888 in her new home on New York's West 57th Street featured dishes depicting scenes from Roman mythology, such as a filet of beef garnished with vegetables resting on the shoulders of Hercules, accompanied by wax cupids. The god Mercury was poised in flight over a piece of ham decorated with truffles. But a pool of water containing real fish and frogs held the most striking display: a two-foot-long salmon nestled in a wax boat, pulled by Neptune driving a seahorse-led chariot made from seashells.

This is just one example of how Gilded Age women were extremely status conscious, competing with each other in just about everything, from their luxurious mansions to the over-the-top dinners they hosted. Amalia's portraits became one of their "must-haves," and indeed she painted portraits of many well-known women from the era, including Alva and Consuelo Vanderbilt, Louise Mackay, Minnie (Stevens) Paget, and Louisine Havemeyer, whose portrait was Amalia's entrance into the closed circle of New York's elite society known as the "Four Hundred," a select list of the only people Caroline Astor and Ward McAllister deemed socially worthy.

Though her talents likely didn't extend to the culinary arts, Amalia had training in the decorative arts, which included not only painting and drawings, but also embroidery, china painting, and decorated linens. As Langone notes, "both during Amalia's time and in the current art world, miniatures will always be seen as straddling the styles of decorative and fine arts." Amalia was also aware of the classical styles of miniatures but used her expertise to put her own stamp on her portraits. Her success and techniques in painting miniatures became a novel differentiator for privileged and influential Gilded Age society, whom she portrayed as American "royalty." She was essentially a trailblazer able to hobnob with the elite and proved that her artwork was worthy, desirable, and in fact highly coveted—a fitting example of the innovation that embodied the Gilded Age.

Becky Libourel Diamond
Food writer, librarian, and research historian
Author of *The Gilded Age Cookbook*, *The Thousand Dollar Dinner*, and
Mrs. Goodfellow

Introduction

Though I am distantly related to Amalia Kussner through the German side of my family, I didn't learn much about her until five years ago. Like so much of the world in 2020, I had time on my hands and started to do online family research, beginning with Amalia. As a child, all I had known was that she was a miniature portrait artist born in Indiana during the Civil War and that she had risen to fame in the late 1890s and painted the Prince of Wales, just prior to his becoming Edward VII with Queen Victoria's passing. My grandmother described the prince as someone who was "sweet on Amalia" and had given her a piece of jewelry. I had seen that piece before it was unfortunately sold; it was a stunning pear-shaped emerald pendant. I also grew up around three of her miniatures, encased in a gold-gilt cabinet, among the clutter of many other family mementoes.

For most of my adult life, my perception of Amalia as told through these few family stories remained unchanged. The assumption that she primarily produced her artworks in Indiana, with just one trip to Europe, was soon dispelled as I started my research. The first "major" discovery was that she also painted Czar Nicholas II of Russia and his wife, Czarina Alexandra. And not only had she traveled to Russia and done their portraits, but she later wrote a detailed and intimate article, published in *Century Magazine*, on her almost month-long visit to the Romanov family.

I was now on a hunt for everything I could learn about Amalia, and I expanded my research to many online sources (newspapers, digitized materials from libraries and museums, etc.). Her popularity both for her artwork and in the late Gilded Age social circles became evident from the mentions of her in hundreds of newspaper articles and the fashion magazines of the day.

What also became clear was that there was an air of mystery about her—mostly designed by her own efforts. She wanted to be perceived as a child prodigy with no formal artistic training. And when she arrived in New York City during the waning days of the Gilded Age to promote her talents, she claimed to be twenty years old—barely an adult. Both of these self-promotions were blatantly false, as she did have many occasions of previous art instruction and was almost thirty upon her arrival.

Her art style—that being miniature portraits—was likely not seen as fine art and instead was sometimes relegated to decorative art, considered a hobby of women and only seen in homes. Regardless of the label, however, she was fortunate to be part of the resurgence of miniatures around 1890.

Soon after, numerous articles cited Amalia Kussner as the primary person responsible for the revival of miniatures, which would last through the 1930s. Those who supported this art form felt that these dainty paintings captured a person's spirit better than the existing photography techniques could. The portraits could provide realistic coloring of the subjects' faces and a vitality that was missing in black and white photos. Miniatures were often given as a gift to a special loved one or worn as jewelry, such as pendants or tiny bracelet charms. One of Amalia's miniatures was even carried all the way to Alaska during the region's gold rush by a prospector who wanted a painting of the girl he had left behind.[1]

Amalia's earlier career, mostly spent in the Midwest and New York City, had Chicago and New York periodicals showering her with accolades. During this time, she painted Mrs. Astor and many other wives of the Gilded Age tycoons. Her portraits would sometimes bestow upon these women an idealized view of their beauty. Furthermore, the women she painted were posed without the strictures of modest Victorian fashion; instead, they were often clothed in wraps of diaphanous fabric, boldly exposing their neckline and shoulders.

Amalia's star burned bright for almost twenty-five years, a period in history that spanned the end of the Gilded Age into the Progressive Era. During this time, she became friends with the Czar and Czarina of Russia, joined the social circle of Edward VII, and established a brief friendship with Cecil Rhodes, the British diamond magnate of South Africa, during the Boer War. Unlike some artists who were retained by famous men and women but would remain "in the background," Amalia was allowed to establish a more intimate relationship with her subjects and to become part of their lives. She accomplished this not only through her talent as an artist, but also through her charm and a keen understanding of how to navigate the complex social structures of the times.

However, publicity about her turned more negative starting in 1900, with a "hidden" marriage closely followed by two lawsuits. Detractors also began saying she was too self-promoting and aggressive in her manner—certainly unacceptable behavior for a woman at that time. Possibly because of the New York elite society turning away from her, she and her husband increasingly traveled to Europe, eventually settling in England.

Though some accounts say her career ended at this time, Amalia did in fact continue to paint portraits of almost all the key figures of European royalty during the 1900s. Her career as an artist did not truly end until 1911—around the time when the society and lavish lifestyles that had propelled her to international fame and fortune would soon be irrevocably changed with World War I and other historical events. At this time, her life also became more focused on her family, who were frequent visitors to England. In total, she painted at least 110 miniatures (and likely more that went unrecorded).

As I finished writing this book, who exactly Amalia was as a person still eludes me. I find viewing her life much like looking through a kaleidoscope—as you turn it, you see a constantly changing image of the same object. But the more I research her life, notable aspects of who she was remain consistent. She was a "self-made" woman ahead of her time, with a passion and a personality that made her one of the most sought-after artists of the elite women of her time. My hope is that as you read this book, you will become as fascinated as I have been in learning about her art, adventures, and even a few scandals.

CHAPTER 1

Humble Beginnings

AMALIA KUSSNER WAS BORN TO TWO GERMAN IMMIGRANTS WHOSE ancestral homes were in different parts of Germany. Her mother, Emilie Weinhardt, emigrated from Schwabach, Germany, in 1853, at age fourteen. Emilie's father, who was a brewer, may have arrived in America before her in 1850. The Weinhardt family settled in Greencastle, Indiana, and one branch also ran a brewery in Fort Wayne, Indiana. Amalia's father, Lorenz Kussner, arrived shortly before Emilie in 1852, from Hesse-Darmstadt. Lorenz came from a musical background, since his father was a music teacher in Germany, and he became an apprentice in musical instrument repairs after settling in the Midwest.[1] He held this position in Greencastle, working with a manufacturer of pianos. Lorenz and Emilie likely met in Greencastle and married in 1857, both at eighteen years old.[2]

By the time Amalia was born in March 1863, the Kussner household already had a daughter, Louisa (later called Louise), born 1859, and a son, Albert, born 1861. In the year of Amalia's birth, the country was well into the Civil War. Indiana was a Union state but bordered on Kentucky, a Rebel state. Greencastle was mixed in allegiance to the Union, but later in the war, it aligned with the Union efforts.[3] At least one of Emilie's relatives, her brother John, enlisted in the Union Army. In addition, the southern part of the state was invaded in 1863 by Rebel soldiers as part of Morgan's Raid. This certainly would have been a challenging time for the family.

In February of the following year, the family moved to Terre Haute, helped by a direct train route from Greencastle. Lorenz opened his own musical instrument repair and sales business, Palace of Music, at 213 Ohio Street.[4] With the end of the war, his business did well, but his building burned down in 1867; with help from Emilie's parents, John and Babetta Weinhardt, the Kussners purchased the abandoned State Bank of Indiana building. This second store location was nearby at 219 Ohio Street and opened around 1870.[5] A number of Emilie's Weinhardt relatives also moved to Terre Haute in the coming years, including John Weinhardt, who had survived the war, and his family.

The Kussners lived on the second floor of the Palace of Music building, and it was recorded that in one room a stage was built on which the children would perform plays in English and French.[6] Living above a music store, Amalia and her siblings grew up hearing the melodies being played on pianos downstairs, either by potential customers or by Lorenz himself. This environment would inspire Albert to pursue a career as a music composer in the later 1890s and Louise to pursue a career as an amateur vocalist.[7]

The Kussner family first shows up in the 1870 census in Terre Haute, when Amalia would have been seven years old. Intriguingly, this census shows the value of their property as seventeen thousand dollars, but it's listed in his wife's name, indicating the property was owned by Emilie. Ads for the Palace of Music from that time period have also survived.

A map produced of Terre Haute in 1880 identifies many different municipal structures and businesses.[8] The legend for this map indicates no fewer than twelve churches and various industries like iron works and wool mills. Certainly, Terre Haute was well located for the transport of goods, being on the Wabash River and with the Union Station train depot. The Palace of Music is located on this map, identified as building number twenty-two. The Kussner home would have been in more of a business area than a residential area but did border on a park. And the Kussners were only two blocks from the Opera House, where Amalia's Weinhardt relatives were active in the music performances.

Amalia's early years were part of a rich musical environment, listening to her father conduct instrument repairs on the floor below and

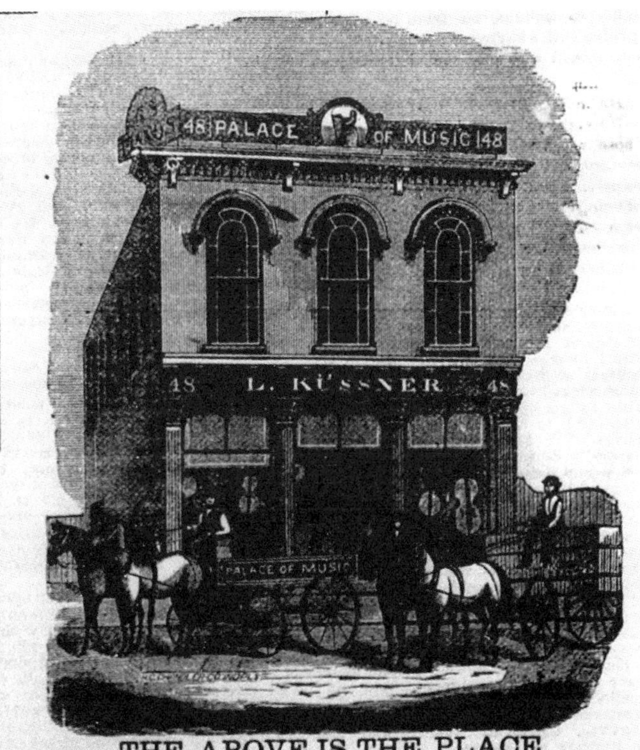

An advertisement for the Palace of Music showing the building, as seen in the February 1878 issue of the *Saturday Evening Mail*.

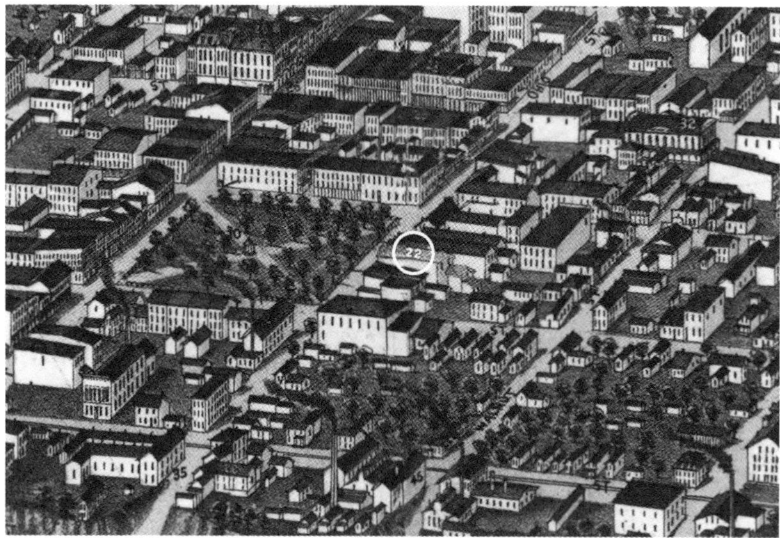

An enlarged panoramic view of Terre Haute, Indiana, in 1880, with the Palace of Music (building number twenty-two) highlighted. *Beck and Pauli (1880), Library of Congress*

sometimes hearing him creating his own musical compositions. One of these was a waltz he composed in 1875, called *Woodland Home.* The front page of the music included his dedication at the top: "To My Little Amalie."[9]

But it was art that would inspire her, and there are various tales of how she became interested in the style of miniature portraits. One account cites that the same year Lorenz Kussner composed his waltz, he gave Amalia a miniature painted on ivory.[10] This was probably her first exposure to the art form. Soon thereafter, she started practicing on discarded ivory piano keys from her father's store.[11]

Her parents appreciated her talents at an early age and sent her, along with Louise, to the local St. Mary of the Woods Academy to get art lessons when she was as young as six years old.[12] This academy was started by a French order of nuns, upon the request of the bishop of Vincennes, to provide education to Catholic immigrants in Indiana. The institution was granted the first charter for higher education of women in the state of Indiana (1846).[13] One of the nuns, Sister Maurice, was a talented artist

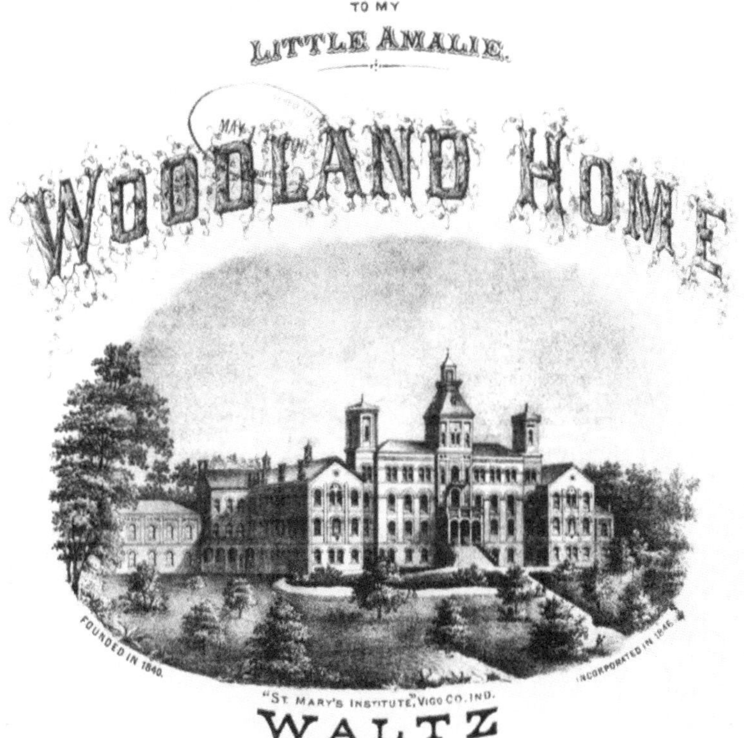

The sheet music cover for *Woodland Home* by Lorenz Kussner (1875). *Music for the Nation: American Sheet Music, Ca. 1870 to 1885, Library of Congress*

and credited with providing lessons to Amalia.[14] Lorenz also became involved with the academy, raffling off one of his organs and providing funds to the school.[15] A pen and ink depiction of the school at this time can be seen on the cover of the sheet music for *Woodland Home.*

Amalia's art lessons continued when she was enrolled in the Terre Haute High School (renamed to Wiley High School a few years later in 1884). Two pieces of her artwork were featured in a collection comprised of fifty-four sketches from the special art classes held on Saturdays. The purpose of this weekend class was described by William H. Wiley in 1876: "This instruction is supplementary to the regular course in drawing. Its design is to furnish more advanced work than is given in the regular courses to all the pupils above the Fourth Year Grade who have any special aptitude in that direction, and desire to pursue the subject."[16]

Her sketches, as seen here, aren't especially remarkable, but there is a bold style to her lines depicting the church and the farmhouse.

Some of her earliest work as a teenager was painting on Minton tiles, which were produced in England and had dimensions of six inches by six inches. Some of these tiles were then used as a decorative accent in some of her relatives' fireplaces. This was a common interior design approach in the later Victorian age. One of her surviving tile paintings (see color insert) is a whimsical gathering of three cherubs around a head, which almost looks like that of a Roman soldier.

Another Minton tile work done around this time was her painting of a Scottish family crest (see color insert), showing a knight atop the crest decorated with bold red and blue flourishes. It is unknown who commissioned her to do this artwork, but it's attributed to Amalia from

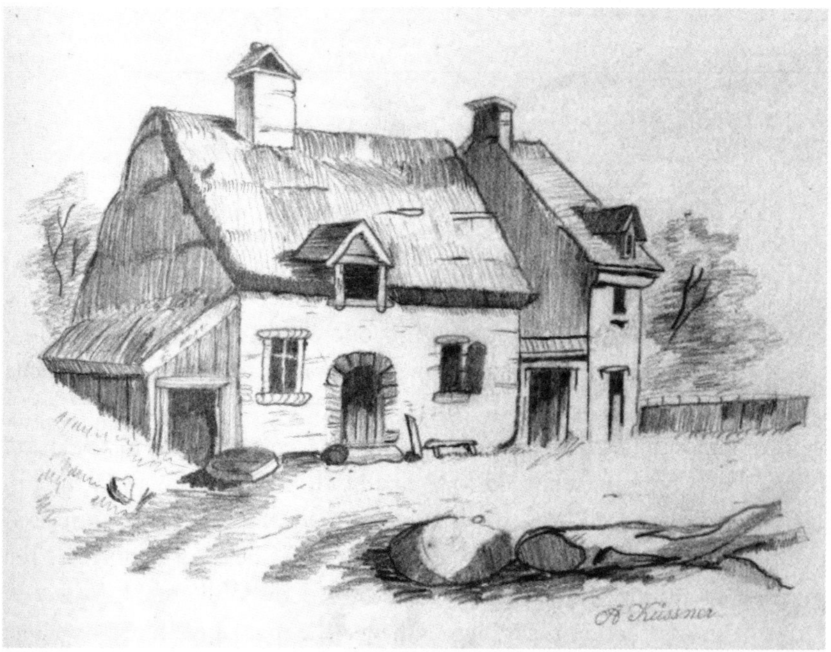

Sketch of a farmhouse by Amalia Kussner (1876). *Courtesy of Vigo County Library, Terre Haute, Indiana.*

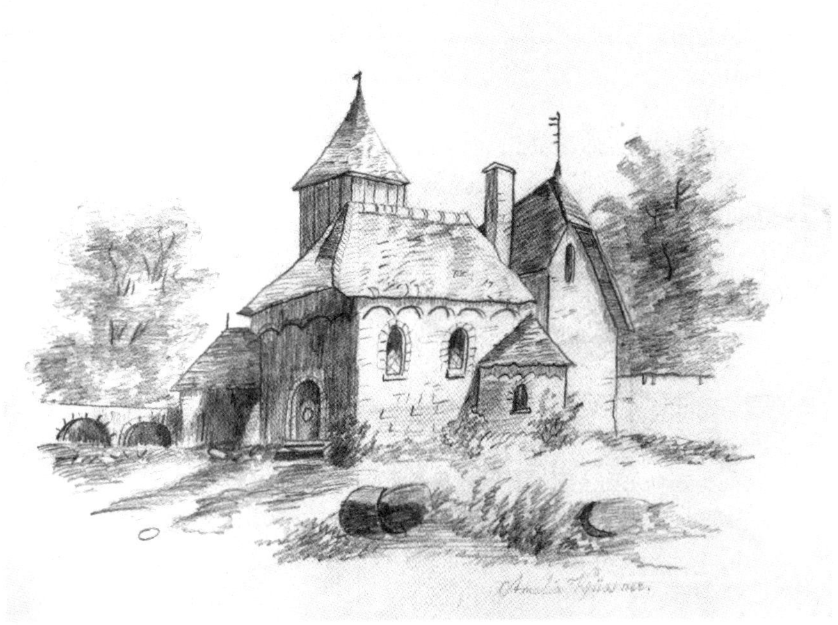

Sketch of a church by Amalia Kussner (1876). *Courtesy of Vigo County Library, Terre Haute, Indiana.*

her initials on the back of the tile. It displays the Gordon family motto, *Animo Non Astutia*, which translates to "Courage not Cunning."

When Amalia graduated from Terre Haute High School in 1881, she wrote an essay that was read to the graduates and audience to a resounding applause. It was entitled, "Money Lost, Nothing Lost, Honor Lost, Much Lost; Courage Lost, All Lost"—a quote by the German writer von Goethe. The local newspaper described how "in composition and delivery, the best performance was that of Miss Amelia [Amalia] Kussner. She commanded the closest attention of the audience and was frequently interrupted with applause."[17]

Shortly after graduation she was sent to Mme. Da Silva's and Mrs. Bradford's school in New York City. She likely traveled east with her brother, who was then enrolled in Phillips Exeter Academy in Exeter, New Hampshire. Though Albert graduated in 1882, she likely returned to New York for another year of schooling.

There were many such finishing schools for young ladies in New York at this time, and they were seen as taking the place of what would later be more formal college education for women. Da Silva's and Bradford's was located at No. 17, West 38th Street and near to Reservoir Square, which just a few years later would become the park Bryant Square. The neighborhood is now the Garment District. During Amalia's years attending this school, numerous grand mansions were being built by the Vanderbilt family, including the Triple Palace (640 Fifth Avenue) and Petit Chateau (650 Fifth Avenue).[18] Alva Vanderbilt and her daughter Consuelo would live in the latter mansion. Amalia likely saw these magnificent structures as they were being constructed, and she would interact fifteen years later with Consuelo, as Duchess of Marlborough, to do multiple portraits of her in England.

The advertisements for the finishing school highlighted teaching multiple foreign languages. Amalia's facility with foreign languages undoubtedly was an asset for her later travels to Europe in the later 1890s. One Terre Haute historian records that while at this boarding school, Amalia also attended New York's Art Institute League,[19] located in 1882 at 38 West 14th Street, between Fifth and Sixth Avenues.[20]

One of her most stunning works that survives today from her early career is what has been labeled *Moon Lady* (see color insert). This was another work painted on a set of three Minton tiles, again to accent a fireplace. It depicts a mysterious, almost mythical woman draped across a crescent moon. The character is clothed in a diaphanous fabric, and it's truly a revealing and sensuous portrait. Amalia's depiction of a full female figure in *Moon Lady* may have been the only one she ever painted. Though she certainly portrayed many women in her miniatures with a sensuous appearance, where the subjects were wrapped in gauze-like fabric with much of their décolletage exposed, these women were only painted from the waist up. *Moon Lady* is not dated, but given the sophistication of the image, it was likely done in the 1880s upon her return from New York.

She also received further art training from Helen Minshall of the Terre Haute Decorative Arts Society, joining as a charter member in 1882 (along with seventeen other women and young ladies). An article entitled "Decorative Art Society" listed Miss Helen Minshall, secretary and treasurer, and Louise and Molly Kussner as members. The article further stated:

> The object of the society is mutual improvement in those things belonging in the realm of Decorative Art, and particularly that branch known as household art—the making of the innumerable beautiful objects which go to adorn our homes, make them so aesthetic, and which can only be made by the deft fingers of woman.[21]

In the theme of decorative arts for the household, Amalia painted a watercolor still life of heliotrope flowers (see color insert), most likely in the later 1880s. As would become a trademark of many of her pieces, her bold signature is prominently placed in the lower right corner of the painting (see color insert).

In 1885, she opened her own studio in Terre Haute and provided instruction in "decorative painting and drawing from life."[22] Her interest and talent for miniatures became her primary artistic medium at this time. She soon started to get commissions from the well-to-do in Terre Haute, painting the prominent residents Crawford Fairbanks (owner of breweries), Charles Minshall (an industrialist), and Stephen Reynolds (an attorney) and family.[23]

With early indications dating back to her high school graduation that Amalia enjoyed being in the public eye, it's no surprise that in addition to her business, she took an opportunity to return to the stage by participating as a dancer in an 1890 Terre Haute play. The production was based on General Lew Wallace's book *Ben Hur: A Tale of the Christ*. This novel is most well-known now from the 1959 movie starring Charlton Heston, and of course for the famous chariot race. But in the context of the culture at the time, the book was a runaway bestseller after its publication in 1880.

Numerous dramatic episodes of the novel were converted into dances, and the performance at the nearby opera house featured Amalia in three routines. One of her dances, termed the nautch, a dance style taken from India, was cited to be the most difficult technically.[24] A preview of the performance declared: "This evening the famous Nautch dance will be given by the Misses May DaMond, Amelia [Amalia] Kussner and Elise Hudson. This will well be worth seeing, for these three ladies are the most graceful dancers in the case."[25] Amalia was never trained as a dancer, but again, the performances gave her a chance to be up in front of the Terre Haute public and were an indication of her almost chameleon-like character to adapt her role to fit the moment.

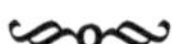

While Amalia's business in Terre Haute was starting to flourish, her father's financial situation was in question. Along with his music business, he seems to have also invested in various real estate purchases both in Terre Haute and Greencastle. However, they were fraught with legal issues. He was involved in legal disputes both in 1880 and 1882, and the local newspaper listed a foreclosure against Emilie and Lorenz Kussner in 1886.[26] Advertisements for the Palace of Music continued up through 1890, but the focus of these later ads was his son, Albert, who seemingly became the primary representative for the piano and organ repairs.

One must wonder: did her father's business failings, which must have been known in the community, instill in Amalia both an economic insecurity and the drive to aggressively push her business as an adult? As will be seen, during her career she demanded commission prices way beyond those of other miniaturists in the 1890s.

At some point in the early 1890s, the Palace of Music closed and major changes were in store for the Kussner family. Albert moved to Chicago, where he could exclusively dedicate his time to composing romantic piano pieces—a career that lasted for at least fifteen years. The rest of the family followed him, but their transition to Chicago coincided with a fateful invitation Amalia received in 1892 from a school friend to join her in New York City. Amalia certainly realized her career opportunities would be more likely to succeed in New York, and she would be returning to a city much changed since her school years there. In a few short years, the elite of that city would know her name.[27]

Chapter 2

The Rise to Fame

With the end of the Kussner family business in Terre Haute and the family shifting their home to Chicago with Albert, it was an opportune time for Amalia to also leave the Midwest in her search for greater opportunities out East. Fortunately, her way was paved by Alice Fischer, a high school classmate from Terre Haute. Alice was already an established actress on Broadway and had at her disposal many contacts among the elite of New York City. Her society connections were further helped by her organization of Twelfth Night Club, a group initially only for women actresses in the New York theater world, formed as a response to the men-only clubs. Twelfth Night Club was dubbed "the woman's club par excellence of the theatrical profession."[1] With time, the club expanded to include other persons of note from the arts, and eventually similar clubs were formed outside of New York.

Alice sent an invitation to Amalia in 1892 to join her in New York, which Amalia eagerly acted upon. Though many references describe Amalia essentially arriving on the city scene by herself, her mother was in attendance to support her new ventures in that city. Emilie, however, returned to Chicago within a year.

Amalia arrived in New York at the beginning of the miniature art revival that was occurring both in America and Europe, especially in the cities of London and Paris. The miniature art form had been around for centuries but had undergone a marked decline in the middle of the nineteenth century. In an article written in 1925, Alyn Williams, founder of the Royal Society of Miniature Painters, stated:

This decline was mainly caused by the introduction of photography, but it was also probably due to poor work. The miniaturists of the Victorian days seem, both in England and abroad, to have grown mechanical and hard in their method of painting. The feeling of making dainty, decorative little pictures seems to have been greatly lost.[2]

Williams went on to bluntly state: "Photography almost killed the art, but the revulsion against the inartistic colored photographs, often masquerading as miniatures, also helped to bring about its revival."[3] Although photography was often seen as a villain in the miniature revival, photographs, through their "critical, black and white view of sitters," helped make the softer, stylized portrayal in miniatures an equally preferred medium once again. However, the re-emergence of miniatures certainly didn't diminish the popularity of photography, and the wealthy of course would often have both miniatures and exacting black and white photographs of their family members.[4]

Art historian Maryann Gunderson, who has studied several miniaturists who were Amalia's contemporaries, also linked the revival to the socioeconomics of the late nineteenth-century United States. New York was "emerging as a key financial and artistic center of this time," which meant the miniature artists who migrated to the city could enjoy higher degrees of patronage from their clientele.[5] "Wealthier Americans could afford both photographs and miniatures, and commonly possessed both."[6] Also, the quality of these miniatures was now on par with life-sized portraits.

Another aspect of the popularity of miniatures was that the wealthy families of New York could easily travel with these cherished portraits reflecting their status and beauty, carrying them to and from their summer homes, such as in Newport, Rhode Island. With the small, elaborate frames, the miniatures could be displayed in their parlors for visitors to see or in their bedrooms for private admiring, whereas larger and often full-length formal oil paintings would have to stay in their stately New York mansions. Later in the revival, "the portrait miniature was referred to as a table portrait," moving away from the art form being seen as just a decorative keepsake.[7]

In New York City, Amalia would find a strong market demand for miniatures and eventually, through fortuitous connections, patrons of Gilded Age New York who had the ability to pay her high commission rates.

⌘

Amalia's first documented work in New York City was as a staff artist at Tiffany Studios in 1892, made possible by Alice Fischer's connections.[8] This is also the year that Tiffany's established a women's "workshop" staffed by the Tiffany Girls, a group of talented women who were employed in the glass cutting shop and were managed by Clara Driscoll. The presence of this staff of women and their artistic contributions has been a recently uncovered piece of history for Tiffany's,[9] and it's intriguing that Amalia arrived there around this time.

She stayed at Tiffany's less than a year and likely left for one of two reasons: first, because those at Tiffany's saw her potential and encouraged her to depart to pursue greater opportunities, or second—and the more likely—because her artwork wasn't getting the attention she felt it deserved.

Soon thereafter, Amalia showed her works to an unnamed art connoisseur. An article from the town of her birth, Greencastle, relates her first and failed attempt to offer her artistic services. Upon taking her artwork to this gentleman, he rejected her pieces, saying that her miniatures were "unsuited to the time" and "too fine, too slow, and above all too costly."[10]

Once again, Alice came to her aid by providing an introduction to Mrs. Louisine Havemeyer, who was already an established art collector. Mrs. Havemeyer promoted the works of Mary Cassatt and collaborated with the artist, receiving guidance from Cassatt in building her European art collection in New York. This association helped expand the American art aesthetic to include the French Impressionists (including Monet, Degas, and Manet).[11]

Mrs. Havemeyer and her husband, Theodore, were well ensconced in the New York Gilded Age society. Amalia's painting of Mrs. Havemeyer's portrait gave her talent exposure to the de facto list of the best of New York's society, the Four Hundred. Though the origins of this list are somewhat hazy, it was a term coined by a gentleman named Ward McAllister, a close confidant of Mrs. Caroline Astor. "There are only about four hundred people in fashionable New York Society," McAllister told the *New York Tribune* in 1888. "If you go outside that number," he warned, "you strike people who are either not at ease in a ballroom or else make other people not at ease."[12] Ironically, McAllister connected with Kussner in 1894 and discouraged her efforts, stating that "her work was too fine and too costly for this age of cheap imitations."[13]

The Four Hundred list was indeed real, but the initial count was closer to 250—a number that matched those invited to the Astor Ball, an annual event in the 1880s and 1890s.[14] This list was made public in the *New York Times* just as Amalia arrived in New York. Those counted among the Four Hundred had to have a long family lineage in America (more than two generations) and be of a certain wealth level, and certain religious groups were excluded, such as those of the Jewish faith and Catholics. "The New York upper class had traditionally been Protestant specifically Episcopalian for the ultra-rich and fashionable. . . . There were a sprinkling of Catholics in the upper class, yet this religious group largely did not belong to the Four Hundred."[15]

The Astor balls were "the highlight of the entire social year" in New York, with people attending not just for the sumptuous dinners and dancing, but to be seen as the accepted elite.[16] Amalia would eventually paint many of the women whose names were found on the invitation list. But first, she needed them to catch wind of her talents.

Alice Fischer advised Amalia that even with a letter of entrée, she should not count on her chances to have a "meeting" with Mrs. Havemeyer, as the esteemed art collector was known not to easily entertain new persons in the arts.[17]

Undeterred, Amalia arrived at the Havemeyer residence, at the corner of Fifth Avenue and 66th Street, to find a stately mansion. Its exterior was missing the Beaux Arts ornamentation popular with other recently built Gilded Age mansions, but its interior was opulent.[18] She walked up the front stairs, carrying a few of her miniatures wrapped in dainty handkerchiefs. At first the maid at the door advised her Mrs. Havemeyer was too ill to receive anyone that day. But Amalia persisted, and her wrapped miniatures were at last brought by the maid to Mrs. Havemeyer for inspection. As Amalia entered the foyer and was escorted to a waiting room, she would have faced the grand staircase, similar in style to the Doge's Palace in Venice. And in the foyer, she would have easily recognized the Tiffany mosaics on the walls. After a lengthy wait, Amalia was advised that Mrs. Havemeyer would receive her, and she was escorted to her room on the second floor. On her way upstairs, and possibly in Mrs. Havemeyer's room, she again would have seen various Tiffany pieces, such as lamps with Eastern-influenced designs.[19]

Amalia's persistence was successful—she triumphantly departed the mansion having garnered a commission to paint Mrs. Havemeyer. The grand dame's connections would lead to others, including Lillian Russell, an American actress, and Marie Tempest, an actress from London. The demand for Amalia's artwork soon greatly increased.

One of the earliest articles to praise Amalia in New York was published in *The Illustrated American* in April 1893; the author describes her work in miniatures as being at a level worthy to be compared to the greats of the past:

> It still remains a matter of surprise that to a female—and a very youthful one at that—should fall the rare genius that must result in the renascence of the most refined form of pigmentary art . . . [her work] will surely restore to miniature painting the vogue and virtue that it enjoyed with Hans Holbein and Nicholas Hilliard to William Ross and Alfred Chalon.[20]

Also by April of that year, her artistic talents had clearly caught the attention of the women in New York who could benefit her career: "Her work was among the class of sitters who would be surest to advance her, les grandes dames de société, who had wealth, position and beauty."[21]

As her reputation for miniature portraits grew, Amalia established a residence and studio at the Windsor Hotel. This hotel was both a popular entertainment venue and an ideal location for travelers, as it was a mere two blocks from Grand Central Station. She applied her artistic taste in personally decorating her suite of rooms, displaying a décor of elegance and femininity. Her rooms were on one of the upper floors, with the studio facing north for good lighting. Her primary decorating colors were greens for the studio, rose pink for her boudoir with roses painted on the ceiling, and white and gold for the receiving room with dominant pink muslin curtains.[22]

Metropolitan magazine photographed Amalia in her Windsor Hotel rooms in 1898. Her opulent decorating style is quite evident, with different types of fabrics draped over various surfaces. The first photograph shows her in a relaxed pose, sitting in front of a fireplace. Behind her on the mantel are flower vases that one can assume are filled with fresh flowers. The table to her right has a heart-shaped frame and is draped with gossamer fabric.

The second photograph was taken in the same room, with her standing to the right of the fireplace, possibly examining one of her miniatures. The table she stands in front of is her worktable and shows some of her equipment, including a magnifying glass on a stand suspended over some works in progress.

Amalia even started providing art lessons from the Windsor; it is documented that she offered lessons to Rosa Hooper, then a young woman just starting as a miniaturist. Hooper would later become a quite successful artist whose career continued the resurgence of the miniature art form.

Early in her entrée into the art world of New York, Amalia chose to present a mythology of being a much younger age than she actually was and of essentially having had no artistic training. Amalia knew that a woman at thirty years or older would be less appealing to society, and she was already thirty-one by 1894. Exhibiting appreciable artistic talent as a young ingenue was also a bit of an amazement to the public. And given her personality, she did not want to be beholden to anyone for her successes—therefore, she wanted no public record of having taken art lessons. This image of herself as a young, untrained prodigy started to be published in newspapers as early as 1894. This was a day and age where falsifying personal facts was still easy to accomplish, and many of the

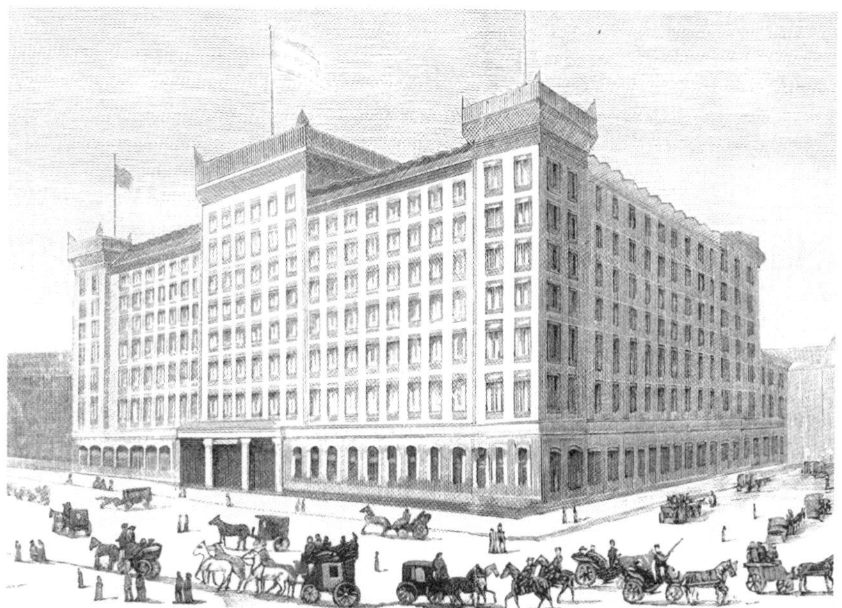

Etching of the Windsor Hotel in New York where Amalia Kussner had her studio (1899). *Creative Commons Attribution-Share Alike 4.0 International license, courtesy of user Kuhn73*

New York papers would not be read by friends and family back home in Indiana.

These myths about her age and background were supported by articles written by Nancy Huston Banks, a noted journalist of the time who published numerous and very complimentary pieces about Amalia. In the *Ladies Home Journal* in 1895, she described Amalia's talent:

> She has studied no master as a model and has apparently given little attention to technique. She paints, if possible, entirely from life, and draws with great ease and rapidity. The richness of her coloring and delicacy of treatment have all the refinement of the French School.[23]

Furthermore, Amalia is documented as a gorgeous, young ingenue in another of Nancy's articles:

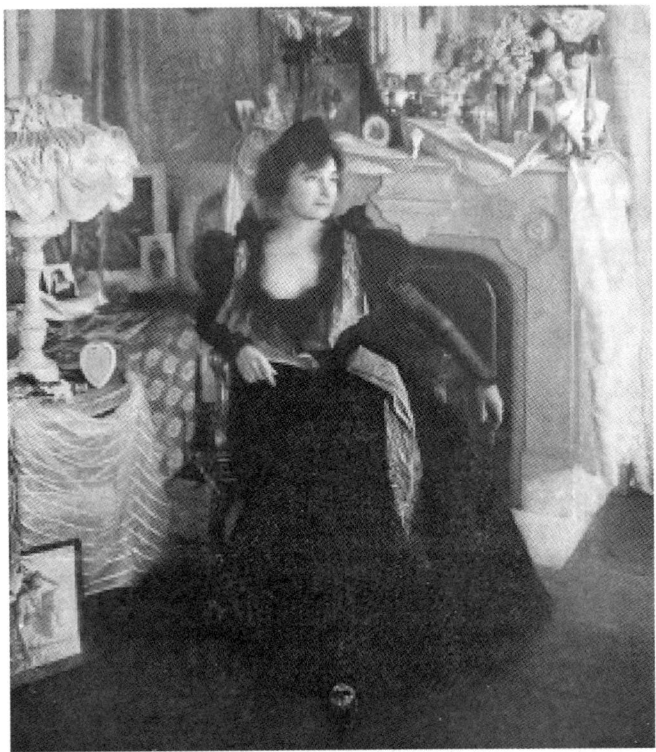

Amalia Kussner sitting in her Windsor Hotel studio (1898). *Courtesy of the Amalia Kussner Papers (Private Collection), Sisters of Providence Archives at Saint Mary-of-the-Woods, Indiana*

She is very small, scarcely taller than a child of 12, with an exquisitely modeled little figure, a perfect miniature woman. Her hands are the smallest that ever wrought magic, her eyes are very large and long lashed and dark, her hair is brown and her complexion brilliantly brunette.[24]

Nancy continues this mythology:

This young girl, then scarcely more than a child, came to New York. She was alone, without influence, brought no letters and was as absolutely unknown as if just descended from another planet.[25]

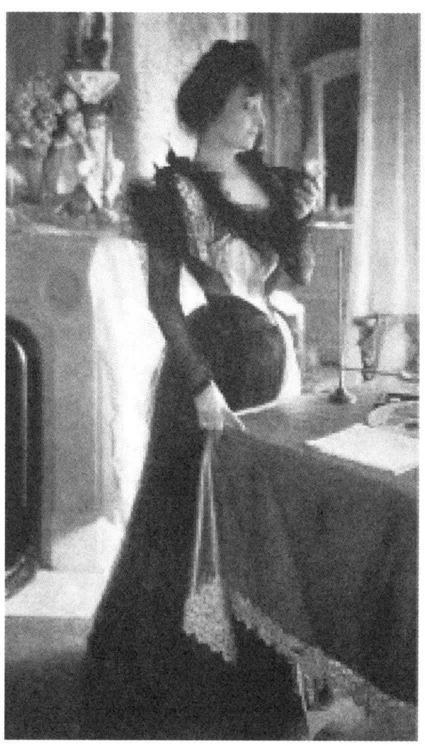

Amalia Kussner standing in her Windsor Hotel studio (1898). *Courtesy of the Amalia Kussner Papers (Private Collection), Sisters of Providence Archives at Saint Mary-of-the-Woods, Indiana*

After these interviews, Nancy Banks and Amalia formed a lifetime friendship. Nancy originally came from Kentucky, in a town near the Indiana border, and grew up in a prosperous household. Her father was a Yale-educated lawyer who later became a judge.[26] Nancy had a brief marriage, and when it ended, she was the object of town scorn. She never remarried, but she did keep her married last name of Banks.[27]

Nancy arrived in New York around the same time as Amalia and in the early 1890s already had an accomplished career as a journalist. In 1893, she had the distinction to be chosen by the governor of Kentucky to serve as a manager on a publicity committee promoting the World's Columbian Exposition, held in Chicago.[28] Soon thereafter Banks became a frequent book reviewer at *The Bookman* magazine, a monthly publication which offered critiques on American fiction.[29] She held that role for another five years, then devoted her skills to writing fiction.[30] She was able to live an independent lifestyle and had sufficient income to follow her career goals as she pleased. It is easy to assume that these two women would have seen in each other a kindred spirit.

Amalia's increasing fame and impressive clientele led to her being an exhibited artist at a number of prestigious art shows in the 1890s. The first, in 1894, was an exhibit of portraits on loan from the National

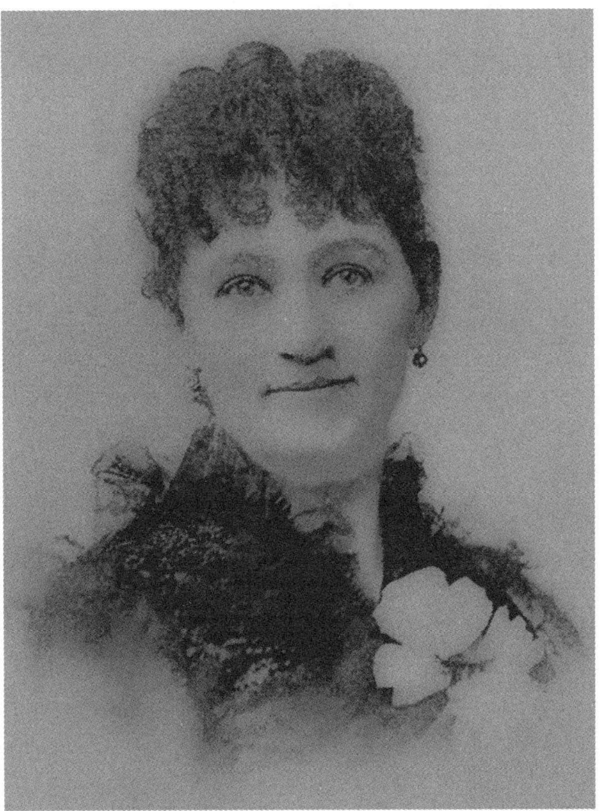

A photograph of Nancy Huston Banks, likely taken for a souvenir booklet at the World's Columbian Exposition in Chicago in 1892. *The Blocker Company, 1892, Library of Congress*

Academy of Design, for which the ticket proceeds supported St. John's Guild and the Orthopaedic Hospital. Twelve of Amalia's miniatures were on display, including her portrait of Mrs. Havemeyer. This exhibit also included works by the American Impressionist William Merritt Chase, showing that Amalia's works were being found on display alongside highly esteemed artists.[31]

Amalia was advised that one of the attendees was the noted art connoisseur who had earlier dismissed her work. This was certainly a triumph for Amalia, as she was known to keep track of those who may have slighted her in the past.

This inaugural exhibit was followed two years later by a show in Cincinnati, Ohio, to benefit the Laura Memorial College and Hospital. Though there was only one of Amalia's miniatures on display, this exhibit had an even more impressive list of artists and subjects from the eighteenth and nineteenth centuries, some of which included Sir Joshua Reynolds, Sir Thomas Gainsborough, and Gilbert Stuart with one of his iconic paintings of George Washington. Amalia's miniature was that of Mrs. Cyrus Hall McCormick, wife of the inventor who founded the McCormick Harvesting Machine Company, later to become International Harvester Company after his passing.

In the mid-1890s, word of Amalia's popularity reached even the highest of the Gilded Age women: Mrs. Caroline Astor. Mrs. Astor was in her mid-sixties at this time and wanted her portrait to be as "kind" as possible. She was quite vain and didn't like being photographed.[32] The likeness presented by Amalia in the finished miniature is a softened image of the woman, and it does indeed portray a more lovely Mrs. Astor. Her face is clearly thinner, and her usually small eyes are made larger and more delicate. Known for her many fine pieces of jewelry, Mrs. Astor is painted wearing a collar-like necklace of large oval gems surrounded by diamonds. Amalia also painted her youngest daughter, Carrie, who became Mrs. Orme Wilson, and her daughter-in-law, Mrs. John Jacob Astor.

Mrs. Astor, in a letter to Amalia a few years later, with an 842 Fifth Avenue letterhead, noted accolades from those with artistic knowledge:

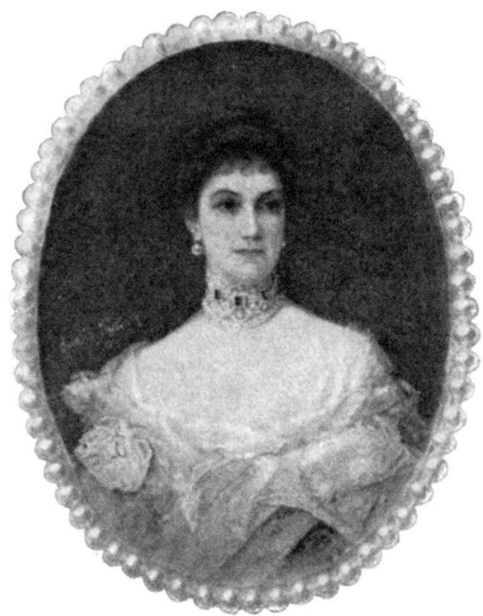

Miniature of Mrs. Astor by Amalia Kussner, as seen in "Amalia Kussner's Miniatures of the Astor Family," *The House Beautiful*, September 1901.

> Your name is well known, and your work is much praised and admired, it speaks for itself, the beauty and delicacy of it are much appreciated by all whose judgement is worth having—The miniature you [did] of me, has been much praised.[33]

This praise from Mrs. Astor is especially impressive given her high standards.

Another important woman on the Four Hundred list who was painted by Amalia was Mrs. Stuyvesant (Mamie) Fish.[34] She was a leader in both the New York and Newport social scenes and was seen as "one of the most prominent society hostesses of the Gilded Age."[35]

Scores of publications throughout the 1890s continued to list Amalia's painting the many women of the highest echelons of New York society. The *New York Journal* in 1896, in a section entitled "Of Interest to Women," showed a trio of such women: Mrs. Lorillard Spencer, Mrs. Van Rensselaer Cruger, and Mrs. Havemeyer.[36]

Soon, her clientele expanded beyond these high society of New York to across the Atlantic. After she was introduced to Mrs. Paran Stevens and did her portrait, Amalia connected with Mrs. Stevens's daughter, Minnie Paget. Minnie, one of the famous so-called dollar heiresses, became the third woman to connect with Amalia in New York and greatly helped her career, ultimately paving her way for international fame.

Minnie's father had been a rich hotelier in both Boston and New York but passed away in 1872, when Minnie (then known as Mary Stevens) was a young woman. Her mother, Marietta Stevens, wanted the ultimate marriage for her daughter: to marry into European royalty. Through her father's international connections in the 1870s, Minnie was introduced to the Prince of Wales, who helped introduce her to suitable and eligible men of noble birth. After some failed attempts with several European royals, she finally settled to marry Sir Arthur Paget in 1878. She was certainly an heiress at this time, given her father's passing, and provided a respectable dowry as part of her marriage to Paget. However, she didn't have full access to these riches until 1895.[37] The Prince of Wales was impressed with "her outrageous American manners," and he allowed her close access to his inner social circle.[38]

There are no known accounts of when Amalia was first introduced to Minnie Paget, but it is known that Amalia initially traveled to London in February 1896, through an invitation from Minnie. So, it is likely the two women met toward the end of 1895.

There is a quite dramatic account of this first journey to London. It describes Amalia leaving New York and boarding a "great trans-Atlantic steamer" during a winter storm. The "fierce, tempestuous gale" continued for most of her voyage across the Atlantic, and upon arriving in London, she was not initially well received. Both literally and figuratively, she waited for weeks in a "London Fog." But her hopes were kept alive by encouragement from Minnie Paget.[39]

The turning point came when Sir John Millais, president of the Royal Academy, praised Amalia's work. In fact, a few of her miniatures were accepted to be displayed at the Royal Academy collection. This vaulted acceptance garnered her numerous commissions, and she quickly became the "new" sought-after artist of London. To celebrate this success,

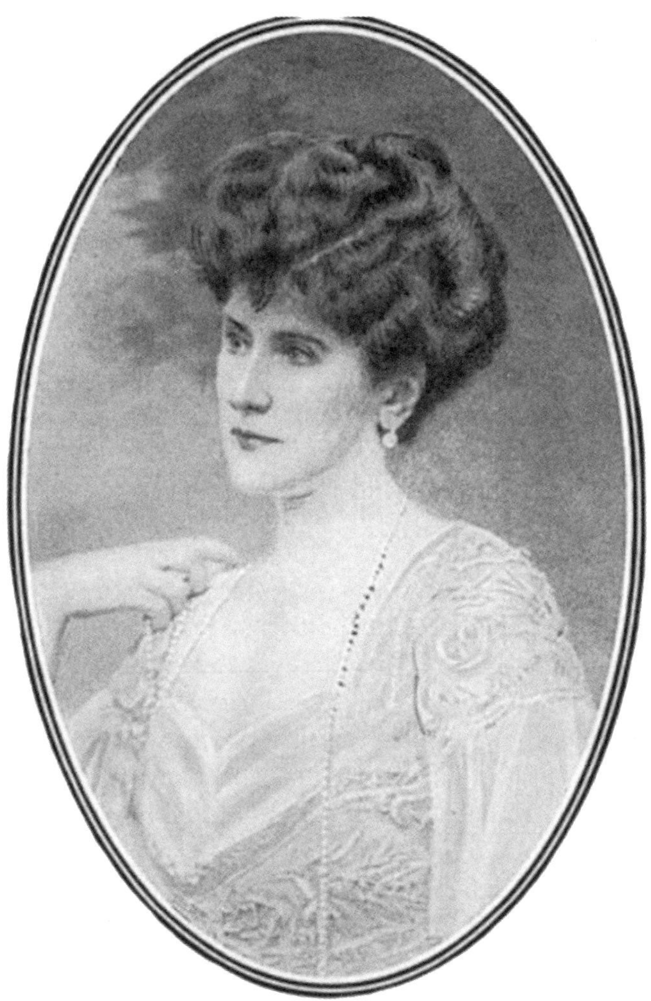

Lady Paget, previously Mrs. Arthur Paget, formerly the American heiress Minnie Stevens (1909). *Alamy Photo Stock*

Minnie Paget hosted a tea to exhibit Amalia's miniatures, with over fifty of Minnie's friends recorded as attending.[40]

News of Amalia's success in London soon reached New York, where a local newspaper reported: "Mrs. Arthur Paget is greatly interested in Miss Kussner's success, and through her the artist has obtained orders for miniatures from prominent social leaders abroad."[41]

The article further recounts Amalia's life as "a romantic one, in which genius conquered every obstacle," and repeats the claim of her having no art lessons prior to her arrival in New York.[42] On the renewed interest in miniatures and how they were valued, the article further states:

> Miniature painting had been a lost art for half a century and had no place in modern portraiture. It remained for the unsophisticated country girl to revive interest in it. Her miniatures at the Portrait Show created a genuine furor.[43]

One of Amalia's earlier commissions, done late in the winter of 1896, was the Duchess of Marlborough, the former Consuelo Vanderbilt. Consuelo at this time had only been married for four months, but clearly was taking advantage of her new role in society to seek the services of Amalia, along with many other women of titled nobility. An article of the time indicated that Amalia had been commissioned to do at least four portraits of Consuelo, two of which were directly ordered by her husband, Charles Spencer-Churchill, 9th Duke of Marlborough.

Most, if not all, of these portraits were done at Blenheim palace, Consuelo's new residence.[44] Amalia was fortunate enough to be a guest at Blenheim, as she communicated to a Terre Haute newspaper: "I write you a letter from the most beautiful spot in England. I never dreamed of anything like it."[45]

This letter was written on palace stationery, with the embossed Marlborough coat of arms. Amalia described the dinners at Blenheim as "served in a sumptuous style. Besides the butler, who is a great personage in this establishment, there are four other men attendants."[46] Following the elaborate evening meal, all would retire to the library and listen to music from a grand organ. During the day, when not creating her portraits, Amalia would walk the palace grounds, including the hot houses and kitchen gardens. She felt at ease in this atmosphere and was clearly welcomed by all.

It's famously known that Consuelo's marriage to the duke had been forced upon her by her mother, Alva.[47] As an independent woman who was traveling the world and solely deciding the direction of her life,

Amalia likely presented a fascinating character for Consuelo. Also, since Amalia portrayed herself as being in her early twenties, she was perceived as only a few years older than Consuelo, who had just turned twenty. However, Amalia by 1896 was in her early thirties. One can only imagine what these two women would have talked about over at least a dozen sittings needed for the four portraits. Certainly, with Amalia in residence at Blenheim, this would have further encouraged a close association.

Through her association with Minnie and her increasing popularity in London, Amalia caught the eye of the British royal family, resulting in one of her most famous commissions, requested by the Prince of Wales. The prince attended the Devonshire Ball of 1897, which celebrated the sixtieth year of Queen Victoria's reign. This event required all guests to wear costumes either of an allegorical theme or from a period of history prior to 1812. The prince chose a costume fashioned after the Knights of Malta, a quite ornate costume. He wanted a miniature of himself in costume, done by Amalia, to be a gift for his wife, Princess Alexandra of Wales. While in London, Amalia received an invitation from the prince's residence, Marlborough House, a few weeks after the ball:

> The equerry is waiting to be desired to ask Miss Kussner to come to Marlborough House on Monday next at 3:45 p. m., about which time the Prince of Wales will be happy to see her. 24th July, '97.[48]

Amalia took the liberty of requesting the prince sit for their session alone, without any of his courtiers, to minimize distractions. This was clearly a bold move to make such a request of the British royalty. However, the prince obliged, and she later documented that of the many famous people she painted, he was one of the most patient and easy to pose.

> At my request, he came unattended, and, in order that nothing might distract my attention from the portrait, no others were permitted to enter.... I have never had an easier subject.... all sittings took place in his private drawing room at Marlborough House, all about us beautiful armor and valuable gifts.[49]

In comparing a photograph of the prince in costume with her miniature, we see an example of how Amalia took artistic liberties in painting her subjects and chose what was most important about them to either minimize or highlight. In her rendition of the costume, she placed the cross of Malta off to the side of his tunic and made it much smaller, which helped to then emphasize his face better.

The prince later commissioned her to paint some of his family in the early 1900s, when he became King Edward VII. In a daring move for the times, Amalia even did a portrait of his mistress, Alice Keppel, in 1903.[50]

> It is the town talk in London that Mrs. Keppel gave the King her miniature, by Amalia Kussner. This present also is shocking to the Britishers.

By the end of his association with Amalia, the Prince of Wales had given her at least two pieces of fine jewelry. One was a necklace made of an emerald suspended in a frame of pavé diamonds, designed by René Lalique,[51] a renowned French jeweler and glassmaker. The other was a fine-jewel-encrusted representation of the prince's prize racehorse, Persimmon, complete with mounted jockey wearing the king's colors. The pin was engraved on the back:

H.R.H. The Prince of Wales
Amalia Kussner
August, 1897

This Persimmon pin (see color insert) may have been handed out to several favorites of the prince, as he gave the same pin design to the Earl of Coventry in 1897 to celebrate the victory of the horse at the Ascot race.[52]

Amalia's opportunity to paint the prince exposed her to an established social group called the Marlborough House Set, sometimes just termed "the smart set." The prince founded this group in 1869, and it became "a social clique of fashionable men and women that revolved around the course of Albert Edward, prince of Wales."[53] Though not a true political

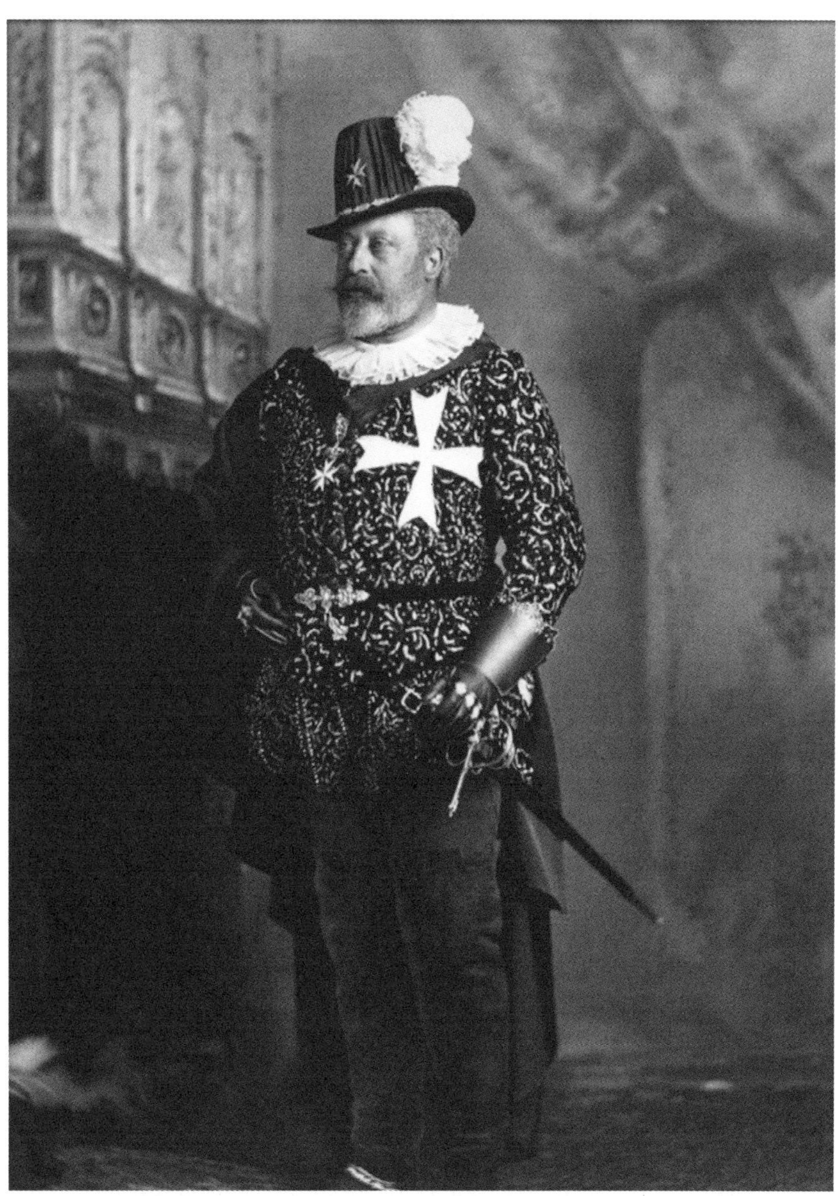

HRH Prince of Wales in his Malta costume for the Devonshire House Ball in 1897. The costume was used as a model for Amalia Kussner's miniature. © *The Victoria and Albert Museum, London. Used with permission.*

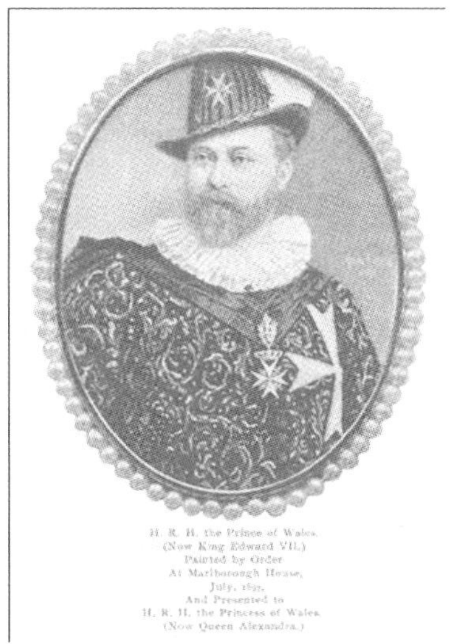

Miniature of the Prince of Wales by Amalia Kussner, as seen in "H.R.H. The Prince of Wales in the Costume of a Knight of Malta," *Century Magazine*, September 1900. *Courtesy of HathiTrust Digital Library*

governing body, those in this circle were aligned with the prince's positions, "especially on foreign policy and dynastic issues."[54] There were many men of wealth and standing, including those of English royalty, politicians, and businessmen, but women were allowed to be members also. Some of these women were known to have a "close association" with the prince.

The talents of the American miniaturist became well known in this group, which garnered many commissions for Amalia, either from the wives of the members or from the female members themselves. Those associated with the Marlborough House set whom she painted included Minnie Paget, Lady Alington (wife of the 1st Baron of Alington), Constance de Grey (wife of the 4th Earl of de Grey), Lady Naylor-Leyland (née Jennie Chamberlain), and last but not least the prince's mistress, Alice Keppel. It's important to note that when the Prince of Wales became Edward VII in 1901, upon Queen Victoria's death, his new court was formed with many members from the Marlborough House Set.[55] This might have further strengthened Amalia's position in London and reinforced how British society viewed her.

Her list of London luminaries that she painted also included those outside the prince's circle, such as Muriel Wilson, one of the most renowned beauties of the Edwardian period and an amateur actress.

Miss Muriel Wilson is probably one of the most admired "daughters of hostesses" in London. She is dark, with beautiful wavy hair, the softest of eyes, and a lovely colouring. There is not a more popular young lady in London.[56]

As in New York, Amalia always welcomed commissions from London's women of money, prestige, and beauty.

❧

While Amalia was establishing her business in New York and London, her brother in parallel was establishing his career as a music composer in Chicago. Albert's Opus 2, *Moon Moths*, was published in 1897 and dedicated to Amalia. This composition sold quite well, and by December of that year a second edition was printed.[57]

In the initial publication, the sheet music included one of the then-famous photographs of Amalia (see color insert) by London photographer Alfred Ellis, with lovely, romantic printing at the bottom. A later printing of the music's cover had an art nouveau design by E. Mulier (see color insert), which matched the green and yellow colors of the actual moon or luna moth.[58]

Albert's Chicago connections would lead to a number of commissions for Amalia, including the Philip Danforth Armour family, owners of the premier meat-packing company of the late nineteenth century. She painted Mrs. Philip D. Armour twice, with one portrait cited as being done in 1894, while visiting her brother in Chicago.[59]

❧

Aside from her miniatures traveling between city and summer residences, one of her works accompanied a man on an adventure to find his fortunes. *The Atlanta Constitution* recounted a journey that took one miniature far from where Amalia had painted it on the East Coast. She

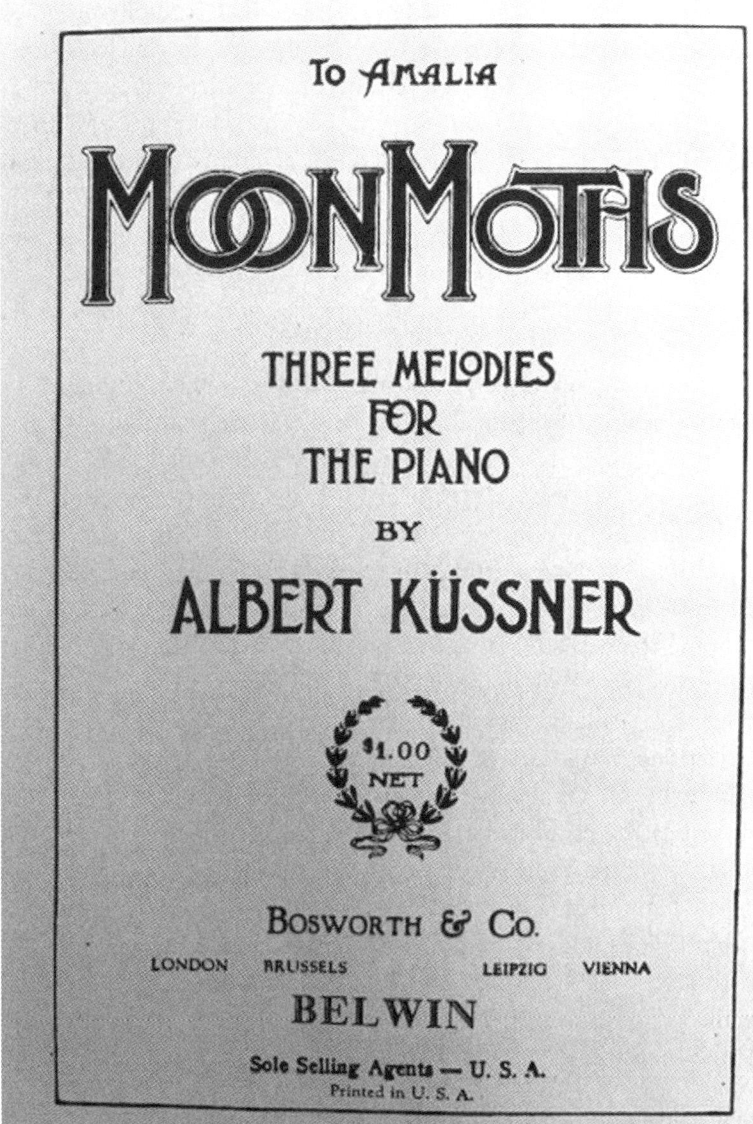

Moon Moths sheet music with Albert's dedication to Amalia. *Author's collection*

painted a young woman named Dolly, whose portrait was set in a frame of turquoise. Dolly's true love, Jack, got the gold rush fever and left his Washington, DC, job as a civil servant. He headed out at the start of the

Alaska Gold Rush in the spring of 1897. Before he left, Dolly provided him with her miniature, a keepsake to remember her by that was small enough to travel across the country with his other critical supplies. It was recorded of Jack's time in Alaska: "His companions during this stay there were not the devil's servants—women, wine, cigarettes and cards—but instead, a miniature by Amalia Kussner."[60]

Jack eventually returned, with riches from his expedition, and was reunited with Dolly. This story emphasizes how miniatures were always seen both as tokens of affection and as keepsakes or status symbols easily taken on travels.

Amalia not only provided her portraits to the women in New York City, but also traveled to paint them at their preferred summer destination, Newport, Rhode Island. Specifically, it was recorded that Amalia had a commission to paint Mrs. Oliver H. P. Belmont (the former Alva Vanderbilt) late in the summer of 1896. The painting (see color insert) likely took place in Newport, as Alva and her new husband had just returned from Europe and resided for the summer at Belcourt, "their country home thereafter."[61] A second portrait was done in early 1897 at Mrs. Belmont's New York home at 24 E. 72nd Street.[62]

Evidence of Amalia's popularity in Newport in the 1890s appears in a novel titled *The Décadents: A Story of Blackwell's Island and Newport*, written by C. W. de Lyon Nichols and published in 1899. The novel describes the estate belonging to the fictional family of Mr. and Mrs. Josiah Singleton Yeoman, whose fortunes started with earlier generations in the New York tannery business. Their estate, called "The Pillars," has the prestigious address of Bellevue Avenue, bordering on the Cliff Walk with a view of the Atlantic Ocean. Amalia's works were included in a detailed description of the fine belongings found in the reception room of the mansion.

> Amid chairs inlaid with brass and red tortoise shell were disposed Renaissance stools, while near by stood a buhlwork cabinet, beside a Verni Martin one, and furnishings from the Ottoman empire, such as one could see on this side of the Atlantic only in the Turkish room of the handsomest, costliest and best appointed hotel in the world—the

Waldorf-Astoria. Other articles of virtù were ranged here and there in bewildering prodigality—Tiffany favrille glass butterflies lighting on lamp shades, a coppó de monté plate near a jade snuff box, a collection of Amalie [*sic*] Kussner's miniatures beside an Egyptian obelisk of Lilliputian dimensions; a piece of Royal Meisen chafing against a field glass of quaint pattern, a trophy of our war with Spain, just sent on from the captured Spanish warship, the Christobal Colon at the victory of the destruction of Admiral Cervera's fleet in the harbor of Santiago de Cuba on July 3d.[63]

⚮

By early 1899, Amalia was very well established both in New York and London and had truly become a sought-after artist by the elite on both sides of the Atlantic. An 1896 New York article even stated she "might be called painter to the 400."[64]

Amalia's now extensive success emboldened her to demand certain standards as far as how her materials would be displayed. At a New York portrait exhibition held in late 1898 at the National Academy of Design, she claimed to be "offended by the unfavorable conditions in which her work was to be shown."[65] Her abrupt withdrawal from the show was also documented in a *New York Times* article:

[The] recent withdrawal of her miniatures from the exhibition is much regretted by the committee. It was due to a misunderstanding which it is claimed could easily have been adjusted had there been less haste in Miss Kussner's actions.[66]

In another New York newspaper, Amalia further explained her reasoning in abruptly removing the objects:

"After removing them I realized that I really had no legal right to do so," said Miss Kussner last night, "but I felt so outraged at the slight shown to my art that I could not help acting as I did. I do not complain especially of the place where my miniatures were hung, for I think mine were perhaps the best placed of any. What I do resent is the fact that the miniatures were placed in a room which has heretofore not been con-sidered fit for anything but photographs. By daylight nothing can be seen there because of the glare and at night because of the darkness."[67]

There is an implied dislike of photography, which at the time was certainly in competition with miniatures. The article further supports this: "she considers that her branch of art has been slighted in placing the examples of it in a poorly lighted room, where their beauties cannot be appreciated."

However, around the same time a visual testament to her accomplish-ments was seen in 1898 in the *New York Journal and Advertiser*, owned by William Randolph Hearst. It was entitled "Great Beauties of London and New York by Miss Amalia Kussner, the Famous Miniature Painter" (hereafter referred to as the "Great Beauties collection"; see color insert) and featured fifteen of Amalia's miniatures. Such supplement sections "featured colorful layouts and covered sporting events, pseudoscience, and popular culture."[68] The format and content of these pages were expressly designed to bring in readership, since Hearst was in competition with another local New York newspaper.

The fifteen women's portraits displayed were done by Amalia over a five-year period, and each was either associated with American wealth or English nobility. The collection included dollar heiress Minnie Paget; a soon-to-be dollar heiress, Miss May Goelet; and a noblewoman, Lady Sophie Scott. Those from New York included various names that would be found on the Four Hundred list, such as Mrs. Van Rensselaer Cruger, wife of Civil War officer and well-known New York businessman Ste-phen Van Rennselaer Cruger.

The display of these portraits was further accented by a detailed background of tile patterns framing each oval. Possibly to align with the British connection of four of these women, the center portrait of Miss Atherton Blight was bordered by two lions in profile, very reminiscent of designs found on European coats of arms.

The Great Beauties collection followed a previous display in the same newspaper a year earlier that had highlighted Amalia's accomplishments and her triumphant return from England, late in 1897. Featured at the

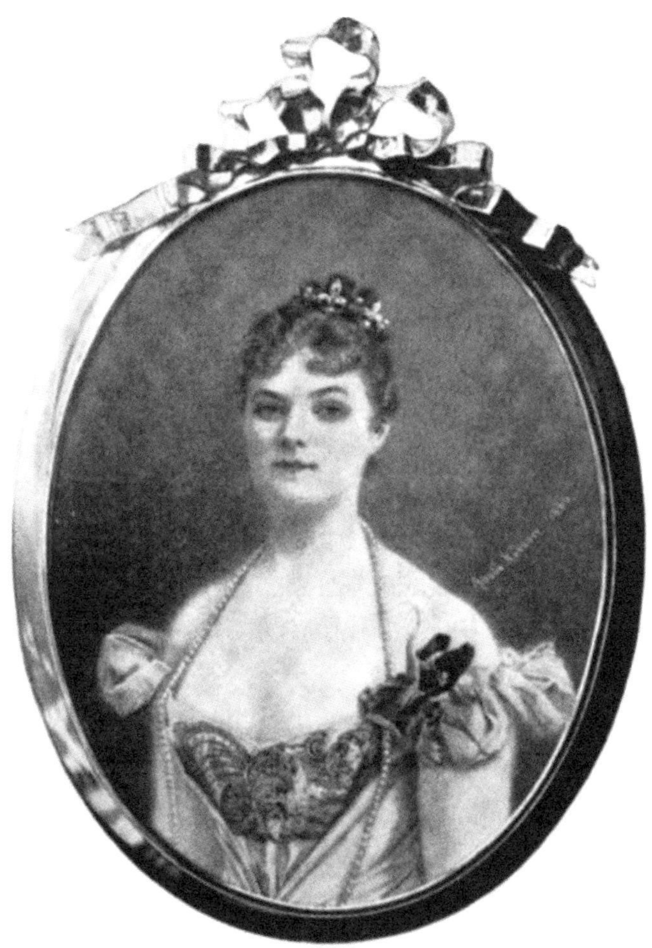

Miniature of Mrs. Van Rensselaer Cruger by Amalia Kussner, as seen in "Modern Miniature Painting," *Munsey's Magazine*, December 1894.

top of the page were five miniatures she had painted in England, all of well-to-do women or those of nobility, and "all belonging to the charmed circle known as the 'Prince of Wales' Set."[69] Since this newspaper coverage was part of the campaign to increase sales, it is easy to state that Amalia was of keen interest to those in New York at the time.

Looking back on Amalia's career at this point, she existed in her world as a singular person. Rarely would any family members be mentioned in the stories of her rising career. In published accounts, there are only very few references to the exposure she received from Mrs. Havemeyer, and none to Alice Fischer. This further supported the mythology of her being a young prodigy who, through incredible efforts, reached this level of success and fame alone.

Nor were any assistants mentioned, even though she likely would have had at least one or two to handle the "business" side of her artwork. No matter where she traveled prior to her marriage, it was her and her alone. It was certainly an accepted—and to some degree a necessary—practice for well-to-do women at that time to travel with a maid. Society did not view well a woman traveling alone, without a chaperone along to ward off the unwanted advances of men. And Amalia could have easily afforded a maid to assist with the daily dressing and all the other tasks involved in her many travels.[70]

There is one documented exception, in her passport application filed in February 1899, which listed a maid, Isabel Walker. But record of the maid's name or even mention of the role of a maid is never seen again.

∽o∾

With Amalia's artistic accomplishments in New York and London, this could have been the zenith of her career, but she had her sights set on painting even more prestigious persons and on traveling beyond the confines of these cities. She would have those opportunities in the last year of the nineteenth century.

CHAPTER 3

Techniques and Commissions

IN EXAMINING THE POPULARITY OF AMALIA KUSSNER WITH SO MANY OF the New York elite and European royalty, what were her artistic strengths and appeal?

"Miss Kussner Learned the Trick of Drapery" declared the heading of an 1898 newspaper.[1] Indeed, the most distinctive feature of her miniatures was the style in which she posed her subjects. She would wrap their upper bodice in a variety of fabrics, such as silk and tulle, usually in an off-the-shoulder fashion. This use of her signature "wrap," or "drapery," started to be recorded in newspapers as early as 1894. Of the fifteen women portrayed in the 1898 Great Beauties collection of portraits, at least nine of the poses use the "wrap" technique (see color insert). For instance, the miniature of Mrs. Frank Tilford, which is seen in the top row (portrait number fourteen), shows a wrap of satin-like fabric with the layers fastened just below her left shoulder with a cluster of silk flowers.

An 1895 article giving early praise for the revival of the miniature style featured a miniature of Mrs. Lorillard Spencer, another early advocate of Amalia in New York City shortly after Mrs. Havemeyer.[2] In this portrait, Amalia not only used her drapery style, but also has the cloth seemingly trail off to the right, as if floating. This makes the portrait more reminiscent of Baroque paintings of gods and goddesses that were typically shown draped in rich fabrics.

As Amalia brought her signature style over to the English women, she was at first met with some resistance to her more provocative styling seen in the American miniatures. The British women's preferred fashion

41

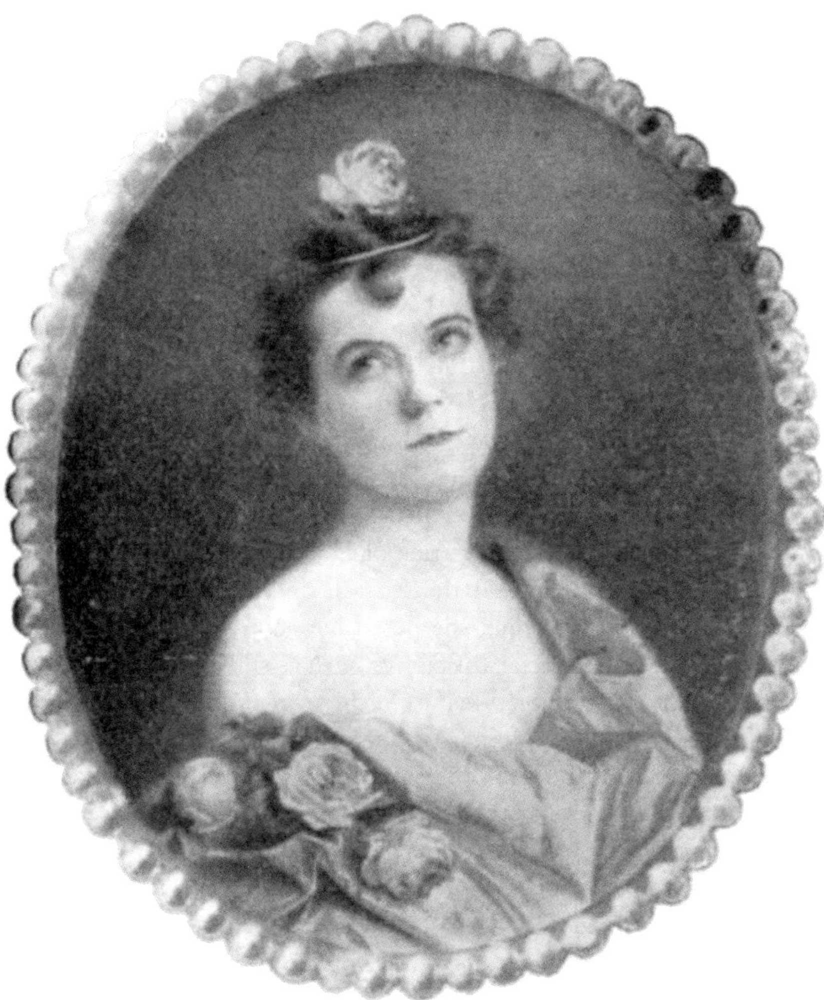

Miniature of Mrs. Frank Tilford by Amalia Kussner, as seen in "Modern Miniature Painting," *Munsey's Magazine*, December 1894.

for these portraits was to be painted without jewelry and with a more modest use of fabric, rebelling against the "décolleté dress."[3] Eventually, with much effort, Amalia was able to persuade them to accept her approach and have their necks and shoulders exposed, assuring them that for women "there is nothing as beautiful as skin."[4] Some also accepted

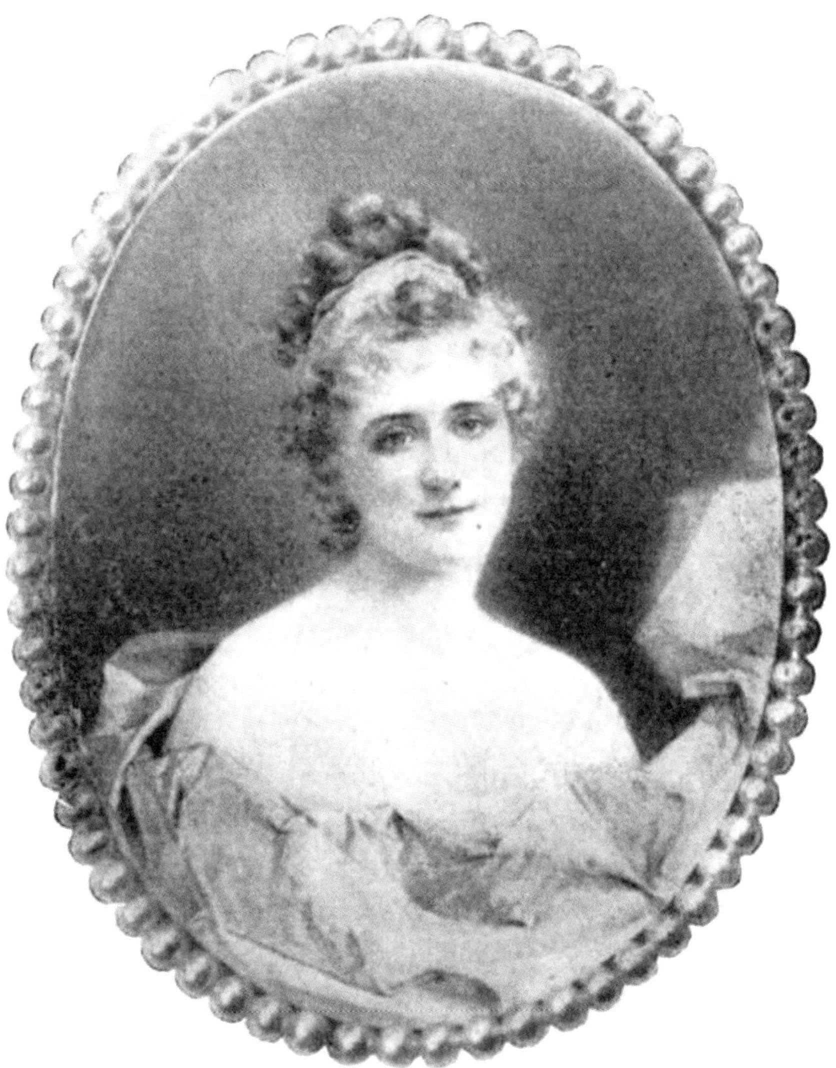

Miniature of Mrs. Lorillard Spencer by Amalia Kussner, as seen in "Modern Miniature Painting," *Munsey's Magazine*, December 1894.

displaying their jewelry and using those pieces as fasteners for the layers of fabric, as was done with American women.

Proof of Amalia's persuasion that English women accepted her styling techniques appeared in *Elite Magazine* out of Chicago in 1896:

All her sitters wear picturesque garments—now a mantle clasped on shoulders with gems, or a drapery that, indefinite as it may be, suggests a Romney or Gainsborough style.[5]

Romney and Gainsborough were part of the eighteenth-century group of painters who produced the "British grand manner portraits."[6] The use of fabrics was seen in Romney's early career, with his "bright colour and precocious skill with drapery."[7]

Elite Magazine also documented her "styling" techniques popular on both sides of the Atlantic:

Perhaps a little of Miss Kussner's success is due to her talent for dress. . . . She imagines for her sitters a wreathing of airy, fairy white tulle caught together and held down with roses.[8]

When women came to her studio for their sittings, Amalia would provide "costumes and draperies" for them to choose from—if they were adventurous enough to do so.[9] One of her more fascinating uses of the wrap was with Lady Feodorovna Sturt, whose husband was "the Hon. Humphrey Sturt, eldest son of Baron Alington" and also a member of Parliament.[10] Amalia chose to drape her in pink curtain fabric from the lady's own home as part of a 1902 portrait. This had to have been a heavy rich fabric of velvet or even a brocade.

Her depiction of these fabrics could vary greatly in the finished portrait—from an exacting rendering of the fabric's texture and color to a more diaphanous approach, with just the edges of the fabric highlighted and using likely a semi-transparent tulle.

This use of sheer fabric is especially evident in the portrait of Leila Hardie Moore (see color insert), with her shoulders visible, and a white bow in her hair and a matching bow at her bodice. Similar sheer fabric wrap is seen on a miniature of an earlier portrait of Lady Feodorovna (1897).

Amalia even dressed herself in this style, as can be seen in one of the classic photographs of her used in the *Moon Moths* sheet music (see color insert). She is wrapped in what appears to be tulle, and her lap is

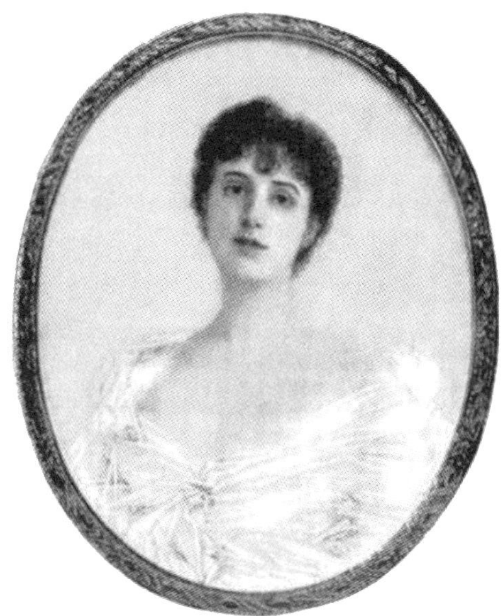

Miniature of Lady Feodorovna Sturt (later Lady Alington) by Amalia Kussner (1896), as seen in "Types of Fair Women," *Munsey's Magazine*, June 1897.

covered by some sort of striped fabric, which could even have been a thin tablecloth.

Many of her American—and later her British—subjects wanted to display their fine jewels and pearls as symbols of their wealth and status, and Amalia was only too glad to oblige. This can be seen in Mrs. Astor's portrait (see page 26), with the large oval gemstones, and in the portrait of her daughter Mrs. Orme Wilson (née Carrie Astor), with the dominant and elaborate necklace.

These ladies' fine jewelry could also serve the purpose of fasteners and holding the draped layers of fabric together. This is shown in the mid-1890s miniature of Mrs. (Mary) William L. Scott, in which a sapphire and diamond piece of jewelry is securing the layer of a fabric wrap described as a rose silk stole.[11] The miniature shows just a segment from a larger necklace designed for Mrs. Scott by the jewelry house of Cartier, using Kashmir sapphires. The stunning necklace was actually designed in connecting pieces that could be used in multiple ways, including as a bracelet or as a shorter necklace.

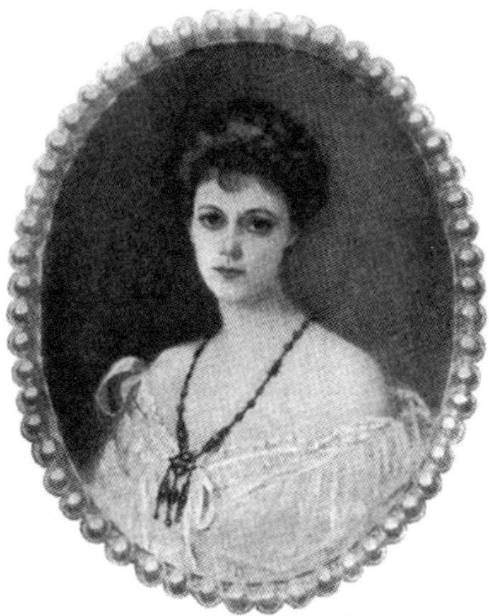

Miniature of Mrs. Orme Wilson (née Carrie Astor) by Amalia Kussner (ca. 1897), as seen in "Amalia Kussner's Miniatures of the Astor Family," *The House Beautiful*, September 1901.

Amalia's technique of using jewelry as a fastener is also seen in the portrait of Mrs. Havemeyer, which was wonderfully detailed in the *Chicago Inter Ocean* newspaper:

> In the miniature of Mrs. Theodore Havemeyer the artist had instilled into her work an atmosphere as regal as that of any pictured queen among the antique miniatures. The soft mass of velvet draped across the bust is of a rare coral, changeful in its luster, and held in place by a band of rubies, emeralds, sapphires, diamonds and pearls, which are so faithfully reproduced in the portrait as to defy the attempts of the eye to detect the lack of shimmer and sheen of real gems.[12]

Another clever trick to secure the drapery was the use of silk flowers, often attached at the midpoint along the neckline. This was a fashion accent but also would hide fasteners used to hold together the folds of fabric. One or more silk flowers were often prominent on the front of the

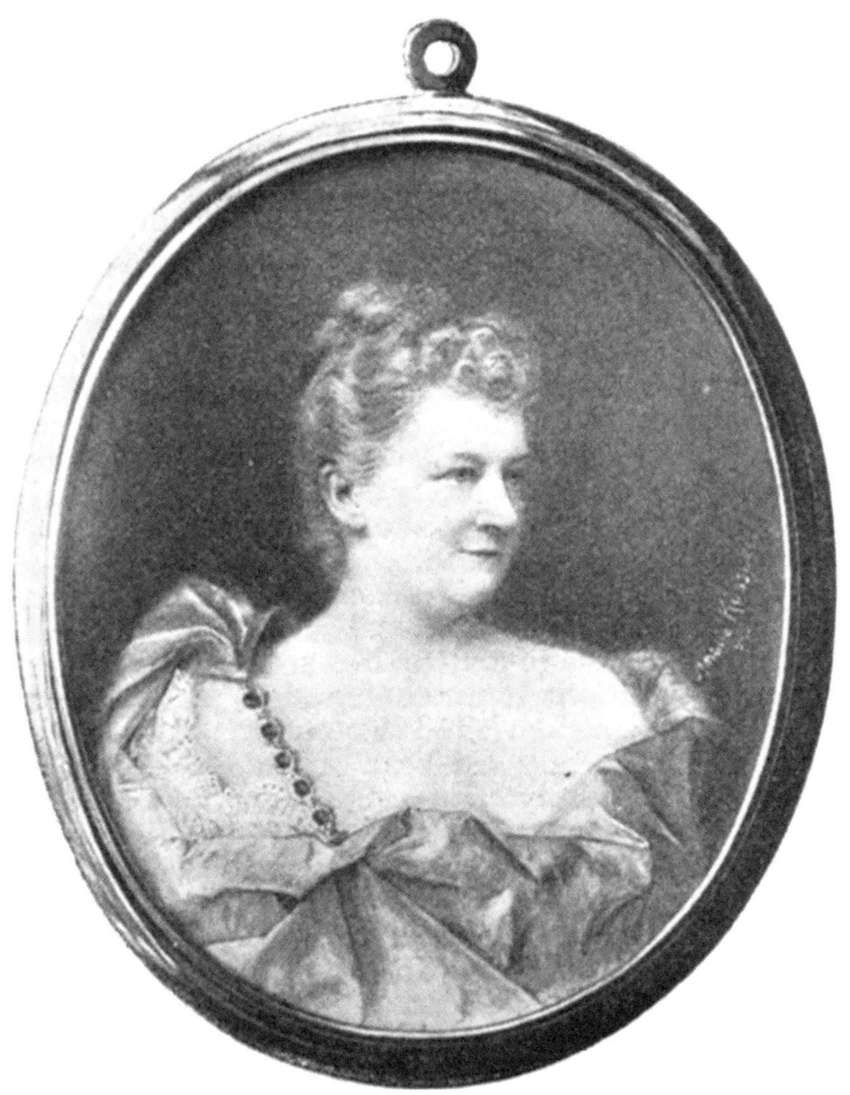

Miniature of Mrs. Richard H. Townsend (née Mary Scott), showing her necklace used as a fastener, by Amalia Kussner (ca. 1894), as seen in "A Painter of Miniatures," *Ladies Home Journal*, October 1895.

women's bodices. As an example, Minnie Paget "is pictured with a veil of tulle about her shoulders, fastened with a cluster of pink roses."[13]

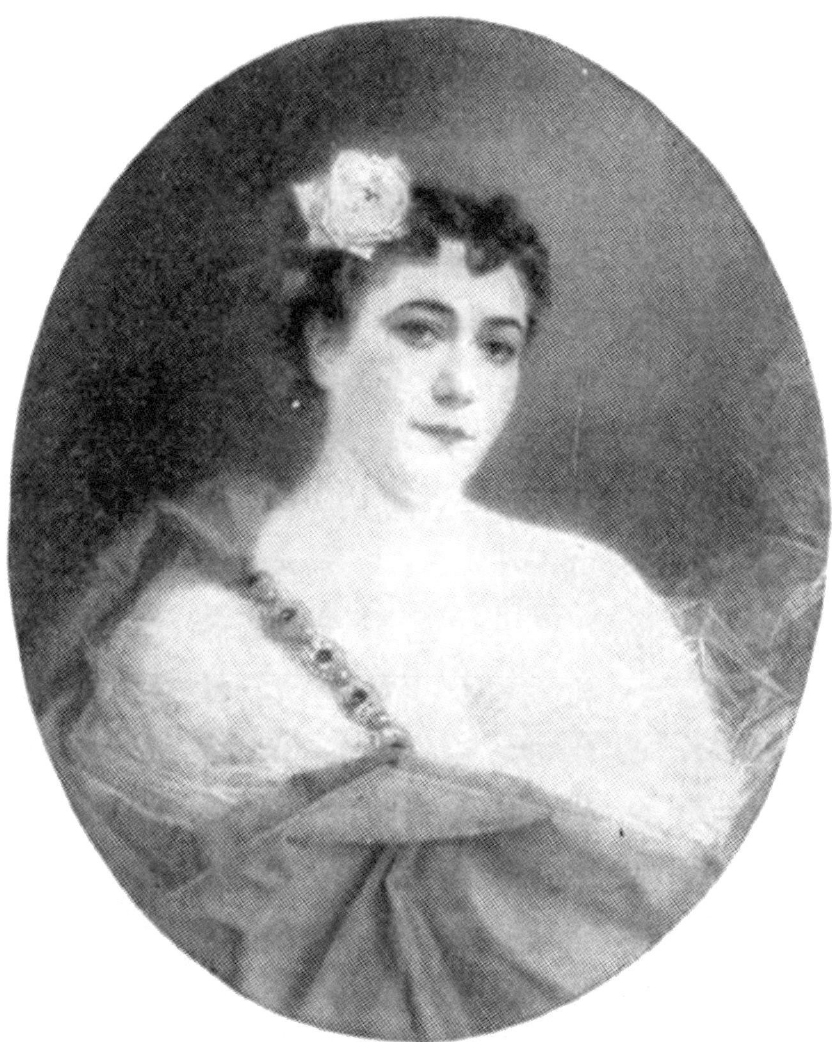

Photo of Mrs. Theodore Havemeyer showing her jewelry being used as a clasp (ca. 1894), as seen in "Modern Miniature Painting," *Munsey's Magazine*, December 1894.

* * *

How faithfully Amalia painted her subjects could vary greatly. Both through her own artistic decisions and likely based on particular requests

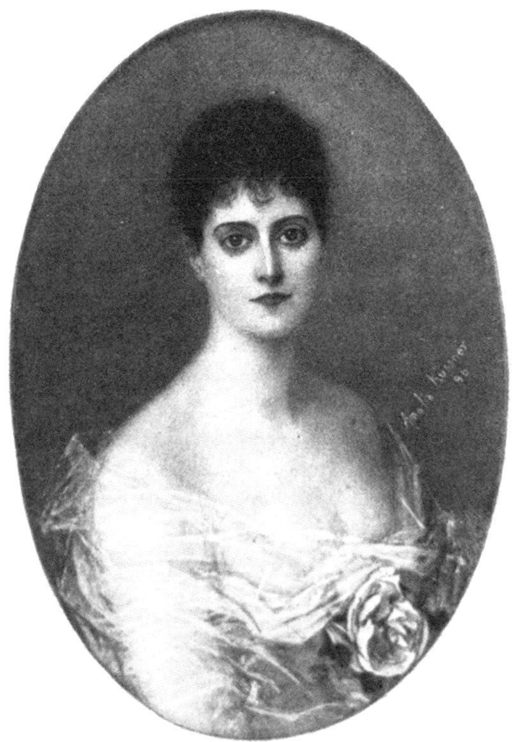

Miniature of Minnie Paget by Amalia Kussner (ca. 1896), as seen in "Amalia Kussner Coudert," *Ainslee's Magazine*, May 1902.

from those who sat for her, she often did enhance their looks. But there are numerous examples, in looking at photos contemporaneous with the portraits, that show Amalia fairly accurately captured her subjects' images.

In looking at the face of Mrs. John W. Mackay in a photograph from 1895, there is a good likeness of her prominent eyes and rounded face in the portrait done by Amalia.

Amalia had a long association with Mrs. Louise Mackay, whose husband's great wealth in part came from mining ventures and his telegraph company.[14] Mrs. Mackay spent much of her time in Paris and London, hosting lavish soirées, which might have helped Amalia's business.[15] Amalia helped create a unique gift for the bride at her son's wedding in 1898: she painted a series of miniatures small enough to be

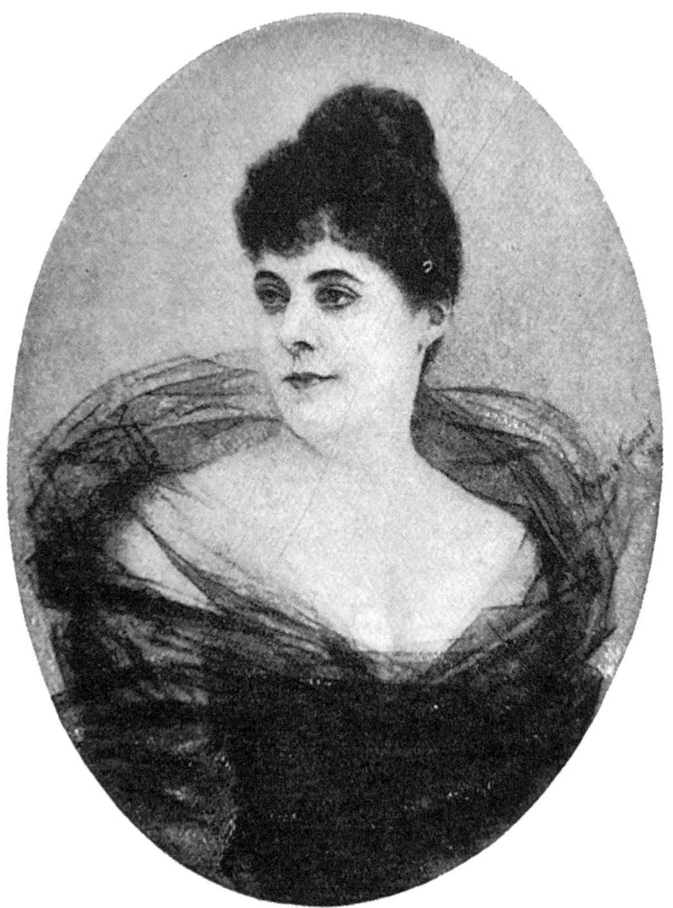

Photo of the miniature of Mrs. Mackay by Amalia Kussner (ca. 1900), as seen in the US edition of *The Book of Beauty*, edited by Mrs. F. Harcourt Williamson (J. B. Lippincott & Co., 1902). Author's Collection. Photo by Edward Ray

used as charms on a bracelet.[16] These charms were connected with gold links, and the miniature ovals were surrounded by diamonds.

In comparing Amalia's front-facing portrait of Mrs. Perry Belmont to a profile photograph, the miniature done in 1899 accurately captures her profile and eyes. Also visible is the classic wrap, with possibly a silk flower in the center.

Amalia was sent a thank you note from Mrs. Belmont's husband:

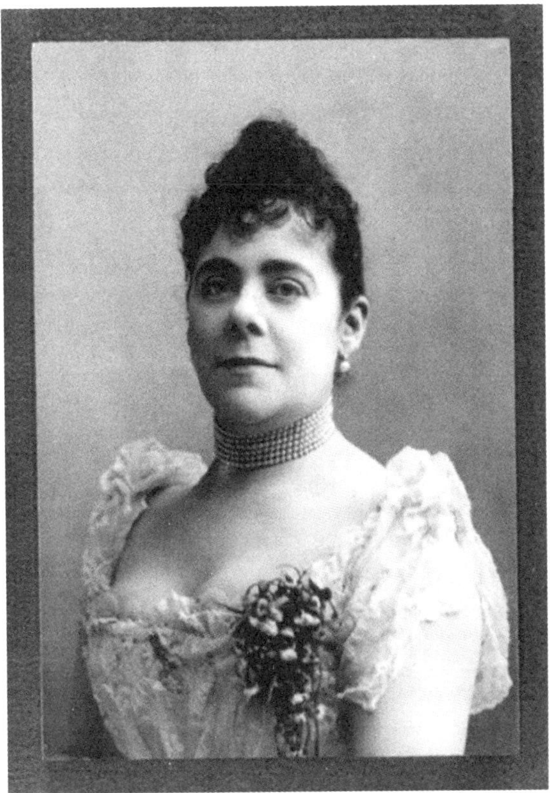

Photo of Mrs. John W. Mackay (Louise Hungerford Mackay) (1895). *Creative Commons, courtesy of user Djmaschek*

My Dear Miss Kussner,

I am delighted with the lovely miniature of my wife which is by far the best likeness of her that has been done, and we are most grateful to you for it—Believe me.

Very sincerely yours,
Perry Belmont[17]

A complimentary description of the Duchess of Marlborough's pose is documented in *The Delineator* magazine and describes how

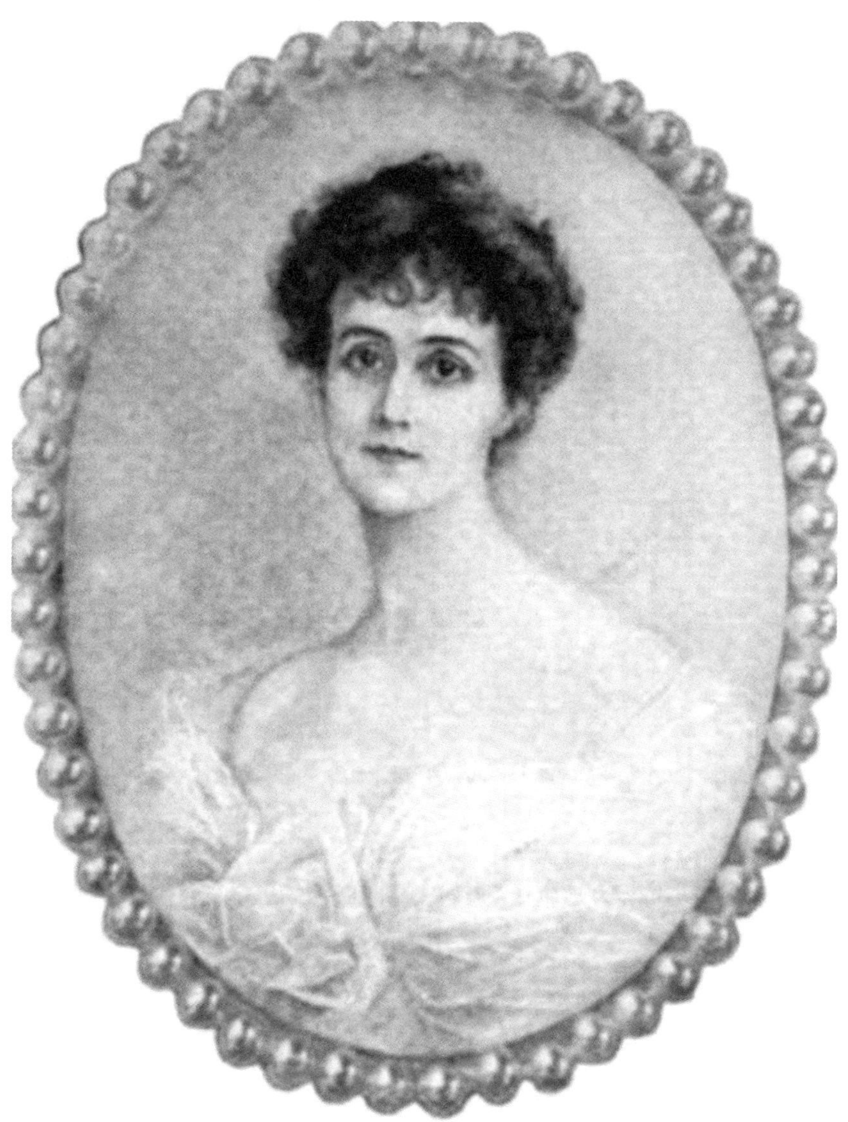

Miniature of Mrs. Perry Belmont by Amalia Kussner (ca. 1897), as seen in "Amalia Kussner Coudert," *Ainslee's Magazine*, May 1902.

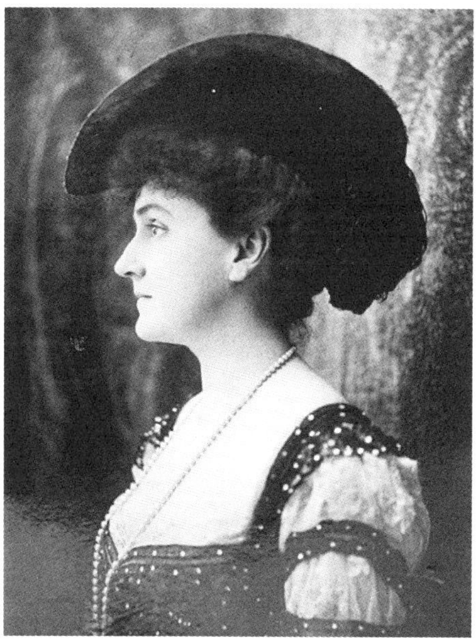

Photo of Mrs. Perry Belmont (ca. 1900). *Bain Collection, Bain News Service, Library of Congress*

Amalia clearly captured both the woman's wistful personality and long, swan-like neck:

> A charming portrait is of the young Duchess of Marlborough, formerly Miss Consuelo Vanderbilt. She is represented looking over her shoulder, and the pose of her head and slender neck is very graceful. She wears a white ribbon, and a white ribbon is twisted in her dark hair.[18]

The portrait matches a lovely black and white photo done of the duchess.

A description of Lillian Russell's painting highlights Amalia's skill at capturing the subject's features:

> Of the examples of Miss Kussner's skill that come under my observation, a miniature of Lillian Russell is, perhaps, the most notable, by reason of its perfection of portraiture and its qualities of technical adroitness.[19]

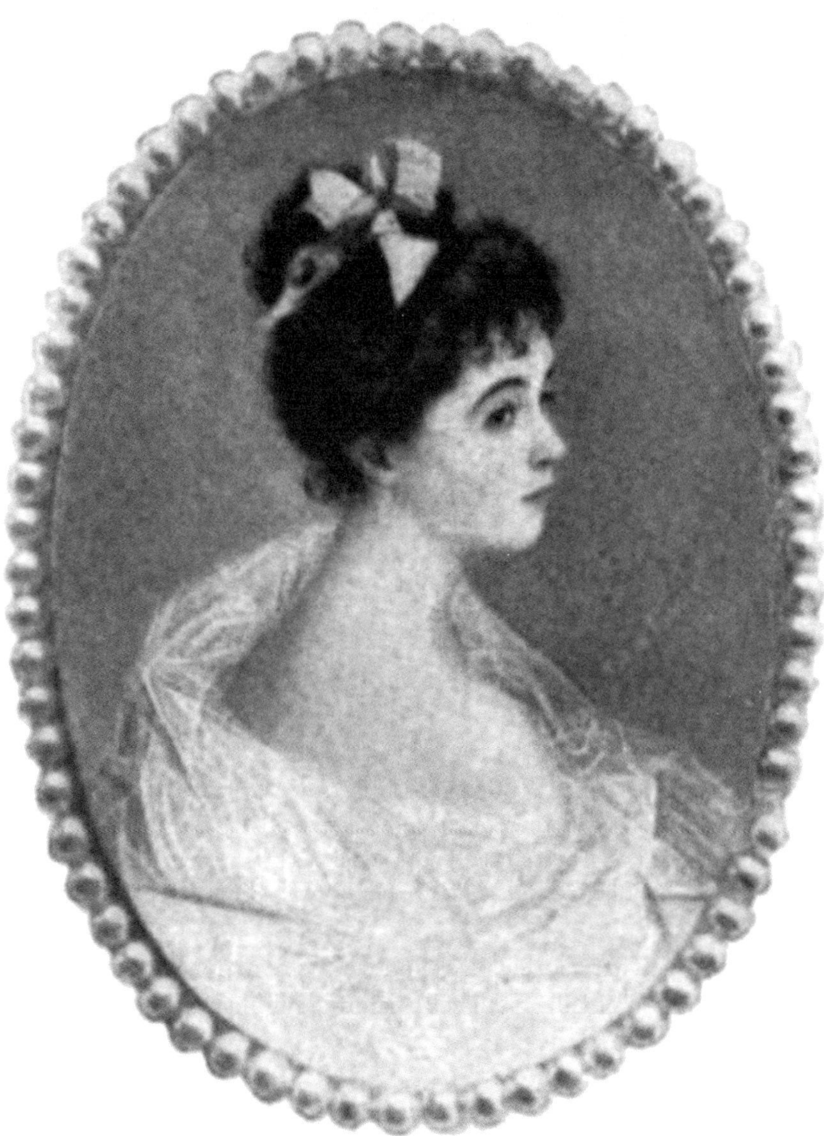

Miniature of the Duchess of Marlborough (née Consuelo Vanderbilt) by Amalia Kussner (1896), as seen in "Amalia Kussner Coudert—Miniaturist," *Ainslee's Magazine*, May 1902.

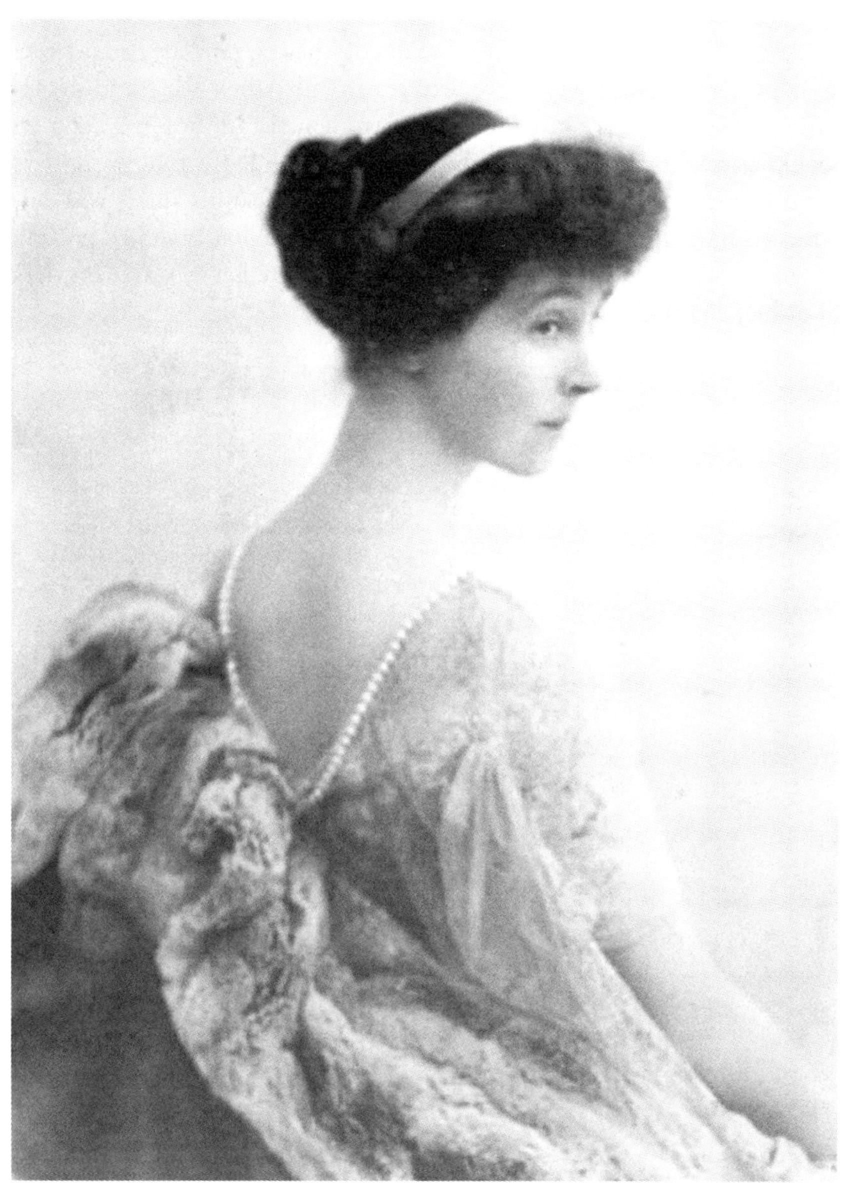

Photographic portrait of Consuelo Vanderbilt, Lady Spencer-Churchill, Duchess of Marlborough, by an unknown photographer (ca. 1900–1905). *Creative Commons Attribution-Share Alike 4.0 International license, courtesy of user Thyra*

Though many of her portraits are of impressive quality and good representations of their subjects, Amalia did have a tendency sometimes to darken her sitters' eyes too much or to render their faces and figures rather indistinct. Certainly, having her women sitting in semi-darkness would cause their eyes to catch the light and become the more dominant focal point, but she at times overly accented this feature, and it was detrimental to the portrait. This can be seen in the previously shown portrait of Mrs. Havemeyer with the jewelry fastener, where her eyes are very dark and there is little else defined about her face.

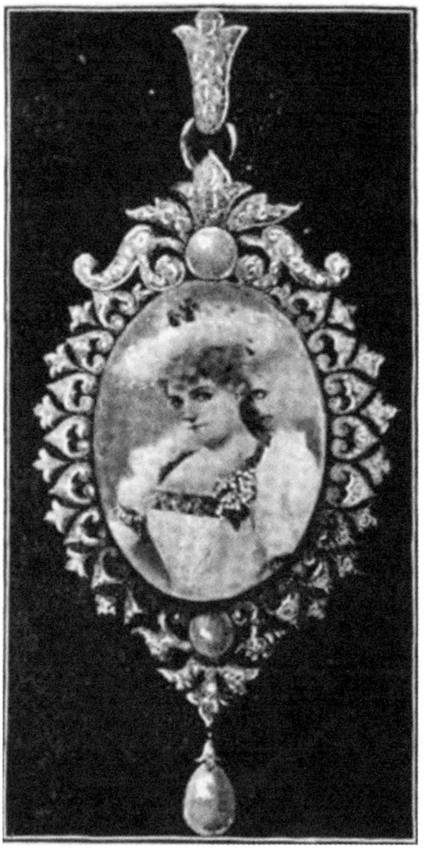

Miniature of Lillian Russell by Amalia Kussner (1893), encased in an ornate frame, as seen in "Of A Certain Painter-In-Little," *Illustrated American*, April 1893.

Amalia's studio had a secluded corner with a place for the women to sit and pose against a background of satin cloth in green and blue.[20] Her finished portraits usually have a nondescript background using shaded variations of a soft, pastel color, but no discernable patterns or shapes. In a portrait of May Goelet, "a cloud of white tulle is about her shoulders, and in her hair is a scarlet ribbon. The background is pale yellow,"[21] an appropriate choice of pastel to frame the white fabric used in the wrap.

In describing the miniature of Lady Naylor-Leyland (née Jennie Chamberlain from Ohio) done by Amalia: "Her fair shoulders are enveloped in tulle. She wears no ornaments, and her brown hair is worn high. The background of blue seems to accentuate her deep-blue eyes,"[22] artfully highlighting her most striking facial feature.

And one cannot overlook not only how the miniatures captured the spirit of her subjects, but also how this artwork needed to convey their prominent roles in society. In three of her Astor family miniatures, Amalia "has caught and given to the personality of her subjects, to the light that radiates from within them, to eye and mouth and ear and pose of head, the unmistakable sign of the patrician," wrote *The House Beautiful* in 1901.[23]

Each of the three portraits referred to in this article shows the artist's trademark features of the wrap and jewelry: Mrs. John Jacob Astor in a profiled wrap pose, with a prominent silk flower in the center; Mrs. Astor (Caroline) in a wrap pose and the silk flower off her right shoulder; and Mrs. Orme Wilson (née Carrie Astor) in an off-the-shoulder wrap with lace and again with a prominent piece of jewelry overlapping the fabric. In these three portraits, Amalia highlights only the edges of the fabric and leaves the texture undefined, making it hard to discern what type of fabric was used—be it tulle or satin.

The decision of how her subjects were ultimately draped and posed wouldn't occur until after the required introductory meeting with her subjects. Amalia used this initial time to both learn their portrait requirements and to understand their personalities, which would influence her composition. She would not only study at length the physical features of her subjects but also try to obtain a more detailed and intimate sense of their personalities. In an 1898 interview, she revealed: "I am absolutely absorbed in the personality of my sitter. I study her, think of her, actually dream of her until the miniature is done."[24]

She usually needed four to six sessions to complete a portrait. Sometimes, if her subject became unavailable, she would use a photo of them to complete the work, though this was a rare occurrence, especially with her dislike of photography.

For the exacting technical aspect of her painting, she often would use brushes with only three to six bristles in order to "make strokes so fine that most of the painting must be done under a magnifying glass. . . . the smallest mistake may destroy the characteristic translucence that constitutes the miniature's greatest charms."[25] Since she usually posed her subjects in semi-darkness, she herself would sit by a light source, such as a window. She was often quoted as saying that having her subjects in this soft light best accented their features.

Ivory was the preferred base for miniatures, but it was not the easiest medium to use. "Water painting on ivory required special talent as the untreated material is a little greasy and does not hold paint well," describes one historian. "Each artist developed a recipe for treating the ivory with chemicals, abrasion, and sunlight to prepare the surface to accept their uniquely processed water paint."[26]

After completing her miniature, the painted ivory was covered by a fine-quality glass shaped to fit over the piece and provide protection.[27] Many of these miniatures would later be placed in frames embellished with fine gems and intricate metalwork. Amalia was likely not part of that process, but it highlights the high regard the owners had for these miniatures. An example can be seen in the framed portrait of Lillian Russell from 1893 on page 56.

In examining Amalia's portraiture style, it is instructive to look at her paintings of the Strong family of Erie, New York, likely done around 1894, of a father, mother, and daughter, and how her style differed with each family member. Charles Hamot Strong was a model Gilded Age businessman, with interests in the coal industry, the local railroads, publishing, and even the new technology of electricity. Their stunning mansion was actually inherited by his wife, Annie Wainright Scott, upon her father's passing. They made the mansion their home, and their only child, a daughter, was born in 1881. Given that Amalia painted all three family members, for convenience she probably would have traveled to stay at their residence in Erie for the duration of the commission.[28]

This mansion was located on the edge of what was referred to as "Millionaires Row" and had a staff of forty to fifty servants. The soirées held by the Strongs were said to rival those of New York City. And given Charles Hamot Strong's connections, the family hosted three presidents: Teddy Roosevelt, William Taft (Charles's former Yale classmate), and Grover Cleveland.[29] Mrs. Strong, who clearly lived a lavish lifestyle, was also instrumental in donating funds to start a nursing college in Erie. She, like many other wealthy women of the Gilded Age, practiced *noblesse oblige*: the feeling that they had a responsibility to those less fortunate.

The miniature of the father (see color insert) is every bit the visage of a Gilded Age tycoon, with his determined stare and strong chin jutting out over his suitcoat. There are very few surviving examples of Amalia's portraits of men, and this is one of the best. This miniature, along with those of the rest of the family, also shows her artist's signature, prominent on the right side of each painting. Although good marketing, this trademark can be a visual distraction from her otherwise fine works.

The miniature of his wife (see color insert) is far more regal and surprisingly revealing. The wrap approach for her is distinctive, appearing to be a satin fabric topped with ermine fur. White ermine fur, with its black accents from the animal's tail, was widely used by royalty to adorn their cloaks and robes, dating back to medieval times. To dress in this manner during the Gilded Age was a perfect example of how those at the higher echelons of society wanted to be considered the royalty of America. The mid-1890s also saw ermine documented as an accent piece and "in better taste" for women's evening attire.[30] Ermine was also used as a "smart" fashion trim on the cuffs of carriage coats.[31]

On the lower right of Annie's bodice is the slight hint of her bosom. The fur and fabric seem to be only held up by the back of her chair and her arms in the front—no visible clasps or strategically placed flowers appear in this painting. It is interesting to note that Mrs. Strong was the sister of Mrs. Richard Townsend (née Mary Scott), who had the wrap with the exquisite sapphire necklace as a clasp (see page 47). The portraits of these women were done within two years of each other. In Annie's portrait, however, she is wearing no jewelry except for a long string of pearls intertwined among the golden curls on the top of her head.

In looking at an enlargement of her face (see color insert), Amalia showed impressive precision in the painting of the individual strands of Annie's hair and even in how realistic her eyes appear. The physical size of this enlargement is approximately one inch by one inch, which makes the exactness of the much smaller original even more remarkable. A faithful copy of this miniature is listed as one of Amalia's pieces that was on display at London's Royal Academy collection in 1896.[32]

Finally, their daughter, Matilda (see color insert), a young teenager at the time, is shown wearing a more modest dress, rather than the ethereal wraps used on the women subjects. Something about the tilt of her head and her pursed lips suggests she may not have enjoyed these sittings and was restless. Sometime later, Amalia did a second portrait of Matilda as a young adult (see color insert).

Amalia painted very few men; when she did, it was usually as part of a family commission, rather than single portraits. In one instance, her rendering of a gentleman of wealth (see color insert)—possibly Richard Townsend—renders his features almost effeminate; his eyes appear especially delicate, which is not natural for male features.

◦◦◦

Another important aspect of Amalia's approach as an artist was how she presented herself as an individual. She dressed as though she belonged in a class above how society then would have placed her—not as an artist, with possibly plainer clothes, but assuming the role of an equal, with very expensive and fashionable outfits. A description of her fashion style was published in a Chicago newspaper, which listed every accessory in great detail:

> A closely fitting tailor-made gown of pale fawn colored cloth, over which was a big collar of white cloth and silver bullion embroidery.

. . . and the picture hat of black velvet and plumes was tilted just the least bit. Her shoes were black patent leather, and her gloves were white suede. The short cape, which completed the costume, was a fluffy mass of black chiffon, and had a great bunch of real violets pinned at the throat.[33]

She was also documented as wearing gowns designed by Charles Frederick Worth, of the famous House of Worth line.[34] One of its lavish stores was in Paris, and "women of means" traveled there from America and from all over Europe. Worth was "one of the premier fashion designers of the Gilded Age"[35] and was preferred by some of the Vanderbilt women.

Amalia also chose to be photographed for her magazine coverage by a somewhat avant-garde photographer, Jacob Schloss. He specialized in photographing women in the performing arts, including Alice Fischer. His posing of women was more exotic for the time, showing them in elaborate costumes and sometimes with provocative expressions. He would also adjust the photo development process to best display their skin tones.[36] The Schloss photograph of Amalia from *The New Peterson Magazine* (1896) shows her posed in front of a hanging drapery and standing with a confident posture, with a hand on her hip.[37] His portrayal of her was not a stilted Victorian image, but instead exuded her bold personality.

Even though Amalia chose to pursue a career, she did not want to be viewed in any way as part of the working class; rather, she wanted to be seen as on par with these high society women. Her approach might have further put her subjects at ease and encouraged conversation while she worked. Gauging by the multiple portraits she did of many of the same women—often three to four portraits of each—she most certainly had an approachable personality and must have been a good conversationalist.

And Amalia would have had to carefully navigate some of the many scandals that were going on in these well-to-do matrons' lives. As an example, she painted Alva Vanderbilt Belmont after the woman's divorce from William Kissam Vanderbilt and subsequent marriage to Mr. Oliver Hazard Perry Belmont in January 1896. Both these events were headlined in all the New York newspapers. Similarly, three years later Amalia would have had to refrain from any discussion of how the new Mrs. Perry Belmont had married Mr. Oliver Belmont's brother immediately after getting a divorce from Mr. Henry T. Sloane. The ink had barely dried on the legal paperwork when later that day "newly single" Jessie Robbins went to Connecticut to marry Perry Belmont. (Their marriage could not take place in New York, since she was found at fault in this case for her divorce and was forbidden to legally marry in that state again.[38]) Both of these divorces and remarriages were well-publicized scandals, and avoiding such topics in conversation during a sitting was a skill Amalia must have mastered.

In a Chicago interview, while visiting her family in October of 1895, she reflected on painting women in America: "They have an independent spirit that pleases me, and they pose with a freedom and abandon I can make much of."[39] That *abandon* she referenced can certainly be seen in the many portraits of women posing with gauzy fabrics precariously wrapped around them.

A master's thesis on the miniature's revival in America during Amalia's time highlighted the influences of "the decorative, fine and photographic arts" on the new style of miniatures.[40] Certainly Amalia had training in the decorative arts, having studied with Helen Minshall in Terre Haute during the 1880s. At an 1886 annual exhibit for Minshall's students, items defined as *decorative arts* not only included painting and drawings, but also embroidery, china painting, and decorations on linens.[41] Both Amalia and her sister Louise displayed their recent works of painted dinner plates and a painted silk pillow, respectively. The collection of items at this exhibit clearly included predominantly household items.

In summarizing Amalia's style, the use of the wrap in her portraits in some ways had influences from both decorative and fine arts. The less-defined use of diaphanous fabrics is more decorative, as it diverges from the restrictive miniature portraits seen prior to 1890 and their need to be in a more classic, European style. But some of her portraits do have a sense of the fine arts—such as the portrait of Annie Wainwright Scott Strong with the use of ermine fur and a more precise rendition of satin cloth. Not surprisingly, that miniature was one of the few that became part of a London Royal Academy collection in 1896.

Ultimately, both during Amalia's time and in the current art world, miniatures will always be seen as straddling the styles of decorative and fine arts.[42]

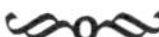

Amalia's commissions during the 1880s in Terre Haute started out modestly at forty dollars.[43] However, her commissions started quite high upon her entry into New York society. At first, her subjects were aghast at an essentially unknown artist asking for over three hundred dollars, which was seen then as the "upper end" for miniature costs. Yet Amalia was firm in her request early on of three hundred to five hundred dollars in 1894, and this amount would soon increase. A commission of five hundred dollars for a portrait in 1895 equates, using an inflation calculator, to over eighteen thousand dollars in 2024. In looking at her commissions over a five-year period, 1896 to 1901, her commissions doubled; she started to get one thousand dollars per portrait, and sometimes even above that, by 1901. This may have been due to her prestige in painting European royalty.

> She is personally liked in England, and when painting miniatures of the Countess of Warwick and the Duchess of Marlborough she was invited to stay at Warwick Castle and at Blenheim. She receives large amounts for her portraits.[44]

One article described Amalia's diminutive size and large commissions with a bit of humor, referring to "that little woman, who weighs less than 100 pounds, quietly plodding along with her brushes and banking a larger revenue each year than that for which our highest city officials fight and struggle."[45]

When she became the sought-after miniature portrait artist of London and was painting royalty and those of noble birth, many people assumed that her commissions would only be paid in jewelry or other costly items. Amalia took this as an insult and assured her followers that there were always payments of cash—though often there might have also been the extra trinket or two, such as the jewelry from the Prince of Wales. These *extra* gifts could have easily exceeded the cash value of her commissions.

In comparing her commissions to other miniaturists of that time, Amalia did indeed receive more than her fellow artists. The upper-end commission amount was three hundred dollars in the 1890s; her rates started there and were soon to appreciably increase. In a 1910 miniature exhibition of forty-four artists in New York, prices were listed in the show's catalogue, and even though it was more than ten years after Amalia's success, the average amount was still in the range of $150 to three hundred dollars.[46] The highest sale price of one thousand dollars was shown for only a few works at the exhibit, one of which was done by Lucia Fairchild Fuller, whose miniatures are now in the Smithsonian.[47]

Amalia's obtaining high commissions on both sides of the Atlantic, from the families of wealthy tycoons and royalty alike, was certainly not always due to her talent as an artist, which at times came into question. There were four factors that distinguished Amalia from her other contemporaries. Her exotic use of her signature wrap was a distinguishing trait, allowing women a degree of self-expression uncommon in the late Victorian age, bordering on today's boudoir photography. Coupled with that was Amalia's willingness to display many of these women with their finest jewels. Secondly, the status-conscious women of the Gilded Age were in a constant competition with each other, from their Paris-designed gowns to their opulent mansions. Amalia's portraits became part of their "must-haves." Thirdly, she lived a lifestyle that, as best she was able, matched that of the women she painted, from her expensive gowns to maintaining lavish surroundings in her home and studio. To some degree she appeared to be *like them*. Finally, and quite simply, she would not accept less than she felt was due for her commissions, starting at an "inflated" rate which grew along with her business in New York City. Regardless, when combined with all the other factors, her clients readily accepted these rates.

Amalia achieved a prominence in both the New York and London societies that was unequaled to any other miniature portrait artist at the time. This privileged position was soon to be even further magnified by her adventures in 1899.

CHAPTER 4

Great Adventures of 1899

As the new year of 1899 began, Amalia was the reigning queen of miniature portraits and was quite well established in both New York City and London. However, her impressive clientele was about to expand with an invitation from the Grand Duchess Maria Pavlovna, the wife of Grand Duke Vladimir, Czar Nicholas II's uncle. She hastily made all necessary travel arrangements and departed from London for St. Petersburg in March 1899. Much of this adventure was recorded in an article that would later be published in *Century Magazine* in October 1906.

St. Petersburg at this time was surprisingly culturally progressive, and early in the reign of Nicholas II "[was] a period of such glittering intellectual and cultural achievements . . . known as the 'Russian Renaissance.'" This included sophisticated accomplishments in music and the arts. As an example, Amalia would have likely known about exhibits in that city of the French Impressionists, such as Cézanne and Gauguin.[1]

Amalia arrived in St. Petersburg just two weeks after having received the request. Upon getting settled in her hotel room, she looked out her window and amid the continually falling snow observed: "the first impression is singularly depressing."[2] Later, the grand duchess supported this impression and said that the landscape in winter created "the melancholy that is the marked characteristic of the Russian temperament."[3]

Shortly after her arrival, Amalia was summoned to meet with Grand Duchess Maria at the Vladimir Palace, on the River Neva. Amalia was dismayed that she was only wearing her travel clothes, since her trunks were delayed in arriving at the hotel. She departed the hotel wearing a long coat to hide her less-than-elegant traveling outfit. Upon her arrival at the palace, since the interior of the royal residence was so warm, the palace staff almost forcibly removed her outer coat.

Amalia was then received quite warmly by the grand duchess in the drawing room, with the duchess extending her hand and speaking not Russian but English. Amalia was impressed by Maria's renowned beauty. In her process of determining the best portrait pose, she realized that the duchess's features reminded her of Queen Louise of Prussia (1776–1810), wife of King William III. There were multiple paintings of this beautiful queen in either gowns or with a royal cloak edged with ermine fur, and many of these had a gauzy fabric wrapped around her neck and trailing off to the right as if floating. Maria then revealed that the resemblance in their features was not surprising, since this queen was her grandmother! Amalia decided then and there that she would pose the duchess in a similar fashion to Queen Louise's, using a brown tulle, to which Maria readily agreed.[4]

The next day, as Amalia was about to leave her hotel for the first sitting with the duchess, "a thunderous noise arose in the hall outside my door."[5] A messenger had come from the Winter Palace bearing a summons that she was to now go and paint a miniature of the Czarina Alexandra instead. She hastily went to Maria to advise her that she would have to delay her portrait; luckily, the duchess was understanding.

Amalia's ride to the Winter Palace was somewhat unsettling, with the horses going quite fast and her carriage being saluted by groups of police as it rode past. Prior to coming to Russia, she had heard "dreadful tales of the way all strangers are watched in Russia."[6] This certainly seemed to be true.

At the time of Amalia's arrival, Czar Nicholas II had been the leader of Russia for five years, following the death of his father, Nicholas I. He had been married to Czarina Alexandra for the same number of years. They already were the parents of two daughters—Olga and Tatiana, four and two years old, respectively. Though it's never mentioned in Amalia's article about her visit, Alexandra was about five months pregnant with their third child, a daughter Maria, to be born in October. With her voluminous royal gowns and her height, possibly this was not evident to Amalia.

Czarina Alexandra was the granddaughter of Queen Victoria, through Victoria's daughter, Alice, and a niece to the Prince of Wales. She was shy by nature, possibly never adjusted to living in Russia, and missed her life before marriage. She was also the favorite granddaughter of Queen Victoria and was especially close to her, having lost her mother when she was only five years old. She most likely welcomed a visit with someone like Amalia who had a familiarity with the British royal family.

As Amalia's carriage stopped finally at the palace, she recalled "leaving the carriage at the overwhelming entrance . . . and walking through the big guard room full of officers and soldiers."[7] She was then greeted by an usher attired in a "gorgeous uniform, the detail chiefly impressing me being the absolute magnificence of the great plumes in his hat."[8] A lady-in-waiting just beyond the entrance was next brought to escort her further into the palace. Amalia told the servant about being saluted and watched by police on the carriage ride over. The lady-in-waiting provided a frank reply, saying: "They know who you are, why you are here, and the time of your arrival. They also know exactly when you are to leave the palace." She ended by saying that any variation from this known schedule would alert the staff that something was amiss.[9] "You are at the Winter Palace every day, coming in close contact with the [royal family]," the local chief of police later told Amalia—hence the need to keep her under close observation.[10]

It was a long walk to reach the Romanov family's private apartments, and Amalia had to first pass through the czar's personal rooms. At their entrance were three "fierce-looking Cossacks, armed to the teeth." When she finally reached the czarina's rooms, they too had a guard, a tall man with a long knife extending from his uniform sash.[11] She finally found the czarina standing in the center of the large room. Amalia found her greeting very similar to her first one with the grand duchess, with Czarina Alexandra showing kindness and speaking English. She was simply dressed in what Amalia described as a "tea-gown," with two prominent pieces of jewelry: "large pearls in her ears, and a splendid star ruby ring, the star ruby being her favorite jewel."[12]

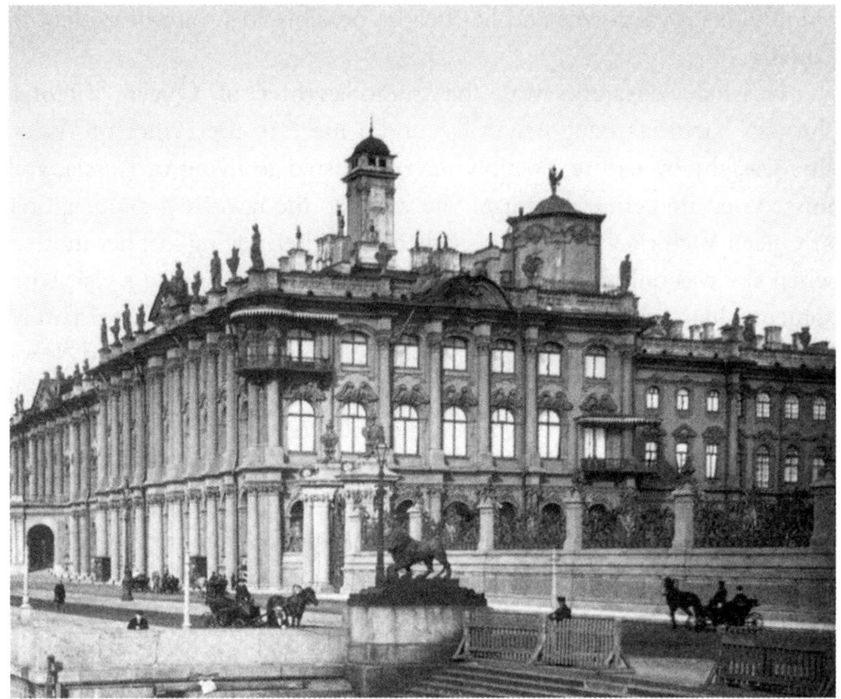

Facade of the Winter Palace in St. Petersburg on the banks of the Neva River (1917). *Süddeutsche Zeitung Photo / Alamy Stock Photo*

Though most of the portrait work of the czar and czarina was done at the Winter Palace, a few sessions were held at the Tsar's Village (*Tsarkoë Seloe*), "the royal summer residence sixteen miles outside the capital."[13] With two structures as grand as the Winter Palace, the Tsar's Village was set up to be an independent town. Amalia mentioned opulent features, such as one room with an ebony floor with inlaid mother of pearl. But in a sentimental observation, she noted that "here the Czar and his bride spent their honeymoon."[14]

Amalia, as she would always do with her first visit to a subject to be painted, recorded in great detail both the appearance and personality of the czarina. Photographs of Alexandra were far less common in America or Europe as compared with other monarchs in the late nineteenth century. Amalia was impressed by the color of her hair, a brown-gold, and her large gray-blue eyes, which would not have been portrayed in the black and white photography. She was most struck by her facial expression: "as singularly wistful and [with a] sweet sadness that never went away even when she smiled."[15]

A few years before Amalia's arrival, miniatures were done of both the czar and czarina, likely around their wedding in 1894, and set in a diamond-encrusted brooch designed by Fabergé. They are currently in the extensive decorative arts collection at the Hillwood Estate, Museum and Gardens in Washington, DC. The coloring of the royals' faces in these portraits (see color insert) would have likely been very similar to the versions done by Amalia.

Amalia drew Alexandra with her head slightly turned and looking down. She felt this pose best matched her combination of shyness and strength. Amalia would later relate that the czarina was one of the most difficult persons she ever painted, but not due to her nature. It was more due to her constant change in expression, where her face would react to "the slightest thoughtfulness, an entrance, the sound of a voice in the distance."[16]

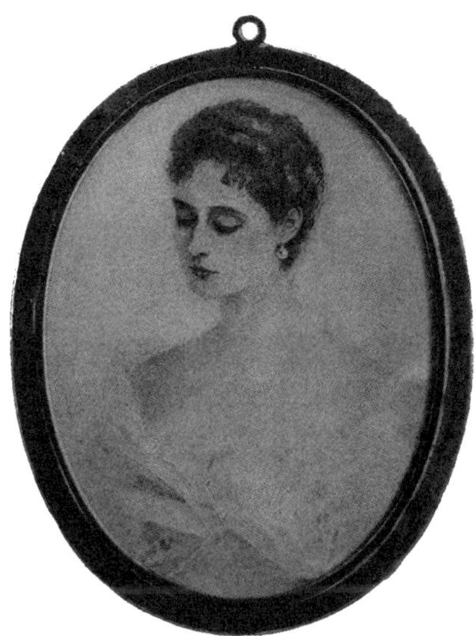

Miniature of the Czarina Alexandra of Russia by Amalia Kussner (1899), as seen in "The Human Side of the Czar," *Century Magazine*, October 1906. Century Magazine, *author's collection*

It is interesting to note that at this first meeting, the czarina told Amalia she had already seen some of her miniatures and was impressed by her work. Though only conjecture, it is possible those came to Russia via Minnie Paget, who was known to be friends with the Romanov family.

The first sitting was the next day, in the czarina's boudoir. Amalia provided great visual detail on the decoration of this room, which was dominated by the color mauve, seen in the silk covering the walls, the rugs, the curtains, and almost every other object. Even the flowers in the room were mauve orchids.[17] Though much more opulent, this likely reminded Amalia of her own bedroom at the Windsor Hotel, which she had decorated in a pink motif and with painted flowers on the ceiling.

The czarina was very cooperative in her posing and sat without moving for most of an hour. Then an interruption came in the clicking of boot spurs on the floor. Amalia saw the czarina look up toward the door and say, "The Emperor is coming."[18]

Amalia turned around, with her heart beating rapidly, and saw Nicholas II. Her first impression was that he looked so young, slight, and gentle. It was hard for her to imagine this man as the ruler of what she declared to be "the greatest empire."[19] He greeted her, very much like his wife and his aunt, the grand duchess, by holding out his hand and addressing her in perfect English. She then realized their use of English explained why, for all of her visit, they referred to each other as emperor and empress, rather than the Russian terms of czar and czarina.

Arrangements were made, after the completion of the czarina's portrait, for Amalia to do the czar's as well. During his sittings with her, Amalia further observed:

> In dwelling upon the Emperor's youthful appearance and gentle bearing, there is no thought of implying any lack of strength. There could hardly be a question of physical bravery in any royal case, since personal fearlessness is part of royal training.

Over the course of around eight sittings with the czar,[20] he was quite the conversationalist, even discussing America's foreign affairs and the ongoing Spanish–American War. She found him well read, and he seemed to be informed on world events and the goings-on with the European royal families. He also spoke highly of America and "expressed his admiration for our national independence of character and opinion."[21] Amalia even went so far as to share some gossip with him—possibly a juicy tidbit she had picked up from London. After sharing this tale with the czar, he found it amusing enough to call out to Alexandra in the next room and have Amalia repeat the whole story.

The czar wanted his portrait done of him in military uniform. After the many sittings were accomplished, "In order to spare him unnecessary fatigue in painting detail, I asked that he send to my hotel the uniform of the Preobrajensky Guard," Amalia wrote.[22] She was granted her request.

When Amalia was at last done with the portrait, an older court valet came to her hotel room to collect the uniform. The valet did a detailed

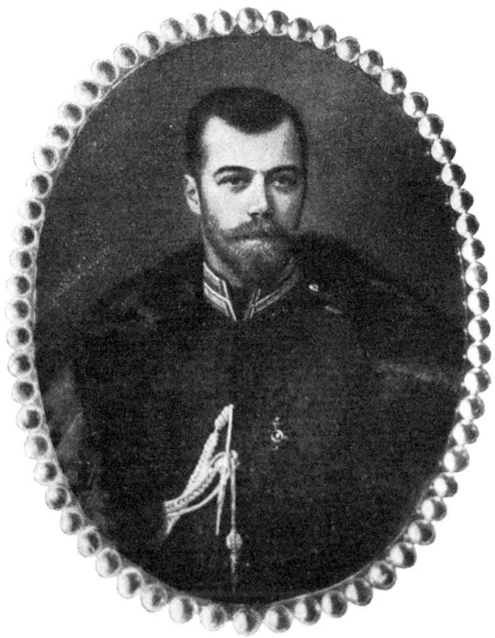

Miniature of Czar Nicholas II of Russia by Amalia Kussner (1899), as seen in "The Human Side of the Czar," *Century Magazine*, October 1906. Century Magazine, *author's collection*

inspection of the uniform, which distressed Amalia, thinking he might be looking for any missing decorations or other such embellishments. But an item *was* actually missing—a large napkin that the uniform had been wrapped in! This fine cloth had a large embroidery of the imperial coat of arms. She reported the incident to the hotel proprietor and advised him that the matter must be reported to the Winter Palace. Not surprisingly, shortly after the proprietor left her room, "a few moments afterward the napkin was handed in at the door without a word."[23]

Through the many days spent at the Winter Palace, Amalia became friendly with the Grand Duchesses Olga and Tatiana, who "quite charmed me with their bright ways." And with her visit extending through Easter, she asked Alexandra if she could provide her daughters with a gift. This offer was accepted, and Amalia presented to them a wire cage in the shape of an egg, with entwined flowers. Somehow, she managed to find a live sparrow to place inside the egg. Their daughters adored the gift but accidentally let the sparrow out; their father came to the rescue, catching the sparrow and placing it safely back in the cage. This scene alone indicates the intimate family access that Amalia had and gave her a sense of their domestic tranquility at the time.

Amalia did go on to complete Grand Duchess Maria's portrait. She followed through on her plan to style Maria with tulle around her neck, to match the various similar portraits of Queen Louise. During her stay in Russia, she also painted the Grand Duchess Helene (daughter of Grand Duchess Maria, later to become Princess Nicholas of Greece).[24] Alexandra's portrait and those of both Grand Duchesses Maria and Helene were all done using the classic "wrap" styling and semi-transparent tulle, though the fabric for Grand Duchess Helene appears to have been a heavier fabric, such as satin.

Later in her visit—and further enforcing the reality of her being watched in St. Petersburg—Amalia learned of an interesting event. While at dinner one evening with the local chief of police, he relayed how the police had been constantly following her and had even recorded her buying a hat at a store near her hotel. They were in close enough proximity to record the actual conversation she had with the store owner, who only spoke Russian, and her issues in trying to communicate what

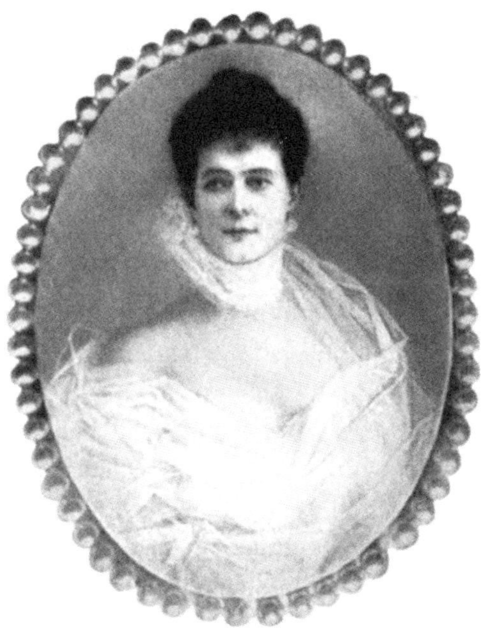

Miniature of the Grand Duchess Maria by Amalia Kussner (1899), as seen in "The Human Side of the Czar," *Century Magazine*, October 1906. Century Magazine, *author's collection*

she wanted to buy.[25] Though Amalia felt quite at ease while at the Winter Palace, there is no doubt she would have been relieved to depart St. Petersburg and the scrutiny of so many watchful eyes.

Before her departure, Alexandra provided a signed photo of herself, in her full regalia as czarina.

The overall tone of Amalia's *Century Magazine* article reflected what she had observed of Czar Nicholas: a ruler in charge of his monarchy and a man of compassion and kindness. This did not match the prevailing view from other countries. Her visit was a point in time in the lives of Nicholas and Alexandra when their domestic tranquility was genuine. However, Amalia really had no exposure to affairs of state and truly could not report on the nature of the politics and the unrest that was already in progress and would greatly worsen with time. She did record the following, which sadly would ring all too true given the assassination of the family in 1918:

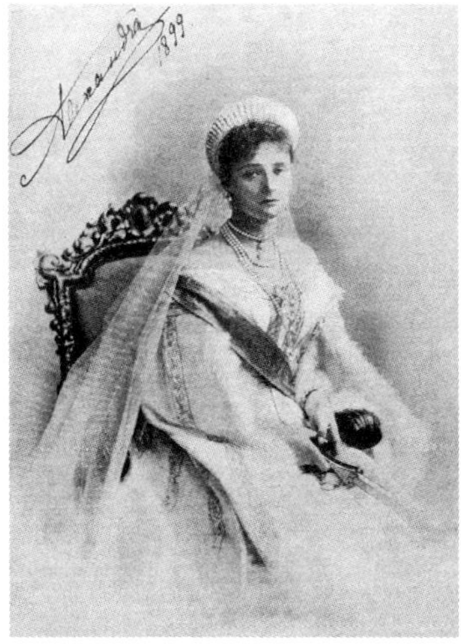

Photograph of Alexandra of Russia, signed by the czarina, given to Amalia Kussner (1899), as seen in "The Human Side of the Czar," *Century Magazine*, October 1906. Century Magazine, *author's collection*

He appeared fully aware of the weight of his destiny, and to be bearing the awful burden with cheerful serenity, always looking at his great danger without one waver of fear.[26]

∽○∾

While Amalia was in Russia, a tragic fire occurred at the Windsor Hotel on March 17, 1899. A St. Patrick's Day parade was in progress, causing crowded streets, which prevented an effective response from the fire department. Escape from the building was also hampered by the fact the fire seemed to start on lower floors. The rapidly spreading fire engulfed the building in ninety minutes; at least seventy-nine people lost their lives.[27] With her suite of rooms being on a higher floor, Amalia's fate would certainly have been in question if she were in the building at the time. Just prior to her departure for Russia, she had "the rooms entirely redecorated, leaving a great many valuables there," including her own collection of other artists' works, such as those of the French painter Puvis de Chavannes. All of Amalia's belongings, including the priceless works of art, were destroyed.[28]

Upon returning from Russia in April 1899, her travels next took her both to New York, where she set up a new residence at the Savoy,[29] and to London, where she attended a charity gala sponsored by Minnie Paget. At this event, she unabashedly wore the three extravagant gifts given to her by the Romanovs:

> [Amalia] was most beautifully dressed in a dress of pale-pink muslin, with a soft toque of pink tulle, and round her neck a necklace of big uncut rubies and diamonds . . . as well as a ruby and diamond bracelet and magnificent pearl and diamond pin, which were gifts of the Czar and Czarina.[30]

Amalia was, however, also paid in cash for her miniatures and given the sum of one thousand roubles.[31]

THE TRIP TO SOUTH AFRICA

The rest of 1899 proceeded with Amalia continuing to do portraits in both New York and London. She settled in the Savoy Hotel, located at Fifth Avenue and 59th Street, which included her studio.

Amalia had a goal to paint most if not all of the social and political greats of the Gilded Age, and one of the subjects on her list was the British mining tycoon Cecil Rhodes, the "Diamond King" worth a hundred million dollars.[32] Rhodes was at the forefront of British efforts in Africa, "with the desire for material gain and power."[33] Four years earlier, he had been deposed by the British government from his position as prime minister of the Cape Colony, but he was still the chairman of the De Beers Mining Company, which by 1891 produced 90 percent of the world's diamond supply.[34]

Rhodes was known for his dislike of having his portrait done, but Amalia was determined to paint him and seems to have contacted Rhodes directly to request a sitting, offering to make the trip to South

Africa. A letter was written to Amalia from Rhodes's home (Groote Schuur) by his secretary, Philip Jourdan:

Groote Schuur,
Rodebosch, near Cape Town
11th Sept. '99

Dear Madame,
    In reply to your note Mr. Rhodes desires me to say that he is and always has been averse to the idea of sitting for his portrait; but if as you say have purposely come out to the Cape to paint his miniature he is prepared to give you a sitting one morning at 10 o'clock sometime next week. It would be well if you will let me know what day you are coming.

I am dear Madam,
Yours faithfully,
P. Jourdan[35]

Perhaps unbeknownst to Amalia at the time she made her offer was that the breakout of war in Africa was imminent. This war, sometimes called the Second Boer War, was the result of complex factors including the targeting of Africa as part of the imperial expansion of Britain and for its untold riches in diamonds and recently discovered gold. Britain was not alone in its goal to gain more territory in Africa; the empire was also competing with France and Germany. The Boers were the original Dutch settlers of Cape Colony, over which Britain had claimed sovereignty almost a century before. Many complex and contentious interactions occurred for most of the nineteenth century, including the Europeans taking the territory from the native populations.[36]

Amalia's friend, Nancy Huston Banks, had been scheduled to return to New York from London in September 1899, even already having a ticket for the steamship *St. Louis*. But *Vanity Fair* of London offered her a generous commission to cover the imminent war in South Africa, and she changed her plans.[37] When Amalia learned that Nancy would be meeting with Rhodes in person, she leapt at the chance to once more approach him by meeting Nancy in Africa and accompanying her as a surprise companion.

By the time Amalia was able to make the trip to Cape Town, she found that Rhodes had gone to his mining compound at Kimberley, a town seven hundred miles north of Cape Town.[38] Nancy arrived in Cape Town around the same time and was also dismayed to see that Rhodes had left. Without hesitation, they both boarded a train for Kimberley.[39] Tensions were already high in the region, and on October 11 their train was forcibly boarded by the Boers. Since those on the train were designated as noncombatants, they were allowed to proceed to Kimberley.

Upon their arrival at the entrance to the compound, Cecil Rhodes "was somewhat dismayed at the unexpected appearance of the young Americans"[40] who had followed him to Kimberley. He reluctantly admitted both Amalia and Nancy to the compound, really having no choice since the railroads south and north of Kimberley were captured by the Boers on October 18.[41]

Amalia and Nancy would have stayed at the Sanatorium Hotel, where Rhodes and his other few guests were housed. It was built and run by De Beers, and the "luxurious semi-private hotel" was in a similar league with some of the best hotels of London.[42] The hotel was located in the central part of the Kimberley compound, which included a hospital and public gardens. The mining operations bordered the area from the south and north, with the "native camp" located in the northeast section.[43]

Soon after their arrival, all aspects of the compound were converted for war efforts, such as the schools and churches being repurposed for hospitals. By late October, reports were coming in that "the Boers were constructing forts around Kimberly for the purpose of shelling the town."[44] At the beginning of the siege, the camp was insufficiently staffed with soldiers, with only half a battalion of the Royal North Lancashire Regiment and two thousand local militia. This number paled in comparison to the five thousand Boers.[45] Workmen who had arrived as miners now had to hastily enlist as soldiers. These former workmen were "literally fighting for the hearths and homes, as most of them had their families with them in the town, the siege having come upon them more or less as a surprise."[46]

With the worsening conditions, the *Boston Post* documented that Rhodes's miniature was executed not at the hotel but underground—surely Amalia's most unusual and challenging working environment—in daily sessions with Rhodes.[47] As the two women from New York arrived in the southern hemisphere's summer, they also endured quite high temperatures during their stay.

Nancy described being able to view the "forces of the Boers gathering on the surrounding hills and planting batteries."[48] Soon thereafter, the Boers launched shells beyond the perimeters of the Kimberley camp, which exploded around both the military troops and the civilian structures. The Boers, knowing that Rhodes was staying in the Sanatorium Hotel, made increasing attempts to have their shelling reach that building. The distance their shells could reach was limited, though; a few

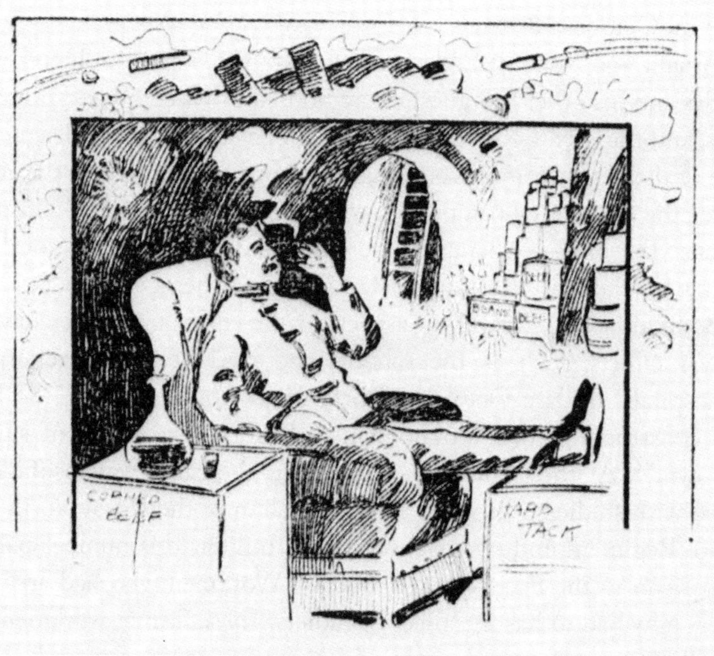

This cartoon depicting Cecil Rhodes underground in Kimberley, surrounded by supplies, accompanied the article "Painted Rhodes's Portrait in a Shower of Bursting Shells" in the *Boston Post* in June 1900.

exploded near the hotel but failed to make a direct hit.[49] This of course still would have endangered Amalia and Nancy.

When there would be a pause in the shelling, Nancy and Amalia "indulged in the pastime of picking up fragments of exploded shells in the streets as mementoes."[50] The *Wichita Eagle* reported:

> The little artist certainly has had an exceptional opportunity of seeing Cecil Rhodes, called the Colossus of South Africa, in his most heroic moods. For when she was not painting she and Nancy Banks accompanied him as he made the rounds of intrenchments [sic], encouraging the soldiers and directing sorties to drive back the Boer pickets and reconnoitering parties.
>
> It is reasonable to suppose that Miss Kussner's portrait of Cecil Rhodes will portray him in a truly Napoleonic aspect. Nancy Banks will doubtless also give to the world the best pen picture yet drawn of this potentate of South Africa.[51]

Yet even amid the dangers and privations of war, Amalia remained focused and determined to continue with her primary task of painting Rhodes. "In spite of the siege, the picture is going on apace," reported an issue of *The Woman's Column*.[52]

Since the compound was cut off in mid-October,[53] food supplies became an issue and rationing was put in place. Even though Rhodes and others had the forethought to stock Kimberley with supplies earlier, shortages started to become serious later in December. However, living conditions and food supplies varied greatly between the British and native inhabitants in the camp. For the duration of the siege, accommodations and food for the guests of Rhodes and the British versus the larger native population were sadly quite different. Many of the native miners and family members died of starvation and disease. Amalia had to have been exposed to some of these horrors of war, including the deaths of a number of British troops.

By the end of November, communications to the outside world became almost impossible. However, Nancy "performed the daring feat of getting the only message out of Kimberley"[54] in the third week of

November. She used the native runners in the camp to deliver her last news report.

In part from Nancy's last briefing and from that of other war correspondents, such as reporters from the *London Times*, multiple articles were published in American newspapers about Nancy and Amalia. One article had the sensational title: "Cooped in Kimberley—Two Distinguished New York Young Women—On Starvation Rations."[55] The writing highlighted the food shortages, describing how the typical resident of Kimberley was restricted to "four slices of bread, three tablespoons-full of beans, three slices of bacon and one cup of coffee." However, the guests of Rhodes and the more senior officers likely had access to better-quality offerings and more plentiful supplies. As an example, later in the siege, to celebrate the arrival of British troops, Rhodes supplied champagne and assorted delicacies to the officers, which was quite "surprising when people had been living on horse meat and other unsavory items for months!"[56]

It was also becoming clear that Banks's and Amalia's lives were further at risk of capture, since they were guests of Cecil Rhodes. All within the camp were aware that there was a twenty-five-thousand-dollar reward offered by the Boers for the capture of Cecil Rhodes. This raised the dire possibility that if captured, the women would be "hustled off to Pretoria, the Boer Capital, like British prisoners, and kept there till the war is over."[57]

The reporting at the time often provided a glowing profile of Rhodes's "strong personality," which was credited to enabling "Kimberley to hold out against the enemy as long as it has."[58] Furthermore, the miners, though hastily converted to soldiers, saw Rhodes as their leader rather than the actual British officer in command. The reality of this situation was that Rhodes actively tried to undermine Colonel Robert Kekewich, the garrison commander. The rationale from Rhodes was that the local forces, many of them the converted miners, outnumbered the trained British forces. This situation "provided the infernally energetic Rhodes with the excuse to interfere in the defense of the town."[59]

Amalia further reported that he encouraged her to be "less extravagant" in her habits. She did indeed observe him living without the

COOPED IN KIMBERLEY

Two Distinguished New York Young Women.

ON STARVATION RATIONS

What Might Befall Them If Kimberley Were Taken.

Headline from the *Wichita Daily Eagle* article about Amalia Kussner and Nancy Huston Banks in Kimberley, November 1899.

trappings of an incredibly wealthy man. His appearance was such that his "style of dress did not command a second look from the casual observer."[60] His home in Cape Town was a "large, simple house, which Rhodes repaired and furnished with country antiques instead of the elaborate furniture of the time."[61] This was a paradox to Amalia, who was accustomed to seeing estates and palaces where every possible excess in architecture and decorations were on display.

Sometime toward the end of December, Amalia was able to leave Kimberley, but she had a long trek to reach a train facility still functioning for passage to Cape Town. At her final parting with Rhodes, he provided Amalia with "a photograph of himself, upon the back of which he had written 'From your tutor.'"[62] Even though Amalia initially arrived at Kimberley for a portrait Rhodes did not want, it seems that they had at least an amiable relationship by the time she left.

What is not documented is how and when Nancy Huston Banks left the compound. News of the perilous situation reached Banks's father, Judge George Huston, in Morganfield, Kentucky. He had advised a local newspaper in late November that he was "en route to Washington, D. C., to have the department take steps for his daughter's safety,"[63] but the results of such a visit are also unknown. Her writings to the London *Vanity Fair* of the war may have been lost to history.

From Cape Town, Amalia boarded a ship back to London, arriving on January 1.[64] Upon her return to England, she found that Rhodes was being hailed as the "hero of Kimberley,"[65] and she must have felt justified in her instincts to risk her life and traveling to South Africa to do his portrait.

Amalia did not immediately return to New York and was welcomed at various social events, where partygoers were anxious to hear about her recent adventures. One such party was given by Minnie Paget in February 1900. Those attending delighted in socializing with "the famous American miniature painter, who narrowly escaped being shut up in beleaguered Kimberley."[66]

Amalia was next documented as arriving in New York just prior to March 1 on the White Star liner *Teutonic* from England.[67] A New York news reporter met Amalia as she disembarked, and she provided a detailed interview that was then published in a variety of newspapers. She related her experiences in painting Cecil Rhodes, and her account of his sittings was not entirely positive, for reasons beyond the war. Though she did state that of all the figures she had painted up to that point, "the personality of Cecil Rhodes made the deepest impression on her," she also described him as having much nervous energy and vitality, to the point that "It was so great as to be almost oppressive."[68] She further compared Rhodes to the Czar, saying that the Russian emperor was a man of peace, whereas Rhodes was a man of war.

Amalia also relayed to the reporter some history of two artists who had tried to paint Rhodes prior to her and had disagreements with him. Due to these issues with Rhodes, such as his critiques of their early efforts, the attempts of these first two artists were not successful and no portraits were completed. Amalia therefore took definite measures to prevent Rhodes from seeing her work in progress. Rhodes did make at least one request for how he was to be painted. He implored Amalia, "Can't you make me look kinder?"[69] But Amalia kept to her artist

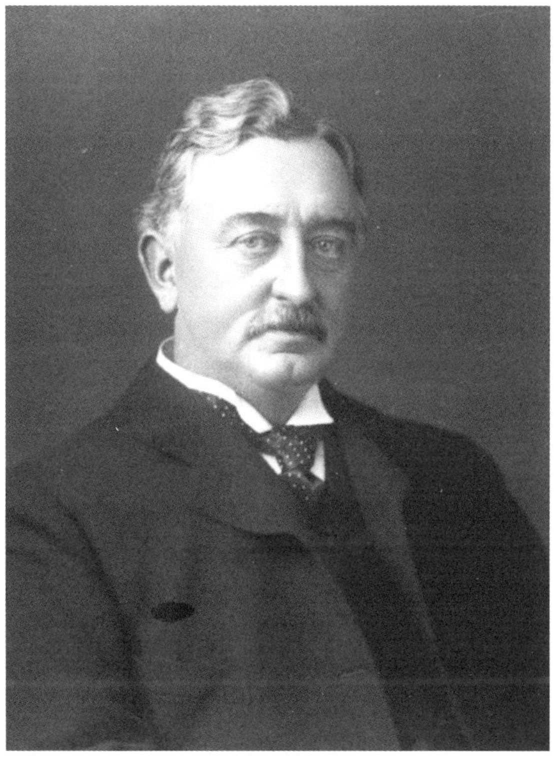

Portrait of the industrialist and politician Cecil Rhodes by an unknown artist (1900). *Creative Commons, courtesy of user Hephaestos*

instincts and informed him that her work appropriately showed the world his accurate character.

In discussing her forced long stay at Kimberley, she said, "I do not think he [Rhodes] had any idea that the troubles in South Africa would lead to such a result as war."[70] Surprisingly, the article ended with her stating that the Boers were both "behind in civilization" but also "a people of wonderfully rugged strength." She also had the opportunity to visit a Boer Village and found it "the most beautiful place she had ever seen."[71]

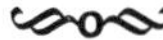

Through both her extraordinary adventures in Russia and South Africa in 1899, Amalia never indicated any fear or hesitation, and seemed to relish being in close company with these great leaders at the end of the nineteenth century. But in the end, Amalia's understandings of the czar and Rhodes, though she captured their personalities and their likenesses, were simplistic. She was either not privy to or simply didn't want to know the complexities of their political situations. Sadly, at this time the whereabouts of the finished portraits are unknown. Eventually finding Rhodes's miniature in a private collection remains a possibility, but those of the czar and czarina were likely to have been destroyed during the tumult of the Russian Revolution.

CHAPTER 5

Personal Life and Marriage

WITH HER RETURN TO NEW YORK IN THE WINTER OF 1900, SHORTLY after being trapped in South Africa and a firsthand witness to war, Amalia immediately resumed her business.

It was at this time that a blatantly negative review of her works was published in an art-focused column in *The New York Times*.

> Miss Amalie [Amalia] Kussner, who has done some very hasty, careless, and even bad work, deserves, at least, the thanks of her fellow-miniature painters in that she has made the art once more fashionable. It is now the hobby of a number of people, and several miniature painters, not always the better ones, have of late been prospering.[1]

This must have incensed Amalia, who had carefully fostered her image in newspapers and magazines, yet she continued to receive commissions from the well-to-do in New York.

She painted Lady Colebrooke in March, who came from London to visit friends in New York and was listed as "one of the reigning beauties of London."[2] This rendering was in Amalia's classic style, with multiple layers of a fabric wrap and silk flowers at the bodice, hiding the fasteners. Also in March she painted Mrs. George Gould and her son, a charming portrait of a mother holding her child, then just two years old.[3] Her husband was the eldest son of the infamous robber baron Jay Gould.[4]

Amalia kept a lovely letter written to her from George Gould, Jr. in June 1900:

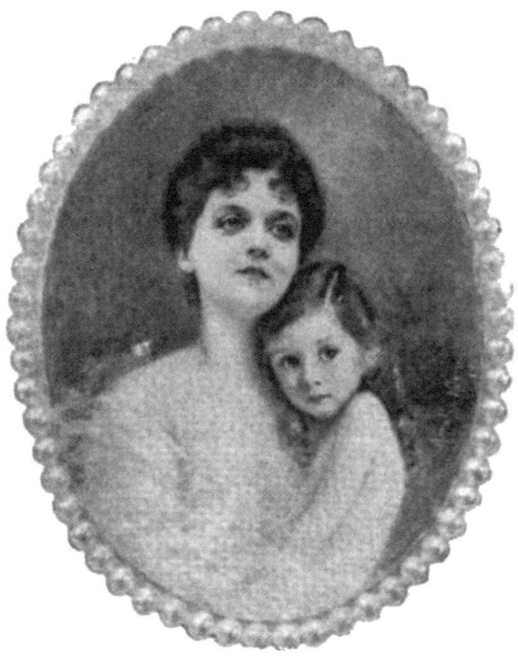

Miniature of Mrs. George Gould and her son by Amalia Kussner (ca. 1900), as seen in "Amalia Kussner Coudert," *Ainslee's Magazine*, May 1902.

President's Office

The Missouri Pacific Railway Co.

New York

Dear Miss Kussner

I want to tell you how much we are pleased with the miniature of Mrs Gould & Georgie.

It's a perfect likeness of both and everyone who has seen it admires it so much also as a work of art.

With kindest regards from both of us

Sincerely yours,

George J. Gould[5]

Monday

18:June

Amalia then traveled to England on the SS *New York* in May, to paint more of the titled women of London.

Amalia's association with Alice Fischer was again highlighted in an early June invitation to join her Twelfth Night Club. The club had expanded beyond the boundaries of the New York stage and became more of a gathering of those accomplished in the arts and literary worlds. Fischer extended this invitation to many distinguished Hoosiers[6] in addition to Amalia. This impressive list included General Lew Wallace, author of the novel *Ben Hur*, and another Indiana artist, sculptor Miss Janet Scudder.[7]

With the numerous newspapers covering Amalia's trip to paint the Prince of Wales in 1897 and the czar in 1899, she had the opportunity to have photos of these now-famous miniatures of royalty published in *Century Magazine*. However, the magazine editors decided to only have the miniatures displayed, without an article, in the arts section of the September 1900 issue. Amalia made her objections clear to the editorial staff, stating: "I don't like the idea of the article—I am sure your idea of placing my miniatures outside (an article) is attractive—but what follows is cheapening."[8] Amalia probably felt slighted that there would be no accompanying article detailing her associations with the royalty. Her objections were not heeded.

Up to this point, her personal life was not well publicized—and that was by intention. She wanted the newspapers to highlight both her artwork and travels, and to maintain an image of her being a young, beautiful, and almost virginal artist. Though not covered in the newspapers, there are a few published glimpses of her activities outside of her artistry. She actually owned a racehorse—Ivanhoe (a chestnut gelding)—that participated in single horse shows and races in New Jersey and New York. Both her name and that of her horse were listed in the Official Catalogue for the Fourteenth Annual Horse Show held at Madison Square Garden in November 1898. This was quite a unique activity for a single woman at this time, especially since some events involved betting on the horses and possibly interfacing with unseemly characters.[9]

The races were quite popular with the Astors and the Vanderbilts, where they were either competing with their own horses or acting as judges. These annual horse shows were recalled by many as "the greatest society and fashionable function of the year" and viewed as the official inauguration of the "winter season" of high society in New York. For those who would have recently returned from their Newport summer mansions, it was the first occasion to be out on public display. Having a suitable horse and the staff to take care of it may have been the only requirements Amalia needed to enter these shows. Certainly, she relished the opportunity to "see and be seen" with the class of people she wanted to be part of.[10]

Her interest in horses was even a topic of discussion with Czar Nicholas II, whose stables had fine imperial horses. One day, while she was in her room at the St. Petersburg hotel, he indulged her by riding past her hotel window at an assigned time to offer a view of his prized horses.[11]

While she was the owner of Ivanhoe, he won numerous awards, including three blue ribbons. Eventually, though, her interest in these races waned, ending with an incident at the Morristown Field Club. There were so many horses entered that not all could be admitted to the race, and Ivanhoe did not make the cut. Amalia was quite indignant and did not hold back in making her displeasure known to the public. By this time, the effort to manage the horse was also more than she wanted, especially with the large number of portrait commissions coming to her, and she decided to sell Ivanhoe to the Gould family, where he was used in part for their daughter Marjorie but also was still entered in races.[12]

But what might there have been of Amalia's romantic life? Though not covered in newspapers of the time, there is an intriguing reference in a biography of Nikola Tesla implying that Amalia was included among his love interests: "Three ladies who interested him were Mrs. Winslow, Amatia [Amalia] Kussner, and Miss Marguerite Merrington. The first, alas, was married; to the second, Tesla wanted to display his inventions at his laboratory."[13] His meeting Amalia is not too surprising, since Tesla was being funded by John Jacob Astor IV by 1899.[14] Amalia had certainly been involved with the Astor family in doing portraits of Mrs. Astor and one of her daughters (then Mrs. Orme Wilson). It is easy to suppose that Amalia also expressed interest in Tesla and his work, as it was so much a part of Amalia's character to be fascinated by new and novel things.

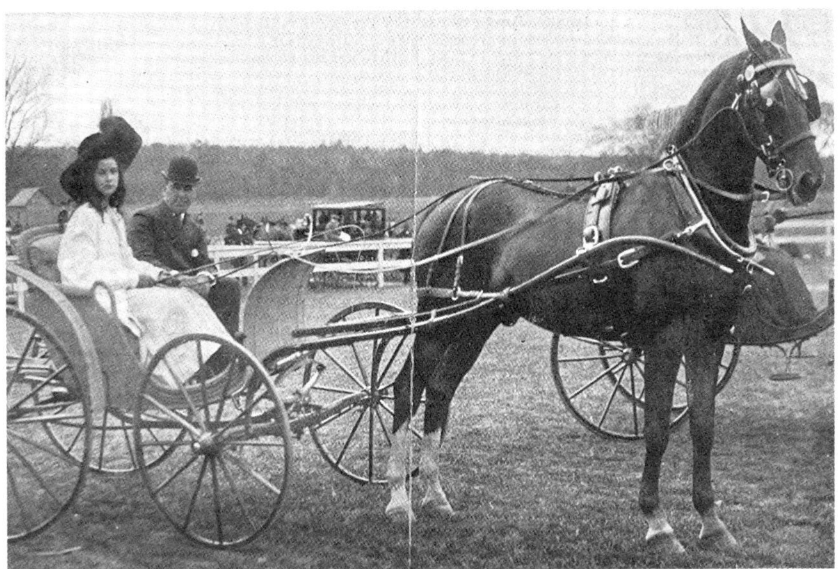

Miss Marjorie Gould in a carriage drawn by her horse Ivanhoe (1903). Photo by C. F. Ross. *Courtesy of the Amalia Kussner Papers (Private Collection), Sisters of Providence Archives at Saint Mary-of-the-Woods, Indiana*

Whether she ever made it to his laboratory is unknown, but if she had, the equipment would have likely resembled something we would imagine in Dr. Frankenstein's laboratory.

Amalia and Tesla might have been seen socially together at least a few times, since both were part of a social and literary group managed by Katherine Johnson, wife of writer and diplomat Robert Underwood Johnson. She and her husband held social functions in New York where "a visitor could dine with any number of luminaries."[15] Katherine Johnson had also been a past love interest of Tesla's.[16] Some others included in this group were the aforementioned Miss Merrington (a playwright) and amazingly Rudyard Kipling and John Muir.[17] Amalia, at this point, was of sufficient social standing that she merited invitations to these sophisticated soirées in 1899. However, Amalia's brief association with Tesla was never covered in any society pages.

Aside from the documentation on Tesla's interest in Amalia, the only other indication of romantic liaisons is a single 1898 newspaper account from Indiana saying she had been engaged to a Mr. John W. Davis, a lawyer in Terre Haute.[18] If indeed this relationship had occurred, she would have been in her twenties living in her hometown, while Mr. Davis would have been fifteen years older. If she had other romantic entanglements, Amalia was careful to keep them out of the press.

Until suddenly, on July 3, 1900, she entered into marriage with Charles du Pont Coudert, known to his family and close friends as du Pont. This was quite an abrupt event; the impending marriage had not been previously announced, and there were not even any notices of an engagement. The sudden nuptials would have raised many questions among society, as basic as "When had they met?" and "When did this relationship become serious enough to lead to marriage?" *The Standard Union* of Brooklyn did state that friends of the couple had some awareness of their close relationship but were still surprised, "for though it was generally known that they were engaged, no formal announcement had been made."[19]

Scores of newspapers reported on their marriage and listed in great detail Amalia's accomplishments, especially her most famous portrait work (the Prince of Wales, the czar, etc.), but mentioned little of her new husband. Du Pont had recently returned from service in the Spanish–American War and was also a lawyer, but there is only a single brief mention of his involvement in the Coudert law firm.

One newspaper described their wedding as a very understated event and reported that the two were "quietly married in the sacristy of St. Patrick's Cathedral."[20] But most articles reflected the astonishment of the New York social circles. "New York Society Surprised: Unannounced Wedding of Miss Kussner and Captain Coudert" read the *St. Louis Republic* headline. The article further stated, "The wedding was absolutely without announcement, and only the mothers of the contracting parties were present."[21] The end of the article cited the impact on the New York social circles: "the hasty wedding of Miss Amalia Kussner and Charles Dupont Coudert made quite a little stir."[22]

In attempting to answer the curiosity of the public, some fantastic tales were spun. Again from the *St. Louis Republic* came the most fictional account of their early meeting: "Captain Coudert and Miss

Kussner were children together, but their courtship had its beginning quite recently."[23] Even with Amalia's being enrolled in a New York school in 1882, she would have been ten years older than du Pont—there was no way for the two to meet in a school setting. And certainly du Pont had never been to Indiana. The most probable account of their meeting was documented in an article written about Amalia's life in 1890 and would have occurred at the end of her first trip to England, during the fall of 1896. Prior to her returning to New York, she traveled to Paris, accompanied by Minnie Paget, to promote her business and shop for the latest fashions available in Paris; Amalia was well known for wanting to stay current with haute couture. With Minnie Paget's extensive social connections, "they were guest of two sisters, Mrs. Frank Glaenzer and the Marquise de Choiseul"—née Leonie Coudert and Claire Coudert.[24] Through this visit, Amalia likely also met their brother, du Pont, who had just graduated from Columbia College. This meeting in Paris was supported by a newspaper article written shortly after their wedding, recounting that they had met in Paris four years earlier, and had been "devoted friends ever since" the fateful introduction.[25]

In terms of how their courtship would have been conducted, assuming their relationship progressed between 1896 and the time of their wedding, it should be noted that both Amalia and du Pont had been out of the country for extended periods. Amalia had started her frequent trips to England in 1896, each of which could be two to four months in length. And she was away from New York at least five months in 1899, with her Russia and South Africa adventures, the year before their marriage. Du Pont himself was physically out of the country from 1898 to the late fall of 1899. There is one account that mentions a "movie-worthy" scene of Coudert meeting Amalia at the New York harbor upon her return from Kimberley and London in February.[26] However, this claim is quite disputable.

Aside from the speculations provided by many newspapers, one article alone stands out to possibly explain at least some aspects of this sudden event. *The Evening Gazette*, out of Burlington, Iowa, obtained content from the *New York Telegraph* and reported:

The stepping off of the young couple was as sudden as anything of the kind could well be, though it was not a case of meet in the morning and marry in the afternoon. The pair had known each other for four years and had practically been engaged most of that time. Up to Tuesday Morning the ceremony appeared to be an event for the dim and distant future, because of the jeopardy in which it might place their careers.

On that day early in the forenoon Mr. Coudert, instead of going as usual to his law office, automobiled to the Savoy hotel, where the Kussners lived, and told the artist and her mother his career was certain to be ruined without matrimony. By having Miss Kussner for his wife, he said, there was some hope of saving it. Miss Kussner confessed that she had come to similar conclusions about her art. It was decided then and there that the wedding bells should jingle within ten hours.[27]

Aside from the abruptness of this event, there was another complication around the nuptials. The service was held in the sacristy of St. Patrick's Cathedral; however, Amalia was marrying a Catholic, and she was a Protestant. Therefore, this meant that the couple would have had to get a dispensation from some higher level of the Catholic Church. Even with a dispensation, their different faiths likely would have precluded a grand church wedding. And despite their well-connected social circles, in attendance were only two people: the groom's mother, Marie Coudert, and Amalia's mother, Emilie Kussner. The most simplistic of celebrations took place after the 7 p.m. ceremony: a private dinner in Amalia's suite of rooms at Savoy with just the four of them.[28]

Those who were able to view and report on any of the related events that day said Amalia appeared in what was termed a "street costume . . . a pearl-gray skirt, white waist and hat of opalescent taffetas." For flowers, the bride only had a simple bouquet, which was small enough to be attached to her outfit. This was so unusual for a woman who usually appeared in the finest of attires. Similarly, du Pont was seen in "ordinary afternoon attire."[29]

A waiter provided what he observed of the couple at their wedding dinner and reported that the whole affair had "none of the conventional bridal trappings."[30] The waitstaff further described this group of people as showing absolutely no indication of the excitement and gaiety appropriate for a wedding dinner. These observations align with what appears to have been a marriage of convenience.

Another controversial aspect of this union that was clearly concealed from the public—and likely a fact known *only* by Amalia's mother—was that Coudert had just married a woman ten years older than him.

Though the *Evening Gazette* reported that du Pont wanted to save his legal career, one would think that any husband of Amalia's would have been relegated to an atypical role, with her career and fame overshadowing his own accomplishments. Time would indicate this eventually would be their arrangement. But who exactly was this mysterious Charles du Pont Coudert?

Du Pont's family was quite well known in New York from the prestigious Coudert Brothers law firm, which was started in 1855. The founders were three brothers: Frederick René, Louis Leonce, and du Pont's father, Charles Coudert Jr. The family's origins went back to France with their father, yet another Charles Coudert, who started his early adult life as a supporter of Napoleon. In the tumultuous years following Napoleon's abdication, Charles Coudert remained loyal to those political edicts and was implicated in a conspiracy and sentenced to death in 1822.[31] A few locally prominent people, still sympathetic to the causes that Charles Coudert supported, were able to get a stay of execution. The political outcast then made a hasty exit from France. He first went to England but decided to immigrate to America, arriving in New York City in 1824.[32] Through various fortuitous connections, and with his ability to speak French and English, he became a teacher. These talents—possibly combined with a dowry from his new wife, Jeanne Clarisse—allowed him to eventually open an academy in New York. His marriage brought four children: the previously mentioned three sons and a daughter, Leonie.

The Coudert children were raised with French as their primary language, and the family's social life initially was relegated to the close-knit community of French ex-patriots in New York.[33] Furthermore, the family continued as practicing Catholics, which would throughout the nineteenth century keep them from being welcomed into elite social circles such as the Four Hundred, whose members were Protestant.[34] In addition, the Coudert family did not have the preferred lineage of the early Dutch and English settlers.

All brothers married within two years of each other in the early 1860s. Charles Coudert Jr.'s wife was Margaret Elizabeth ("Marie") Guion, of French Huguenot descent. This union brought seven surviving children, but only one son, Charles du Pont Coudert (b. 1875).

As a young man, du Pont was most certainly destined to become a lawyer. His cousin Fred, son of Frederic René and four years older, was already a lawyer and working in the Coudert law firm by the early 1890s.[35] The law firm, which for years had a strong foreign clientele from France and Latin America, started to become a renowned international law firm given Frederic René Coudert's expertise abroad in international law. He caught the attention of the senior politicians of Washington, DC, and was involved in various high-profile government legal cases and the Supreme Court. So, du Pont grew up as a member of a tremendously accomplished family, and as the one surviving male of his generation, expectations must have been high for his career.

Du Pont attended Columbia College and was active in a fencing club, organizing annual balls, and as a member of the fraternity Psi Epsilon, graduating in 1896 from the Arts College.[36] The following February was one of the last grand Gilded Age events: the Bradley-Martin Ball. Du Pont and his sister Clarisse were on the invitation list. This ball, given the more open attitude of the Martin family, welcomed a broader set of the wealthy which obviously allowed Catholics. The event exhibited the many extravagances of similar balls given by the Astors and Vanderbilts but was not as well received by the general public. The blatant excesses of this time in history were declining in popularity, since more and more, issues around social disparity were becoming prominent in the headlines.

As was customary, all attendees had to be in costumes of some sort; themes were usually of "times past." Du Pont wore a French magistrate's costume, and his sister attended in a costume fashioned after an old portrait of an eighteenth-century aristocratic young woman. Amalia appears to have had no invitation to this ball, even with she and du Pont supposedly courting at this time. However, this was the custom—guests were not allowed to bring anyone who was not part of the original invitation list.[37] The photo of du Pont in costume is quite unique, since very few photos of him exist.

The year 1897 would also be a period of transition for the Coudert law firm. At this time, there were only two surviving brothers, since Louis Leonce had died in 1882. However, du Pont's father, after years of long workdays and other health issues, passed away in July.[38] Charles Coudert's will, drafted certainly with clarity and purpose before his death, left most of his estate to his children—the six daughters and Charles du Pont Coudert—and what he must have seen as sufficient funds to support his wife, Marie. Both the homes at 53 West 48th Street and in Tuxedo Park, along with all of their contents, were willed to Marie, plus her husband's life insurance policy.

Marie was known to live a lavish lifestyle, however, and immediately found this arrangement not to her liking. Only one week after the death of her husband, she took decisive steps to invalidate his existing will, declaring there was a prior will drafted in March of that year that had provided more than just the properties to her, and that her husband had written the newer May will under coercion.[39]

Du Pont became involved in support of his sisters on this matter, but Marie defended him, saying, "My son is the idol of my heart. Whatever part he takes in this very unfortunate litigation, I know, has been forced upon him. I am convinced he was influenced to act as he is doing." She further implied that an unnamed person—maybe one of the sisters—had exerted undue influence both on her husband and later on her son to change the will.

Aimee Marguerite (at this time Mrs. Brennig, with her second marriage) was the most vocal of the six sisters, claiming that her father had always intended to provide well for his children. Furthermore, she claimed that none of the sisters knew of the contents of either the alleged March will or the May will, and thus there was no possibility they could have been involved in any coercion.

There were other additional unhealthy family dynamics, with Marie being estranged from three of her daughters at this time.[40] The consequences of these disagreements would have long-term implications

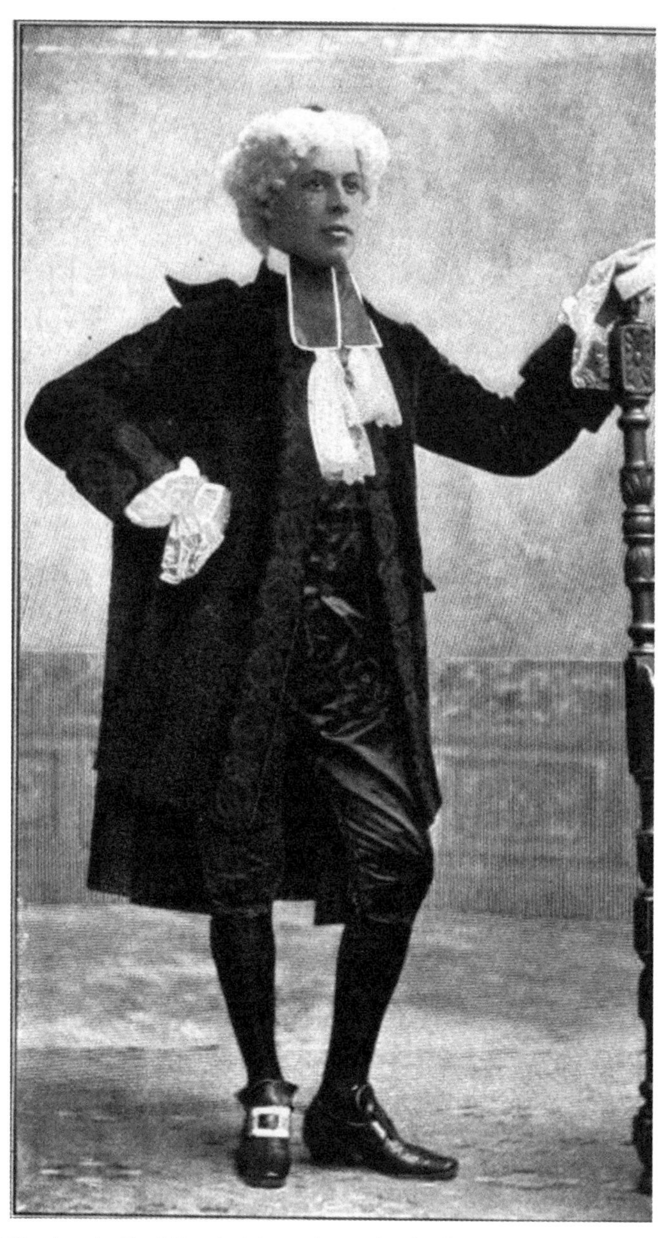

Photo of Charles du Pont Coudert in costume for the Bradley-Martin Ball (1897). *Courtesy of the Richard Jay Hutto Collection*

for du Pont and eventually Amalia's relationships with some of her sisters-in-law.

The last surviving brother, Frederic René, was so distressed by this family matter, and with his own health issues, that he decided to withdraw from this drama. His son Fred started to assume a major role in the firm in his place and worked with outside counsel to represent the children until "an out-of-court settlement with Marie" was reached in December of 1897.[41] Though the matter was seemingly settled, the whole affair was very prominent in the New York newspapers, and Amalia had to have been aware of these events. Furthermore, this would certainly have been a difficult position for du Pont in terms of where to place his allegiances: with his siblings or with his mother.

In the midst of the family turmoil, du Pont attended Columbia Law School and passed the bar in 1898.[42] A natural progression would have been for him to join the law firm. However, he chose to volunteer for the Spanish–American War and enlisted in June of 1898.[43] He was listed as a captain working with the Commissary of Subsistence and served in the Philippines, under General Otis.[44] His role in managing food supplies and other critical resources clearly kept him from the front lines.

After an honorable discharge, he returned to New York in the late autumn of 1899 and did indeed assume the role of a lawyer in the family business. How much he was involved and to what degree he was "wanted" at the Coudert firm is in dispute. This is evident in an excellent history of the Coudert Brothers law firm, where du Pont is never mentioned once in this timeframe. Instead it is his cousin, Fred Coudert, who eventually became the primary family member to run the firm. What is further curious is that cousin Fred also volunteered for the Spanish–American War and enlisted in May of 1898. He was a lieutenant and led a cavalry to Puerto Rico, and likely was more directly involved in the conflict.[45]

This brings the story of the couple to the start of the twentieth century and Amalia's return to New York from London in February following her dramatic months in South Africa. As previously noted, an unpublished biography of Amalia claims du Pont met her returning ship at the docks in New York. This certainly paints a romantic and cinematic image. But in articles already referenced, when Amalia was interviewed

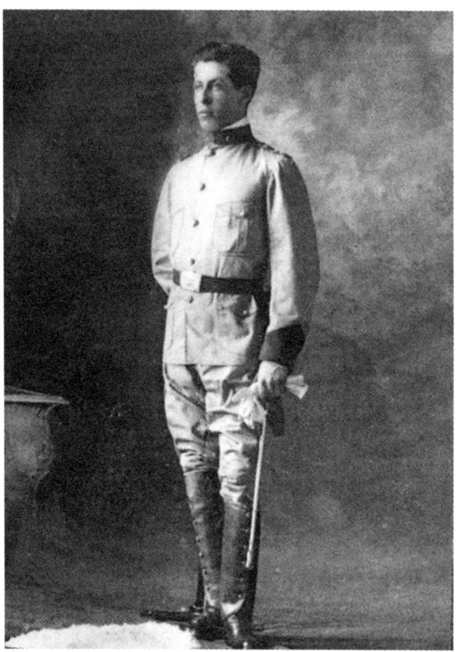

Charles du Pont Coudert in uniform during the Spanish–American War, author unknown (ca. 1898). *Courtesy of the Coudert family; retouched by Edward Ray*

at the docks his presence is not mentioned. Even if he was there, the reporters and likely Amalia chose not to mention his presence. It's also interesting that upon leaving Africa, Amalia arrived in London at the start of January and did not rush back to America, attending numerous social events in Paris and London. Miss Fanny Reed, sister of Mrs. Paran Stevens, "gave a grand dinner in her honor" in Paris, later in January.[46] In February, Amalia was a celebrated guest at Minnie Paget's London charity event, to benefit the families of those at the Boer War.[47] She departed from England as late as February 14, sailing on the *Teutonic*, part of the White Star Line.[48]

Upon her return to America and reuniting with du Pont, just recently home from the Philippines, Amalia likely painted a miniature of him in uniform (see color insert). It's unsigned but reminiscent of her style and was passed down through the du Pont line; she probably didn't see the need for her signature since it wasn't part of a commission.

The couple's honeymoon was also quite unplanned, as Amalia already had passage booked on the *St. Louis* on July 5 to go to England to work on yet more commissions from European royalty. Mr. Coudert was not able to get a larger stateroom on the *St. Louis*, and he booked passage on the *Majestic* for their honeymoon.[49] Amalia wasted no time celebrating and clearly reported to the newspapers that her career endeavors would continue, as was stated in the *Star Tribune*: "While abroad, Mrs. Coudert will paint miniatures of the princess of Wales and the emperor of Germany."[50] This would have been Princess Alexandra, wife of then Prince of Wales, and—Amalia was hoping—Kaiser Wilhelm II.

The couple spent close to four months in Europe. During their time away, late summer newspaper articles announced the publication of her miniatures in *Century Magazine*, but under her maiden name of Kussner, which probably "raised some eyebrows."[51]

Ultimately, what did Amalia gain from this marriage? Clearly, she had made a name for herself as an artist and was already financially well off. And possibly so was du Pont, at least within this timeframe, with the inheritance from his father. The prestigious Coudert family was listed on various New York social registers, and they were certainly one of the prominent, elite Catholic families of the era, with Frederic René on the board of directors at St. Patrick's Cathedral. But they were not among the Four Hundred, undoubtedly excluded due to their religion.

In looking at du Pont, it is also significant that though he seems to have briefly been part of the Coudert Law firm upon his return from the Philippines, later—either of his own choosing or as the result of a decision made by his relatives in the firm—he did not resume his role as a lawyer upon his return from the honeymoon. The only other listing of his activities outside of his legal duties, just prior to his marriage to Amalia, was being on the executive committee of the local badminton club.[52] Though certainly not a challenging sport, this club in New York "became a weekend meeting place for New York's society leaders."[53]

Though little was ever mentioned of du Pont in the coverage of their wedding, a few articles carried a short assessment of him: "Captain Coudert has never cared for society. He has been devoted for several years to Miss Kussner."[54] Maybe having a husband who shied away from the public life, and who seemingly had no career of his own that would detract from her accomplishments, was the best fit for Amalia. But there had to have been a friendship between them, and he likely adored her. Whatever the ultimate reasons for this marriage, as with many other nuptials in the Gilded Age theirs was likely not a marriage of love.

The newlyweds returned to New York in October, and their life fell into a regular pattern of frequent trips abroad and enjoying the New York social life. Such events included a welcoming party that was given for the couple by du Pont's sister Constance and her husband, William Garrison, at their Tuxedo Park home.[55] Surprisingly, Marie Coudert gifted to her son and new daughter-in-law her home at 53 West 48th Street, including *all* of its furnishings. She then moved into a smaller townhouse in New York. Ironically, Amalia and du Pont would spend little time at this residence.

Shortly after her return to New York that autumn, Amalia wrote a letter to one of the editors at *Century*, Mr. Johnson. Whereas originally she had objected to how the editors intended to publish her miniatures of the Prince of Wales and the czar, she was now complimentary on the display of miniatures by themselves:

> I have been ill even twice upon return from Europe, or I should have written you before to thank you for the lovely publications of my miniatures. . . . I got the magazine just before I left England & many of my English friends complimented the artistic way in which you had done them.[56]

Also intriguing about the *Century* letter is the design of the monogram on her stationery: her first name only (not her initials or any indication of her married name) in a circle topped with two wings and a heart with an arrow through it (see color insert). The wings themselves were not uncommon symbols on, for example, European family crests, but combined with the heart, it is more difficult to discern the meaning. This distinctive design would further support how the world viewed her: mysterious and hard to define.

Amalia would not take on the traditional role of a married woman. She was determined to continue her portraits, though she became more selective of her clients at this time. But this life, which seemed to suit both her and du Pont, would be disrupted by unexpected legal issues in 1901.

Chapter 6

Lawsuits and Mysteries

The year 1901 would bring legal issues for both Amalia and her husband. Things started in April, when once again issues were brought up by du Pont regarding the handling of his father's estate. Frederic René Coudert, his uncle who originally had been appointed as the executor of brother Charles Coudert's estate, was asked to provide details of his handling of the deceased's financial and physical properties. The legal filings submitted by Amalia's husband claimed that "his uncle came into possession of about $150,000 of personal property" but that no distributions had occurred either to himself or to other members of the family, including his six sisters and his mother, Marie.[1] Each child of Charles Coudert should have received one-seventh of the overall estate. At the time of this lawsuit, two of the sisters, Claire and Leonie, were already married and living abroad in France. Two other married sisters, Constance and Aimee, were living in New York. And finally, Jeanne Clarisse and Grace were unmarried and living with their mother.

The attorney, John J. Adams, was hired by du Pont not only to file the lawsuit but also to represent the interests of his mother and sisters. The suit was also filed against du Pont's cousin and fellow veteran, Fred Coudert, who had taken over managing the law firm.

Frederic René countered the claim of the missing distributions, issuing an affidavit that stated the effects of the various homes owned by his brother Charles had been provided as instructed to the widow, Marie. He also claimed there was very little that had *not* been accounted for in the way of physical properties, and further insisted that none of the property or belongings had come to him personally.

Attorney Adams countered that further inspection of the reports provided "left them entirely in the dark as to the value of the property,"[2] and therefore with a lack of clarity on the distributions. Also mentioned was that du Pont had filed objections to previous accounting provided by his uncle. Clearly, this had been an ongoing issue.

The only concession made by Frederic René was that he would involve appraisers "to make a report on personal property if necessary."[3] The ongoing legal issues between Charles du Pont Coudert and his uncle and his cousin may have indicated deeper rifts within the family and further highlight the mystery of why Amalia's husband was never significantly involved in the Coudert Law firm. Unfortunately, no evidence of how the dispute was resolved has surfaced.

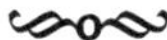

A much more shocking legal affair appeared suddenly in June, with newspapers that displayed the sensational headline of a mysterious lawsuit against *only* Amalia Kussner Coudert. The suit was brought by a "Blanche Lincoln," which by all accounts may have been a fictional name to protect this woman's privacy and identity, as many articles echoed the sentiment, "Who Blanch(e) Lincoln is, no one seems to know."[4]

The only publicly available pieces of information on the lawsuit are the names of the plaintiff (Blanche Lincoln) and the defendant (Amalia Kussner Coudert), who the lawyers were for each of these women, and the financial damages sought: $125,000. This was a significant amount at the time and would translate to over four million dollars in today's currency. Absolutely no other information on the content of the lawsuit was made public.

This strict secrecy agreed to by both sets of lawyers was adhered to, and no newspaper reported much else. Nevertheless, the headlines tainted the perception of the New York society, and it was generally assumed that some sort of indiscretion had been committed. Unfortunately for Amalia, word of this lawsuit also found its way to the newspaper in the town of her birth, Greencastle, Indiana. The *Greencastle Banner* carried the

AMALIA KUSSNER SUED

QUEER PROCEEDINGS AFFECTING
THE NOTED INDIANA ARTIST.

Legal Mystery in the Supreme Court
of New York—Cause of Mrs. Blanche
Lincoln's Suit Not Known.

Headline of a July 1901 *Indianapolis Journal* article about the lawsuit against Amalia Kussner.

suspicion, "The thing has a tinge of romance and mystery about it that has set all New York agog."[5]

There was one tantalizing clue, which was leaked to a single newspaper, the *Indianapolis Journal*, that the lawsuit mentioned a former admirer of Amalia's who was involved. But unfortunately, this name was never publicly divulged. Further adding to the sensational mystery is the single recorded statement from Blanche Lincoln who, when queried on the reasons for the lawsuit, simply said: "wait, and you shall see." The lawyers for both the claimant and the defendant were reported as saying, "We hope the public will never know."[6]

It is worth noting that both sets of lawyers had already been involved in high-profile cases—knowing what those cases involved and their specialties of law could help us infer the type of lawsuit this might have been against Amalia.

John J. Adams and Delancey Nicoll were the counsels for Amalia. Attorney Adams had been retained again, having just recently represented the Coudert family two months earlier. Nicoll had represented George Jay Gould, the eldest son of Jay Gould, three years previously. This was a continuation of the famous Gould blackmail case and involved convoluted legal issues from a woman claiming to be the mother of Jay Gould's child. Nicoll, who in addition to being a civil attorney had also been a former district attorney of New York City, was cited for his "ability to browbeat and gobble up hostile witnesses."[7] A few years after representing Amalia, Nicoll also represented a shady character who was hired by a concerned relative to break up a young man's marriage.[8]

House, Grossman, and Vorhaus, who represented the mysterious Blanche Lincoln, were all involved in cases of bribery and bankruptcy, more focused on financial matters.[9] But shortly after this 1901 lawsuit, they seemed to be almost exclusively involved in legal cases originating from the entertainment world. The name of their law firm can be seen listed in the entertainment magazine *Variety* through the 1900s, where they were hired to provide copyright protection to theatrical productions.[10]

Putting together the specialties of the various counsels, could there have been some sort of "hush-money" involved in addition to accusation of an indiscretion?

The case was scheduled for the end of June, on the docket calendar of the New York Supreme Court, with Judge Henry Bischoff presiding. However, none of the lawyers appeared on the appointed day, and the judge then removed the case from the calendar. Therefore, Blanche Lincoln, or whoever she was in real life, won the suit by default.[11]

Given what few clues there are, and viewing these proceedings from a more modern perspective, what type of indiscretion could this have been, especially with such a huge amount being requested for damages? In looking at other famous legal cases of the late Gilded Age, certainly huge settlements were proffered in divorce settlements, especially in cases of documented illicit affairs, such as the William and Alva Vanderbilt settlement in 1895.[12] But none of those factors seem to be relevant in this case, especially since there is little evidence that Amalia had much of a social or romantic life outside of her career prior to her marriage.

Could these legal proceedings be somehow related to Amalia's motivations for the sudden marriage just a year earlier? Aside from du Pont's career needs to be in a marriage, Amalia's agreeing to this union might also have been related to something that happened in 1900, and she married du Pont in order to appear more respectable and to be associated with a prominent New York family.

Most certainly, those at Coudert Law Firm would have rankled on this negative press, even though the law firm name was not mentioned in the articles. Regardless, the scandal certainly would have had an impact on Marie Coudert and the six sisters-in-law, especially those living in the greater New York area.

And of course, there would have been impact on Amalia's family living in Chicago, including her brother, Albert, who by 1901 had become a publicly acclaimed composer. The sibling relationship would have been widely known, especially since the stunning photo of Amalia graced the cover of one of his compositions.

Amalia had gone to great effort to spin a mythology about her age and artistic training for years, since 1893, and she had enjoyed mostly positive publicity. When useful, she provided reporters with embellished information, such as the timeline and nature of her relationship with her husband prior to the marriage. Therefore, the news coverage of this lawsuit must have been devastating to her. However, through all of the negative coverage, her fictitious age persisted, with one Boston newspaper listing her as twenty-six years old, when she was in fact then thirty-eight.[13]

Not surprisingly, Amalia and du Pont headed for Europe just after the case ended by default. Amalia appears to have departed no later than mid-July, given she was feted at a social event in England on July 27. Her benefactor, Minnie Paget, gave her an elaborate tea that was attended by the Duke of Cambridge and two lesser princesses from Germany. Du Pont left later, on July 24, sailing on the White Star steamship *Oceanic*.[14] Clearly, he departed too late to have been in attendance at Amalia's social event.

At the tea, Amalia advised those attending that she was on her way to the continent and shortly after left England.[15] Records do show that she went to both Germany and France, arriving in Paris from Homburg, Germany, by the end of September. Homburg was the location of Kaiser Wilhelm II's summer castle, and part of her reason for this trip may have been to talk to the Kaiser regarding doing his portrait.[16]

While Amalia was in Paris that fall, she had the honor of being introduced to Madame Loubet, who was "desirous of having the famous

American miniaturist paint portraits of herself, her husband, the President of the French republic, and their son."[17] Madame Loubet entertained Amalia for two hours at the Élysée palace; however, the article in the *St. Louis Dispatch* didn't indicate if Amalia indeed painted the French president and his family. Regardless, this was yet another example of Amalia's connections with the highest society levels of Europe.

As for whether Amalia was shunned by New York society, surprisingly, perhaps, there was a glowing description of her in the New York periodical *The Critic* published in November 1901. Though one can't be sure of the date the article was written, likely the publisher would have had the choice to remove the article prior to publication if Amalia were still persona non grata and the mysterious incident still prominent in the news. The author of the piece stated that Amalia's work was still greatly in demand thanks to her distinctive style, especially favored by the "royalties and titled folk," and that she continued garnering the highest commissions for miniatures.[18] It appears the lawsuit had little impact on her business in the city.

There was very little coverage of Amalia or her husband for the rest of that year, except for a less-than-flattering *New York Times* article, also in November, that had no connection to the recent legal proceedings. The piece covered the habits of women of society with regard to peculiar objects they kept as talismans to protect them and bring them luck. Amalia was quoted as saying that she wore an "ugly bracelet, woven of silvery white horsehairs," given to her by an Arab sheik. The horsehairs were from the sheik's favorite Arab horse. Wearing the bracelet was essential to her when she was painting, she said, otherwise her artwork became "a ghastly daub."[19] Amalia's odd habit was documented along with other examples, such as Queen Victoria's high regard for Manx cats, which she was convinced "brought good luck to the royal household." The article took the derogatory tone that these women, "the superstitious sex," would still depend on such objects and beliefs even when given higher education.

Generally, Amalia's work in New York seems to decrease after 1901, with more and more of her time spent in Europe. But this drop in commissions also could have been due to the fact that European society seemed to accept her more in their ranks of high society and in the social circles of the royalty, whereas Amalia was never to see an invitation to the coveted soirées of New York's elite. In America, she would remain seen as an artist whose job was to paint them in all their glory but who was not on par with their social standing.

CHAPTER 7

A Shift in Focus

Amalia's painting of royalty throughout Europe continued through the 1900s, though her overall number of portrait commissions did decline, with fewer being done in New York and a few other cities in the United States.

Early in the decade, Amalia was commissioned to do a miniature of Miss Marion Cockrell, possibly in Washington, DC. She was the daughter of Missouri Senator Francis Marion Cockrell, and one of the few women painted by Amalia related to an American politician. A photo of the miniature was prominently displayed along with an article that announced her engagement in December of 1903. Miss Cockrell was extolled as a "famous beauty." Below the miniature was a photograph of Miss Cockrell, with the classic hairstyle of a Gibson Girl.[1]

In 1903, Amalia again painted a miniature of Mrs. Alice Keppel, one of King Edward VII's favored women. Mrs. Keppel commissioned Amalia to paint her portrait as a birthday gift for the king, who in turn gave Alice a tremendously expensive coat made of Russian sable fur with a yellow satin lining. To complete this luxurious garment, there was a "sapphire diamond clasp at the throat."[2] Both gifts were seen as somewhat shocking by the London society.

Even with Amalia's having fewer commissions in New York, she was still connected with some wealthy women from America who had started to travel more to Europe and spend extended vacations abroad. Included among these travelers was Mrs. Frank Mackay, who Amalia had painted previously (and who was featured in the Great Beauties collection; see color insert). Mrs. Mackay lived part time in England and was the hostess of well-appointed social events that included the titled men and women of Britain. Amalia painted her again in 1904, producing a "charming miniature."[3]

Though not part of a portrait commission, Amalia and her husband had a most unusual meeting with a figure who in some ways exceeded the highest levels of royalty: Pope Pius X. Likely through the Coudert family's strong associations with the Catholic Church in New York, they were granted a private interview with the pope in 1904. They left the meeting with a large photograph from the pope, with the inscription, "To the little married couple, Amalia and Du Pont Coudert."[4]

One royal woman, Queen Maud of Norway, was most impressed by Amalia's talent and commissioned her multiple times. Queen Maud's life started in England, where she was born "Maud of Wales" in 1869, the daughter of the then Prince of Wales. She was married to Prince Carl of Denmark in 1896.[5] Norway, at that time, was governed by Denmark. However, after many years of wanting to be a separate nation and a series of lengthy and intense political negotiations, Norway became a separate country in the fall of 1905. Prince Carl then was elected the king of Norway and assumed the title of Haakon VII.[6] Maud became the queen of Norway, though she often traveled back to England to visit family, including her father, now King Edward VII.

One such trip was made to Sandringham in the late fall of 1906, to have Amalia do her portrait. The following account comes from "Lady Mary's Gossip," a London society column reprinted in many American newspapers:

> Mrs. Dupont Coudert, better known as Amalia Kussner, has had many royal commissions, so it can be no surprise to her to have received an order for a miniature of Queen Maud of Norway. Mrs. Dupont has an immense vogue over here and commands big prices for her work.[7]

The queen's interests included the latest fashions, and she was one of the most impressively attired women of royalty at the time. With such sophisticated taste in her wardrobe, it's natural that she would have wanted Amalia to paint her in order to get a striking and less traditional portrait. Amalia was commissioned to do at least one more portrait of Maud a few years later, traveling to Norway in 1908 along with her husband.[8] Many of Maud's gowns are today part of a permanent collection at the National Museum in Oslo, Norway.[9]

With the large numbers of royalty and titled ladies and gentlemen that Amalia painted, she almost always spoke highly of her experiences with them. In a 1902 article, she expounded, saying:

> Royalty is not formidable. It is very human. . . . It never disappoints an artist in an appointment. All have their off days, you may be sure, like the rest of us poor mortals—tired, headachy, and all that; but there is never one word of complaint.[10]

She went on to say that she saw them living lives of "generous and kindly self-sacrifice" and observed it being difficult for them to live up to the era's standards of *noblesse oblige*.

Amalia had earnest plans to paint another reigning monarch, Kaiser Wilhelm II, the emperor of Germany, and her intentions were published in newspaper accounts even before the portrait was agreed upon. She had contacted the British ambassador to Germany, Francis Lascelles, requesting a meeting with the emperor and sent along reproductions of her miniatures. Lascelles replied in September 1901 from Berlin that "a long time will elapse before I have an opportunity of seeing the Emperor."[11] Furthermore, he acknowledged that "a personal interview with the Emperor would of course be the most satisfying way of meeting your wishes. . . . I see no hope of this for a long time to come." There is no doubt that Amalia tried several times more to arrange a sitting with him, as she had with Rhodes, but to no avail. Many years later, in a 1913 interview, she revealed that she still wanted to paint him.[12] But with the end of her career and the start of World War I in 1914, it was ultimately never to be.

The 1902 article about Amalia's views of royalty also featured an interesting role reversal, in which an English noblewoman became the artist and Amalia the subject. Following Amalia's arrival in London and introduction to upper-class social circles, she became friends with Violet Manners, who at the time was the Marchioness of Granby and an established artist as well.

Violet, of some titled lineage herself, was married at the age of twenty-six to Henry Manners in 1882,[13] who all knew with time would be part of titled succession. Sure enough, with the passing of his father, Henry obtained the title of the 8th Duke of Rutland in 1906.[14]

Whereas Amalia's earlier connections to the high society of London were through Minnie Paget and those connected with the Marlborough Set, Violet belonged to a different social group called "the Souls." She seemed to embody their culture and was described as "Ethereal, artistic, bohemian, passionate."[15] In some sense, the Souls were in competition with the social group associated with the Prince of Wales, and in other ways they actively rebelled against the Marlborough Set:

It was as a reaction to this pattern of late Victorian society that the Souls developed their new and distinctive style. They were not satisfied with the entrenched, ineffable, unchanging manners and modes of the upper-class world.[16]

Furthermore, "nobility was not an absolute condition of membership of the Souls."[17] Instead, the characteristics that were valued most were wit and intellect. Women were welcome in this group—an opportunity that stood out in a time when "clever women" were usually not admired. In the earlier years of the Souls, Violet was considered the queen of this social group and was probably the most unconventional of the female members, in part because she was also close to those in the acting world of London. Some members of the Souls spoke disapprovingly of her in secret and thought her close association with the group of actors was too bohemian.

Violet was an accomplished artist, especially with pencil sketches, though she never received any formal training. She had her works exhibited throughout her life, starting in 1877 at the opening of the Grosvenor

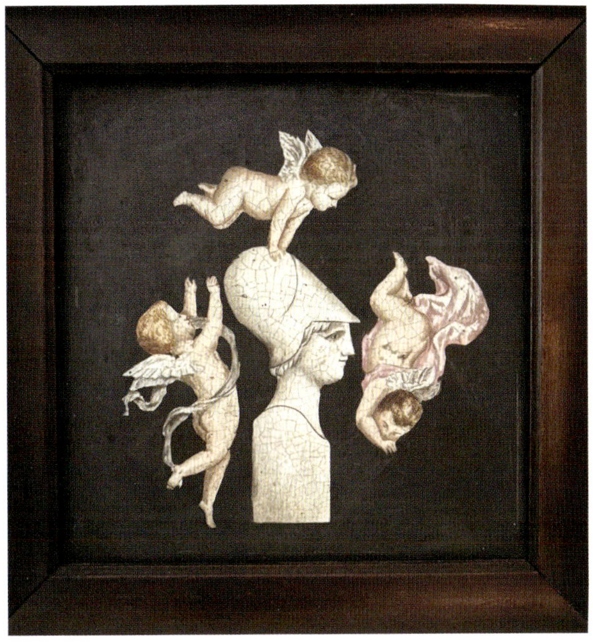

Cherubs Dancing around Head by Amalia Kussner (ca. 1880). *Author's collection. Photo by Edward Ray.*

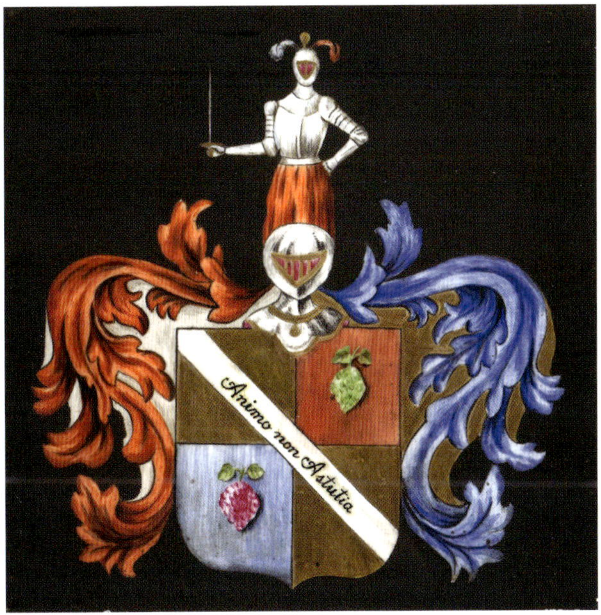

Painting of a Scottish family crest on Minton tile by Amalia Kussner (ca. late 1870s). *Courtesy of the Vigo County History Center, Terre Haute, Indiana. Used with permission.*

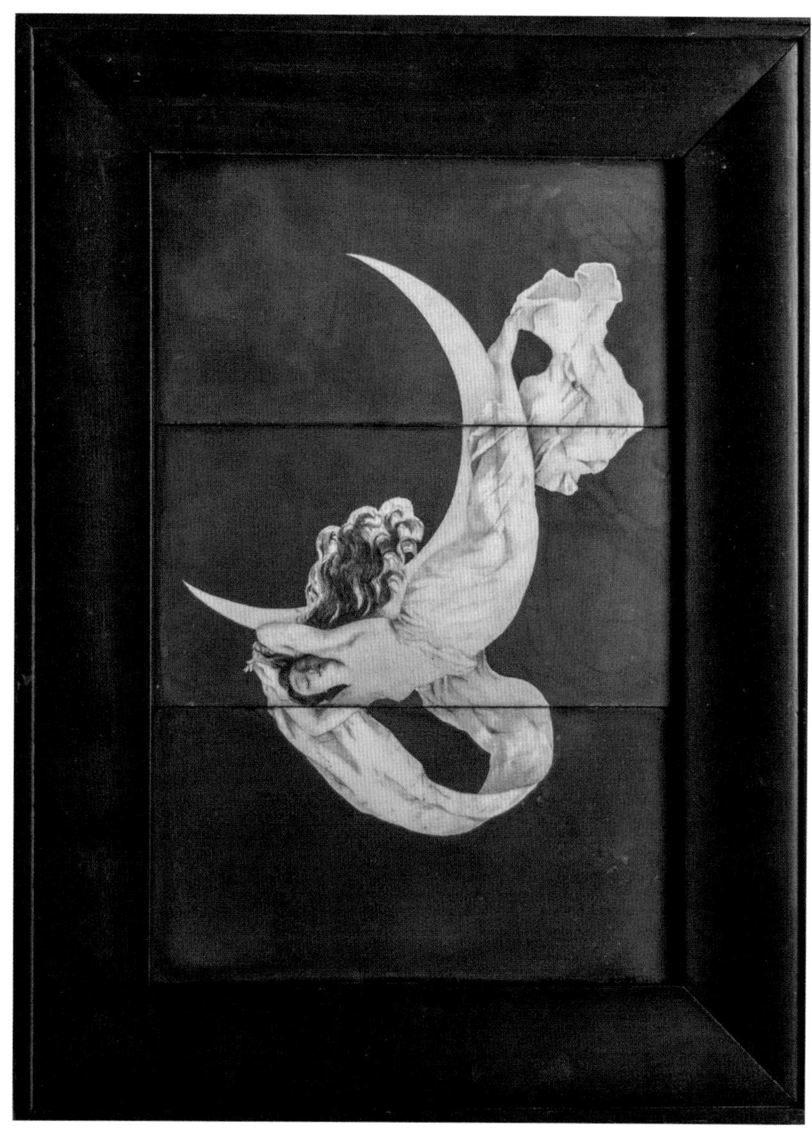

Moon Lady by Amalia Kussner (ca. 1885). Author's collection. Photo by Edward Ray.

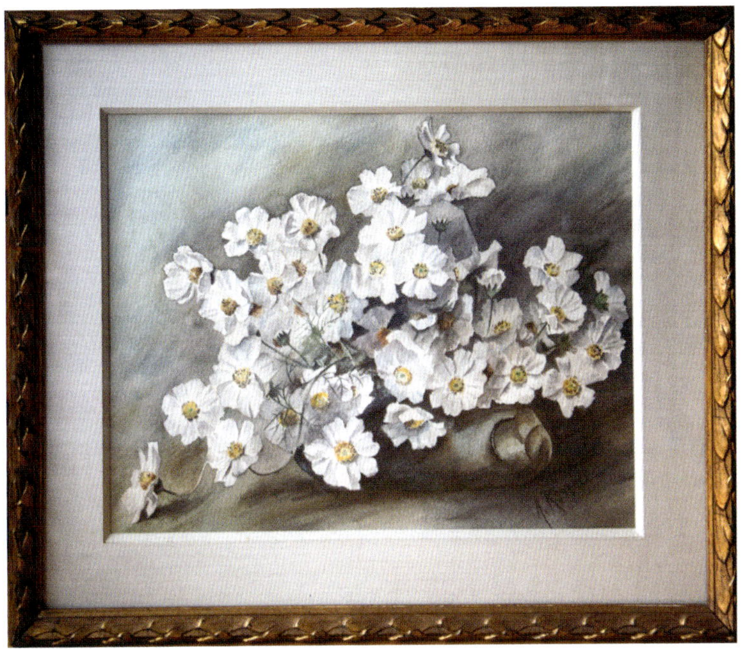

Flowers in Vase by Amalia Kussner (ca. 1885). *Author's collection. Photo by Edward Ray.*

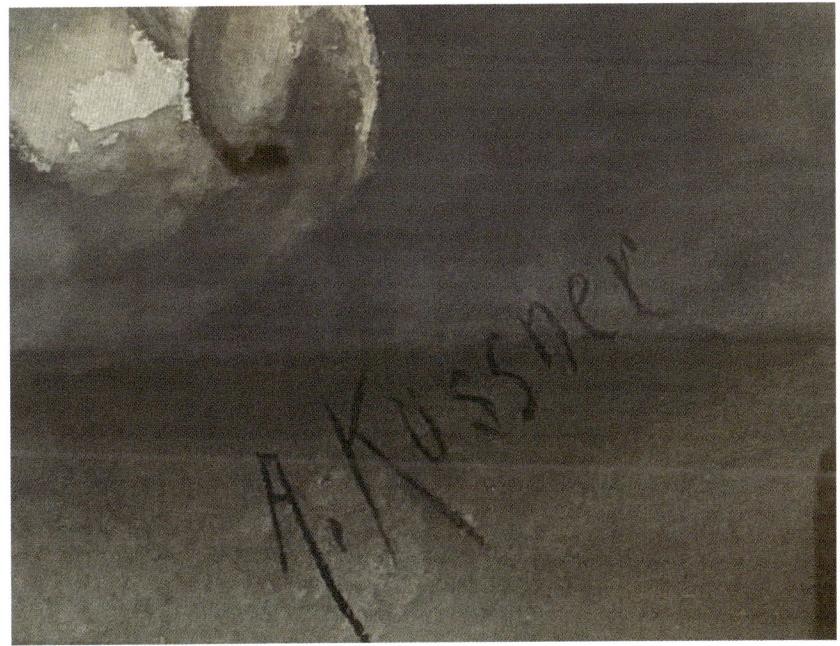

Close-up of Amalia's signature on *Flowers in Vase. Author's collection. Photo by Edward Ray.*

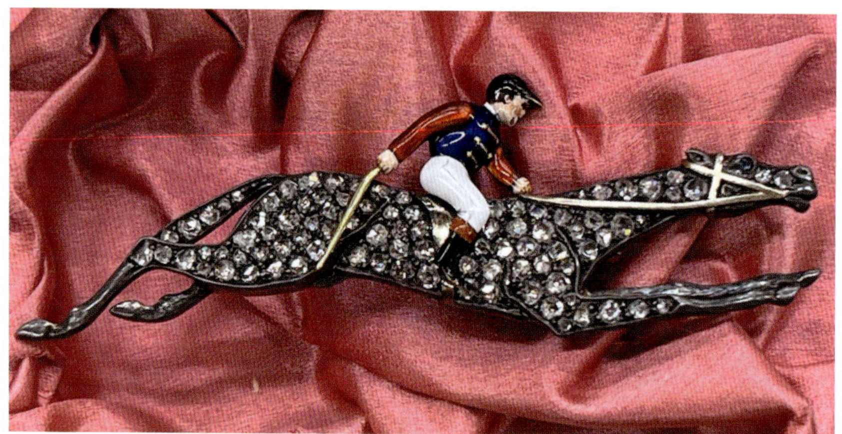

Persimmon pin given to Amalia Kussner by the Prince of Wales (1898). *Courtesy of the Amalia Kussner Papers (Private Collection), Sisters of Providence Archives at Saint Mary-of-the-Woods, Indiana. Photo by the author.*

Cover of *Moon Moths* sheet music by Albert Kussner featuring the art nouveau design by E. Mulier (1905). Bosworth & Co., London, England. *Author's collection.*

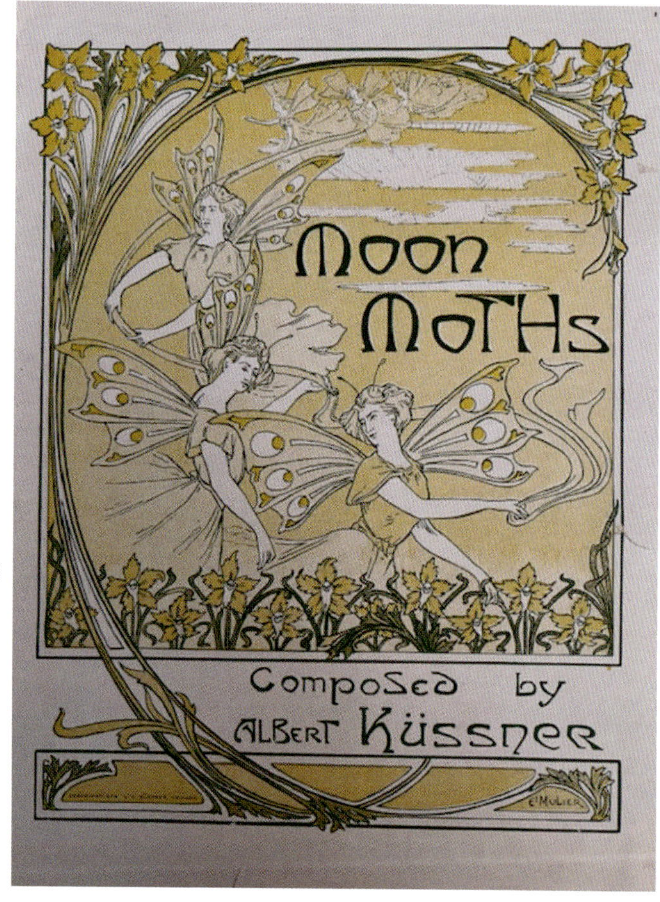

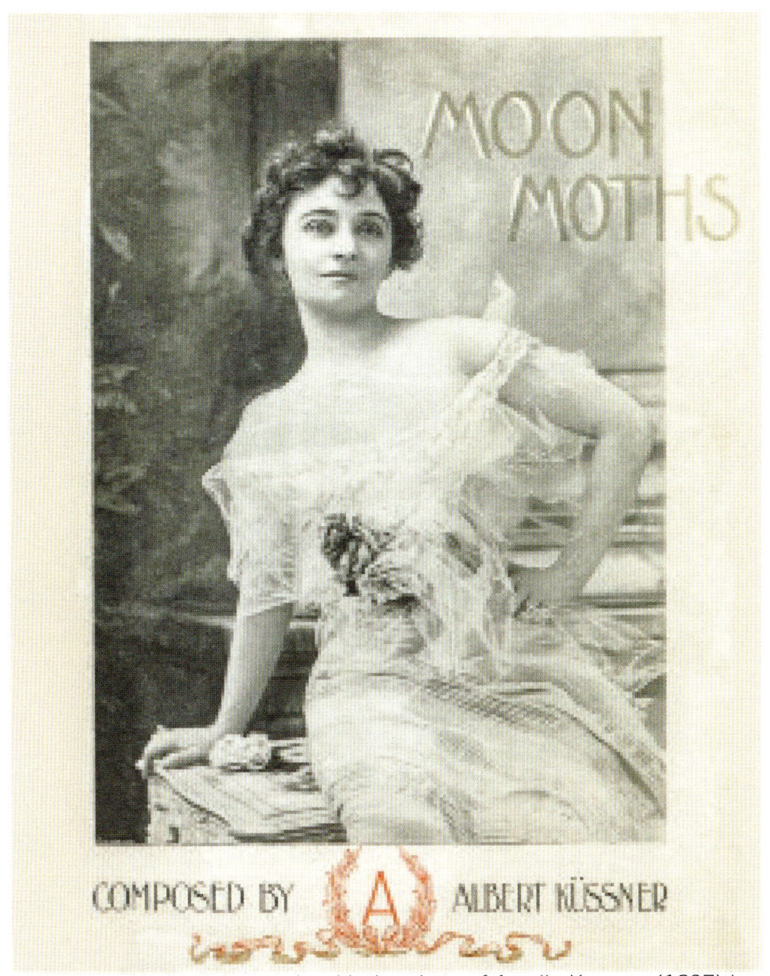

Cover of Moon Moths sheet music with the photo of Amalia Kussner (1897) by London photographer Alfred Ellis. Parlor Salon Sheet Music Collection, *DigitalCommons@Umaine, public domain.*

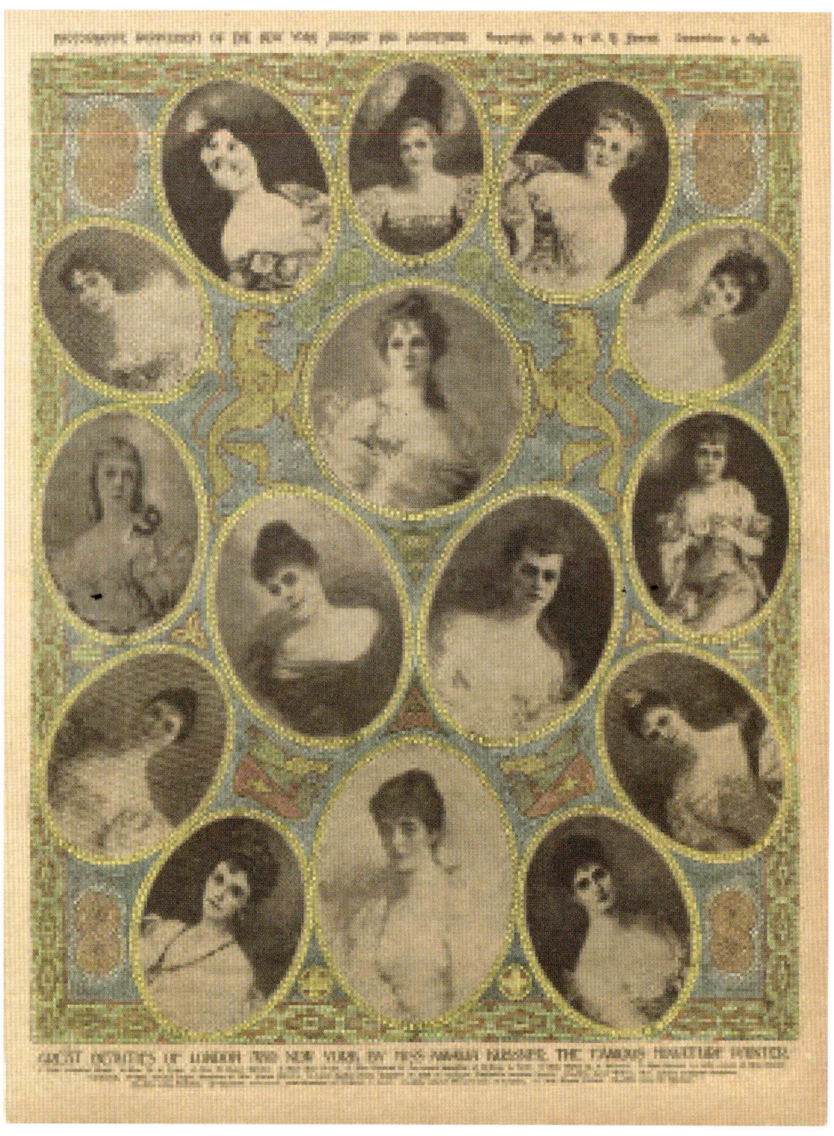

The "Great Beauties of London and New York" display of fifteen miniatures by Amalia Kussner, as seen in the *New York Journal and Advertiser*, December 1898. From left to right: Top group: Mrs. Alfred Harmsworth of London, Mrs. Frank Tilford, Mrs. M.A. Tyler, Mrs. E. Reeve Merritt, Miss May Goelet. Center: Miss Atherton Blight. Middle group: Mathilde Townsend, granddaughter of William L. Scott; Mrs. John W. Mackay; Mrs. Oliver H. P. Belmont; Mrs. Richard H. Townsend, daughter of William L. Scott. Bottom group: Mrs. John Dutcher; Mrs. Orme Wilson, Mrs. Astor's youngest daughter; Lady Sophie Scott, daughter of Earl of Cadogan, England's greatest beauty; Mrs. Arthur Paget, daughter of Mrs. Paran Stevens; Miss Eleanor Le Roy, cousin of Mrs. George Vanderbilt. *Library of Congress*

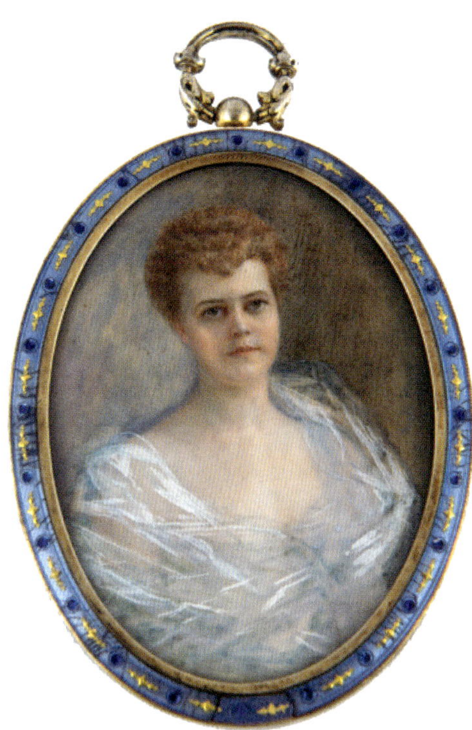

Portrait miniature of Alva Vanderbilt Belmont by Amalia Kussner (1896), paint on ivory, metal, enamel, gemstones. *Courtesy of the Preservation Society of Newport County, collection number PSNC.532a-b. Used with permission.*

Miniature of Leila Hardie Moore (1898) by Amalia Kussner. *Courtesy of The Historic New Orleans Collection, collection number 2012.0205, Gift of Joan Burguieres Brown. Used with permission.*

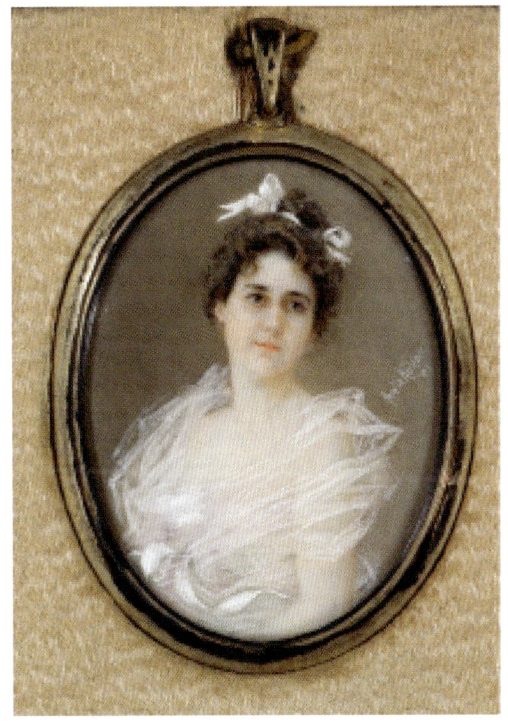

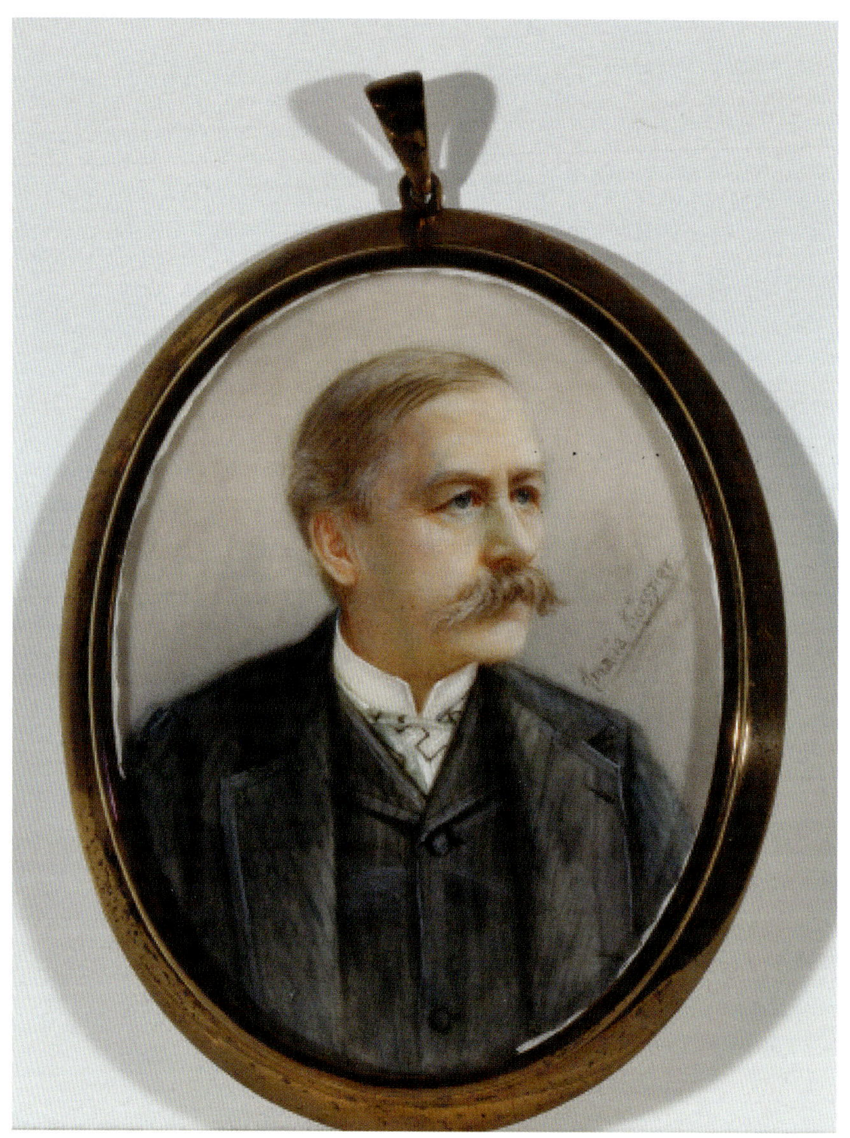

Miniature of Charles Hamot Strong by Amalia Kussner (1894). *Courtesy of Swope Art Museum, Terre Haute, Indiana. Used with permission.*

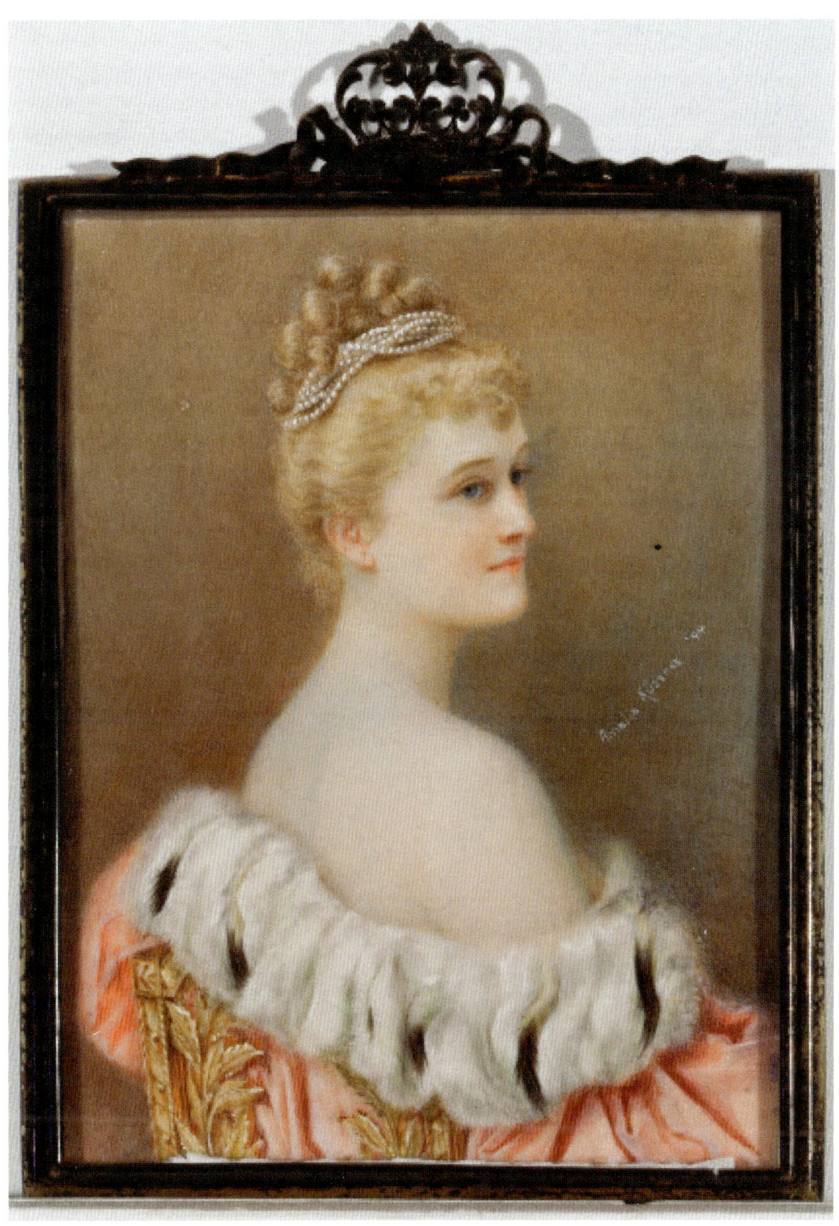

Miniature of Annie Wainwright Scott Strong by Amalia Kussner (1894). *Courtesy of Swope Art Museum, Terre Haute, Indiana. Used with permission.*

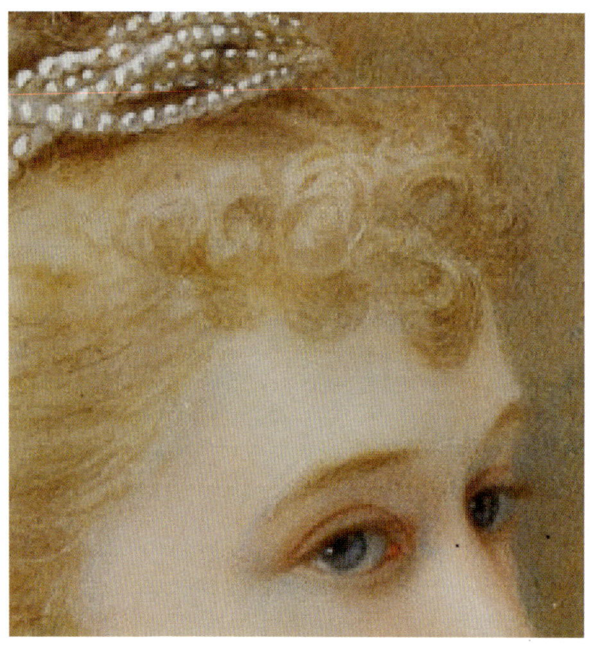

Close-up of the miniature of Annie Wainwright Scott Strong by Amalia Kussner (1894), showing the precision and realistic detail. *Courtesy of Swope Art Museum, Terre Haute, Indiana. Used with permission.*

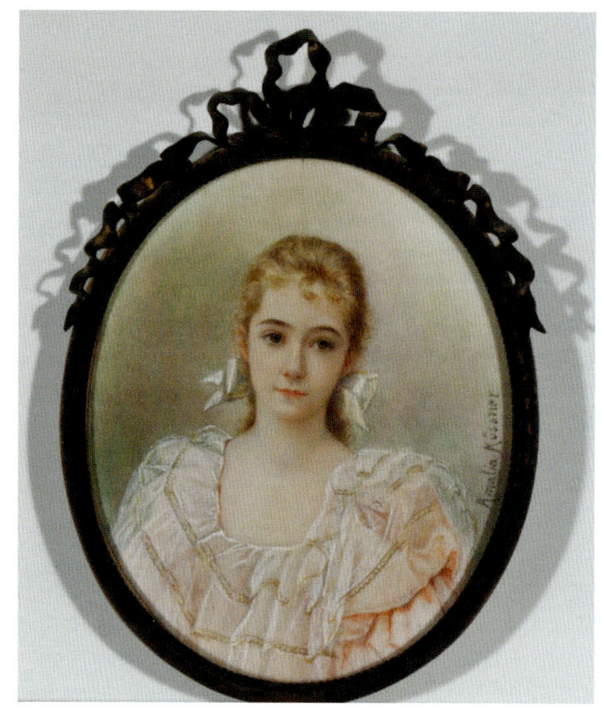

Miniature of Matilda Thora Wainwright Strong by Amalia Kussner (1894). *Courtesy of Swope Art Museum, Terre Haute, Indiana.*

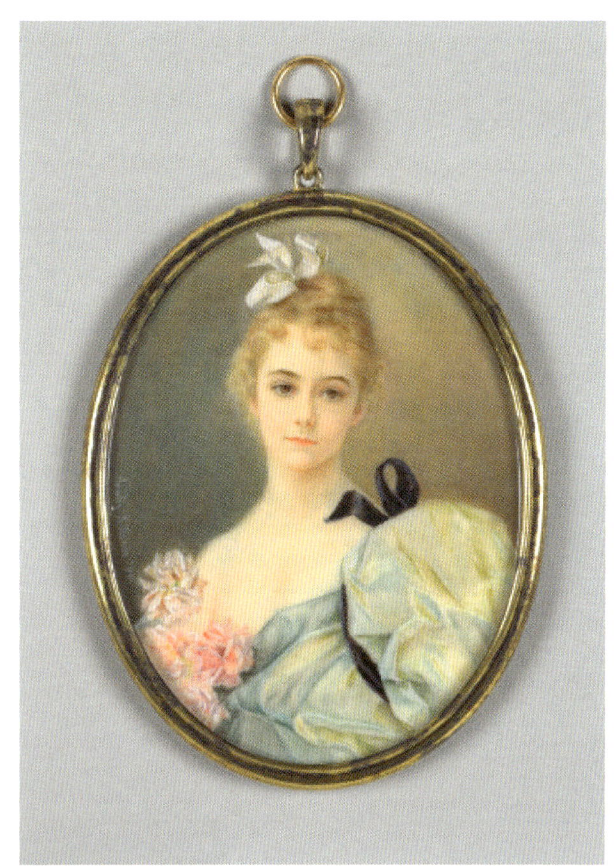

Later miniature of Matilda Thora Wainwright Strong as a young adult by Amalia Kussner (year undetermined). *Courtesy of Cincinnati Art Museum, collection number 2004.493, Gift of Mr. and Mrs. Charles Fleischmann III. Used with permission.*

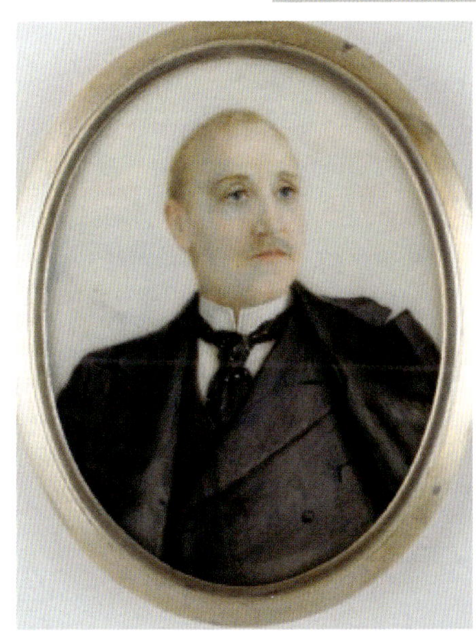

Portrait of a Man, possibly Richard Townsend, by Amalia Kussner (ca. 1897). *Worcester Art Museum/Gift of Lewis Hoyer Rabbage/Bridgeman Images (#WAM8970421).*

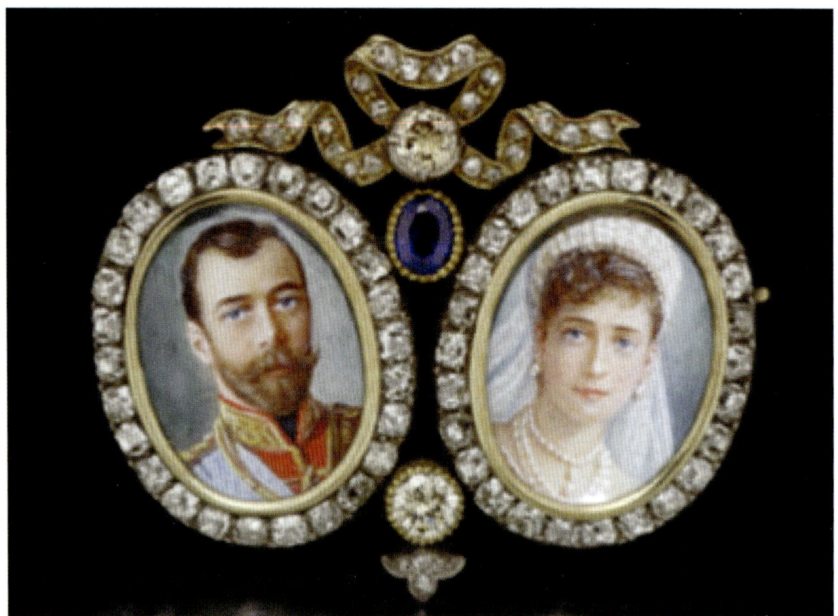

Brooch with miniatures of Nicholas II and Alexandra (ca. 1894–1896). *Courtesy of Hillwood Estate, Museum and Gardens, Bequest of Marjorie Merriweather Post, 1973, photographed by Alex Braun. Used with permission.*

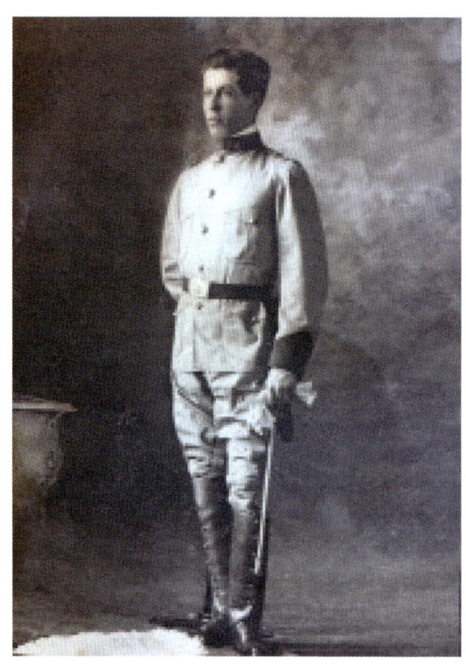

Miniature of Charles du Pont Coudert in uniform during the Spanish–American War, attributed to Amalia Kussner (ca. 1898). *Courtesy of the Coudert family. Retouched by Edward Ray.*

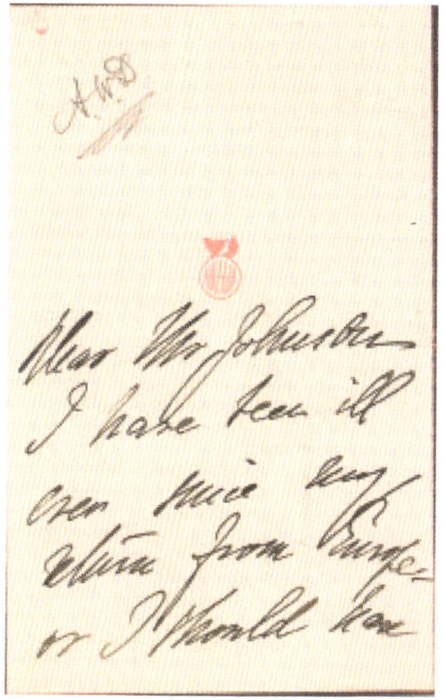

Amalia's monogrammed letterhead, as seen on a note she wrote to *Century Magazine* editor Mr. Johnson (1900). Century Company Records, *The New York Public Library, Digital Collections.*

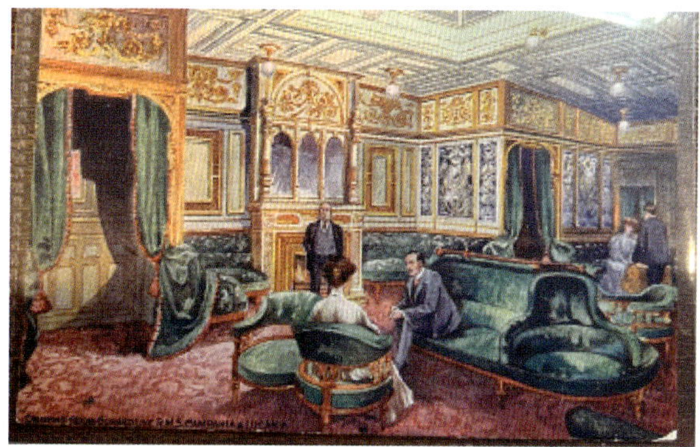

Postcard featuring a color painting of a typical drawing room aboard the Cunard liners RMS *Campania* and *Lucania* (1900–1910). Universal Postal Union. *Author's collection.*

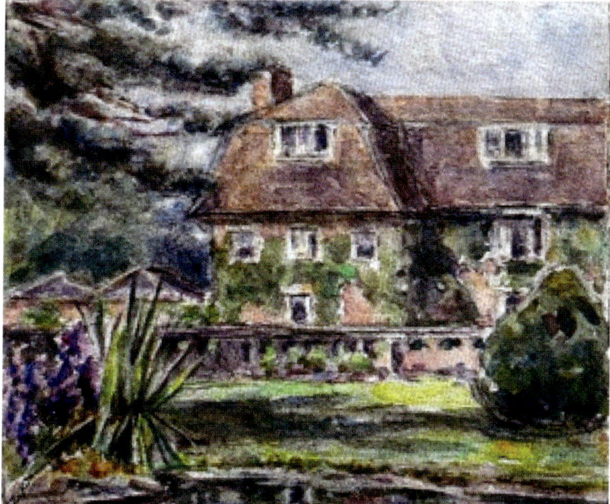

Watercolor of Thankerton House by Amalia Kussner (ca. 1920s). *Courtesy of the Seth Weinhardt Collection*

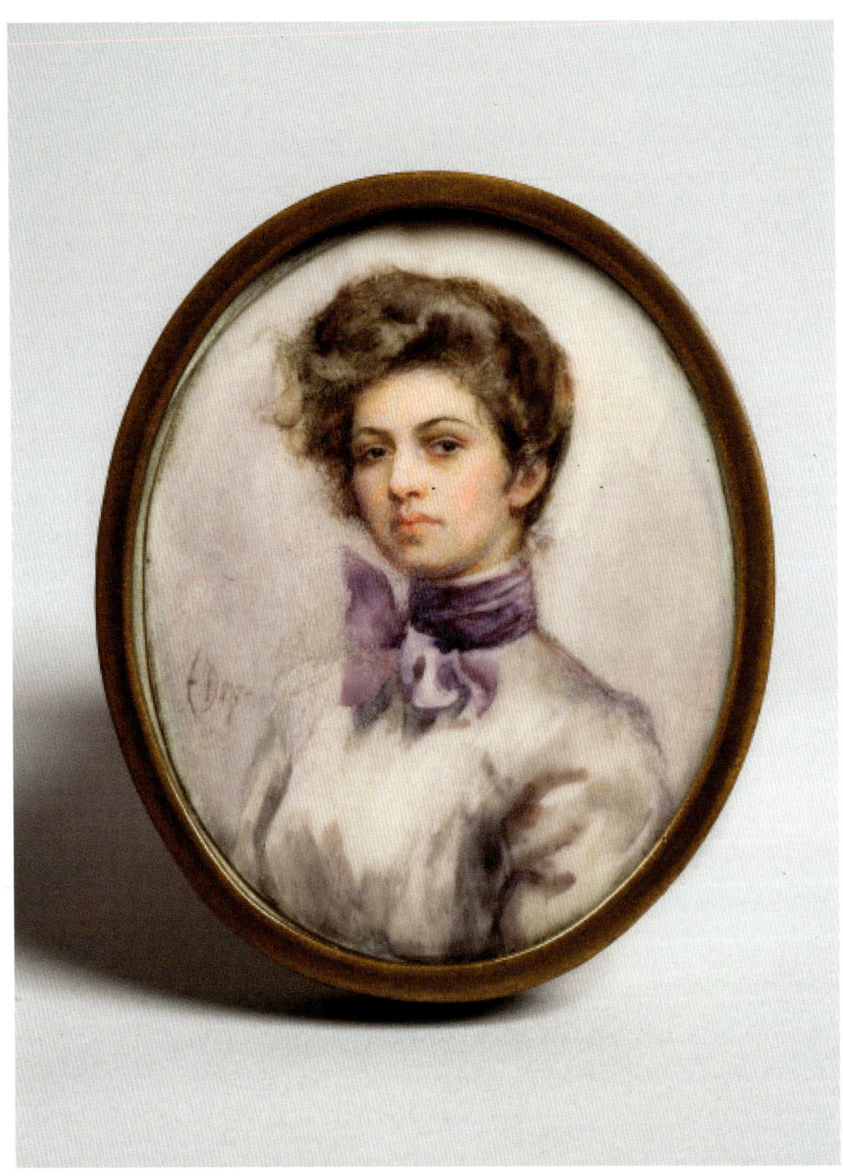

Me, a self-portrait miniature by Eulabee Dix, watercolor on ivory (ca. 1899). *Courtesy of National Museum of Women in the Arts, Washington, DC. Gift of Mrs. Philip Dix Becker and family. Photograph by Lee Stalsworth. Used with permission.*

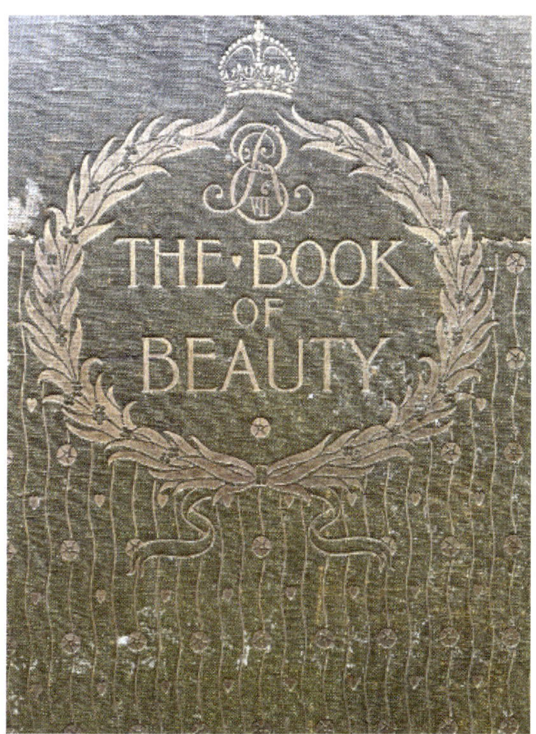

The top portion of the front cover of the US edition of *The Book of Beauty*, edited by Mrs. F. Harcourt Williamson (J. B. Lippincott & Co., 1902), showing the royal monogram (1902). *Author's collection. Photo by Edward Ray.*

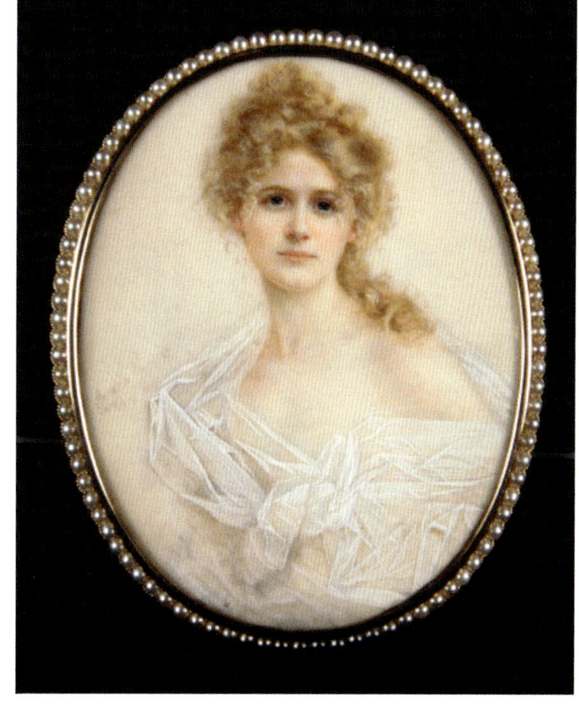

The engagement portrait of Ruth Lee (née Ruth Moore) by Amalia Kussner (1899) that is part of the collection at Chequers, the prime minister's estate. © *Mark Fiennes Archive. All rights reserved 2024/ Bridgeman Images.*

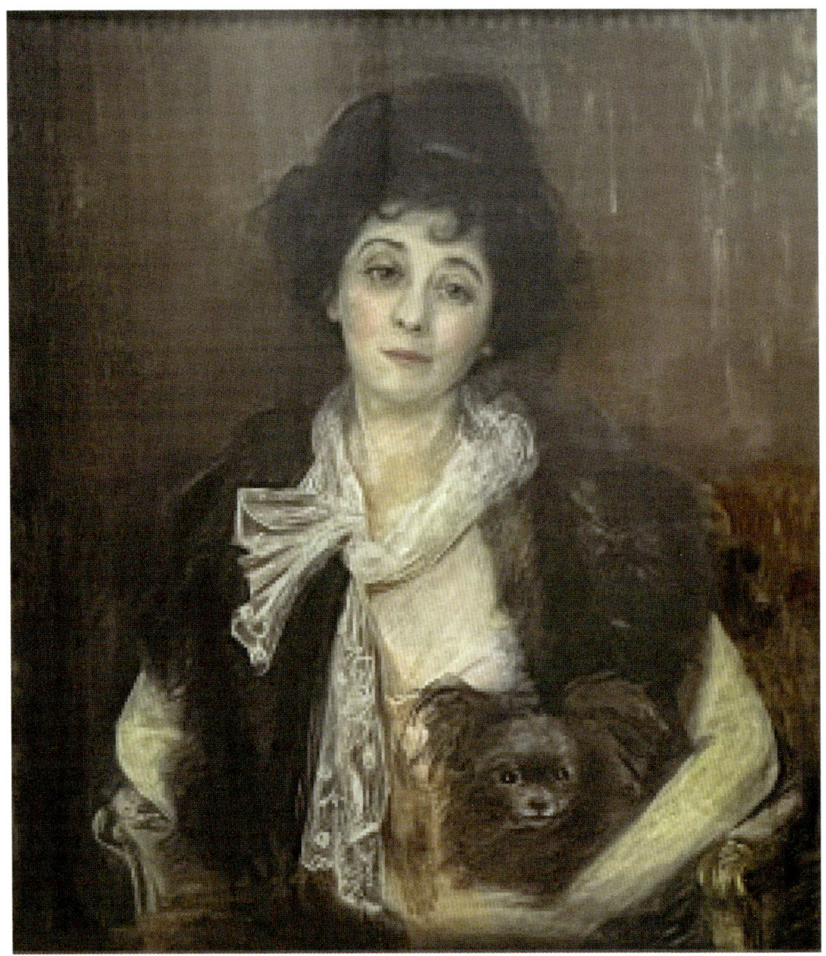

Portrait of Amalia Kussner by Lady Henrietta Guiness (Mrs. Benjamin Guiness), date unknown. *Courtesy of the Amalia Kussner Papers (Private Collection), Sisters of Providence Archives at Saint Mary-of-the-Woods, Indiana. Photo by author.*

Gallery.[18] She was most noted for "her ability to capture the likeness of the subject" in pencil and paper.[19] Like Amalia, this was due to both her skill and her close association with many of her subjects, many of whom were members of the Souls. A number of Amalia's portraits also featured members of the Souls, including Daisy, Countess of Warwick. In Amalia's efforts to paint the elite of British society, it likely mattered not which social group her sitters came from.

Amalia and Violet certainly connected socially and coordinated two events in July 1898, both held at the Willis's Rooms in London, "a new venue for afternoon parties."[20] Violet's party was held in the early afternoon and specifically labeled as a Souls event. Amalia held her tea later that afternoon at the same venue and "most of the party adjourned . . . to Miss Kussner's party."[21] Amalia provided a distinctive atmosphere, with trees brought in and placed around the tables so the guests could feel like they were outdoors. She also supplied novel refreshments and, against the British social convention, omitted their classic beverage, instead offering "all kinds of new drinks—anything, in fact, but tea."

One cannot be sure, but it's likely that Amalia sought out Violet in 1899 to do her portrait rather than Violet approaching her. Amalia would have seen that many of the important members of British society had already been sketched by Violet. The Marchioness created a delicate yet expressive portrait of the miniature painter in 1899, possibly using charcoal and pencil, showing Amalia clothed in one of her signature wraps.[22] For this noblewoman to have taken the time to do such artwork was further indication that Amalia was appreciated and accepted by English society in ways that were never evidenced in New York.

Violet received a commission for the sketch she did of Amalia and in turn sent her a thank you letter dated August 22, 1899:

Dear Miss Kussner,

 It is very good of you to have sent the money—I do hope the frame will be all you like—you are so nice to praise the drawing so much—& it made me contended to take the [money?]

 I will show you some day the reason for my wanting money—this is to pay for my marble monument.—I want it all to be paid for by my

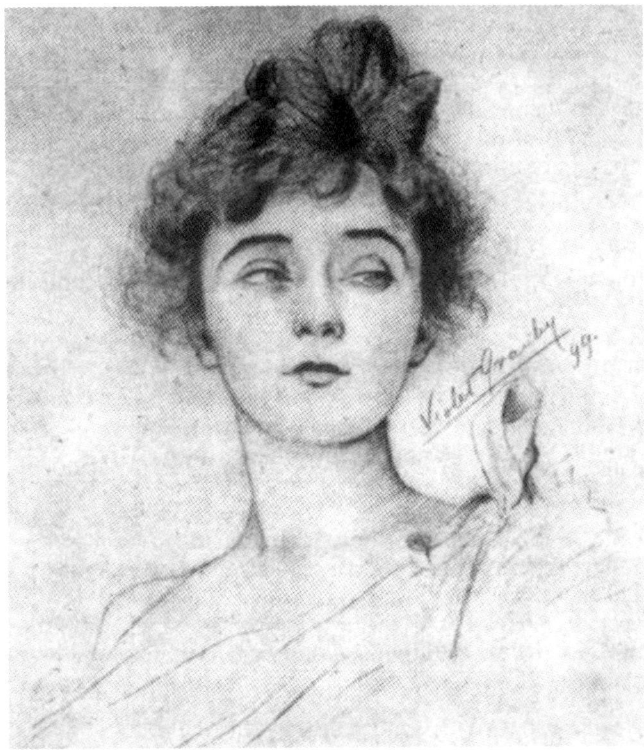

Sketch of Amalia Kussner Coudert by Violet Manners, Marchioness of Granby (1899). *Creative Commons Attribution-Share Alike 4.0 International license, courtesy of user Julian Felsenburgh*

own work—as well as being all my own work—And it's the work of my life and life's blood really. I mention this—as perhaps you would like to have helped me—for that sacred object—

I hope your holiday is going to be delicious.

With many many thanks,

Violet Granby[23]

The aforementioned marble monument was most likely a part of the life-sized effigy that Violet created as a dedication to her son, Robert, who died at age nine in 1894 after a short illness. Violet had a death mask made of her son and used that likeness to start the sculpture, which took her forty years to complete while she lived at Belvoir Castle. Violet, without any training in sculpture, shows her son in a reposed position, eyes closed with hands folded on his chest, and even captured his features in detail, including "the curls of his hair falling across his face, the tiny dimple in his chin, the contours of his neck."[24] The effigy, which is mounted on a marble base, has an inscription crediting Violet with the creation of this "final token of her love."[25]

From the letter alone, it's not clear if Violet ever divulged to Amalia the sentimental purpose of the monument, but one can assume they stayed in touch and that Amalia would have eventually learned how her money helped pay for this special memorial. According to the archivist at Belvoir Castle, Victoria Perry, it is "extremely likely" that Amalia's payment to Violet did indeed go toward funding the monument for her son, especially because there are *no* other recordings of Violet doing artworks of this nature for the rest of her life. Her sculpting endeavor became her sole focus and took many decades for her to complete; the final monument wasn't finished until the 1930s.[26]

A collection of Violet's artworks was published in 1900, titled *Portraits of Men and Women*, consisting of fifty-one of her sketches. Two years later, many of her works appeared in an impressive exhibition at the Grafton Galleries of London that included her sketch of Amalia. In looking at the totality of her sketches, Violet's most productive period was the 1890s, similar to Amalia's career. She expanded beyond just those who were part of the Souls, and especially for the male portraits chose her subjects "on the basis of their public renown."[27] This was certainly evident from the sketches included in her book, which includes portraits of Cecil Rhodes and author Rudyard Kipling. Violet was also sufficiently established at this time to have done a portrait of Queen Victoria, which was included in the *Portraits* collection of 1900.

In comparing Amalia and Violet as artists, though they did portraits of many of the same subjects, Amalia presented a sometimes romanticized vision of her sitters, whereas Violet provided an exactness, as well as more of a texture to her subject's faces, since she did not use color in her sketches. But certainly, the two talented women were sought after by both prominent social groups and important figures during the Victorian and Edwardian periods.

In April 1904, Amalia would be once again plagued by lawsuits and much notoriety. This time it was Amalia who initiated the legal action, brought against Mrs. Claude (Ada) Watney of London. The suit claimed that Amalia was still owed two hundred guineas out of the original agreed-upon fee of four hundred guineas. Mrs. Watney denied that the original commission had been four hundred guineas.[28]

Amalia and Mrs. Watney started their correspondence regarding a portrait late in 1901, while Amalia was staying in London. Amalia offered her services to Mrs. Watney in a letter, listing the many royals she had painted, including the czar and czarina of Russia, and the potential upcoming portrait to be done of the Kaiser. Mrs. Watney was suitably impressed, and the portrait was completed the following year when Amalia was back in London. However, Mrs. Watney wrote to Amalia afterward, stating that "My friends like it very much, but I want you to alter the mouth and chin, which are too pretty for mine."[29] Such a request was quite unusual for Amalia, since often those who sat for her wanted their looks *improved* and to be given a younger visage.

Mrs. Watney further claimed she thought the original price was in the range of one hundred to 150 guineas but that she had sent an amount of two hundred guineas in a measure of good faith, to account for the needed alterations. She had also stipulated that the portrait be completed by her husband's birthday and said Amalia did not meet that date. Mrs. Watney's defense was somewhat weakened since she had sent another note to Amalia in which she provided her with a glowing review of the miniature: "I like your portrait immensely, the coloring is so beautifully soft, and the minuteness of the fine work really marvelous."[30] Now Mrs. Watney claimed this was not the truth and that her husband had at first discouraged her from being critical of the artist.

Though Amalia cited the jurymen's agreement that "she was entitled to the full amount," the judge dismissed the case, possibly due to the good character of Mrs. Watney's husband, a well-to-do brewer from London. The main focus of the news coverage after the dismissal was that Amalia would not allow the legal proceeding to end and wanted to take further action.[31]

Amalia left London and returned to New York with her husband in early May. Amalia's friends suggested she meet with Mrs. Watney, since she too was in New York at this time, possibly in the hope that the two women could have a resolution outside of the courts.[32] Any actions of appeasement between the two women directly never occurred.

Amazingly, through Amalia's persistence and another legal action, the case was won in March 1905. The Watneys ended up paying significantly more than she had originally requested: four thousand dollars in total, a sum which now included Amalia's legal fees.[33]

In comparing this lawsuit to the mysterious case from 1901, Amalia had no qualms about being very public about her grievances with Mrs. Watney. She clearly had strong convictions about the validity of her claims, whereas the Blanche Lincoln lawsuit was completely shrouded in secrecy—further evidence that Amalia may have been found "at fault."

⚕

Du Pont's mother, Marie, started to have health issues in 1902, with a hospital admittance that August.[34] She passed away suddenly at sixty-two years old in September 1903, from what was termed "apoplexy," while she was visiting her second home, a cottage in Tuxedo Park. Du Pont and Amalia were in Europe at the time and could not attend her funeral.[35] Services were of course held in St. Patrick's Cathedral in New York.

With the recent notoriety around the estate of Marie's husband, Charles Coudert, a Chicago newspaper made speculations that Amalia and her husband would now be entitled to an even larger inheritance with Marie's passing.

One of Chicago's most talented and famous daughters is about to be placed in a situation enabling her to spend a great deal more money than she has ever had access to before, and if that isn't good news I want to know what is.[36]

However, Marie Coudert's estate was more likely to be distributed among all the children, as with her husband's estate, so the likelihood of a large sum coming to the couple is doubtful.

The Coudert family then lost Frederic René, the last of the three Coudert brothers, in December of that year. His passing was frontpage news in the *New York Times*, with a multi-column obituary. He had just moved to Washington, DC, looking to live in a milder climate. He had been in ill health for several years and had held a less-involved role in the law firm for some time.

For du Pont's six sisters, the first decade of the twentieth century would bring many other changes to their lives, including various marriages and divorces. One of the most famous marriages was that of Jeanne Clarisse Coudert to Condé Nast, who eventually founded the famous publishing empire along with *Vogue* magazine, in 1902.

∽o∾

Once again, Amalia Kussner would be featured in an issue of *Century Magazine*—but this time as a writer, telling of her experiences in Russia. The article appeared in the October 1906 issue, titled "The Human Side of the Czar."

From the start, the whole premise of the article was to present a sympathetic view of the czar to the public. Her writing begins with this clear intention: "I have hoped that some one [*sic*] free to speak would tell through the American press some of the kind things I know to be true of the Czar."[37]

She then boldly declares that her close association with the czar gave her better access compared to any other writer:

> It is scarcely likely that any of the writers can have had a better opportunity for forming an opinion. It was my rare privilege to see and know him as he is at home, in the private apartments of the Winter Palace, with his family close about him.[38]

Her article also states that her first visit to Russia was only a few years previous, when in fact the publication came out over seven years since her visit.[39] Though she did return briefly in 1901, that visit was never mentioned in the article.

The details she shared of her experiences with the Romanov family were already quoted and discussed in chapter 4, but it's interesting to see how this article was received by the public with the changes in the political and social climate of Russia. One review of the article from the *San Antonio Daily Light* emphasized that her writing provided "a far different and much more interesting idea of the czar and czarina" versus how that monarchy was viewed by "reading the 'yellow journals.'"[40]

Other reviews took a more jaded view and indicated the content had "an element of novelty, often amounting to surprise" in this "personal narrative" by Amalia.[41] The implication was that her perspective did not align with the general public's perception of the czar.

Certainly, at this time in history Czar Nicholas was being viewed as a vacillating and struggling monarch. Difficulties in his monarchy were headlines in *The New York Times* the very month of Amalia's article in *Century Magazine*. The October 6 issue of the *Times* was titled "The Czar's Predicament"; it went on to mention both the political upheaval in the empire and the assassinations of his "trusted counselors," and labeled the czar as a "constitutional weakling."[42]

However, several newspapers copied verbatim a single section from Amalia's article: her description of the czarina, citing Alexandra's beauty and elegant countenance. This excerpt would have been carefully selected to avoid any political observations on the czar.[43]

Many of Amalia's fascinating and intimate observations of the Romanov family were still valid, but it's clear why the public would find her praise of the czar puzzling at this time. However, Amalia's efforts to have this article published had actually started many years before, as seen in a series of letters to *Century Magazine* editor Richard Watson Gilder. She had begun sending queries as early as December 1900, upon returning from her honeymoon.

> 53 West 48th Street—December 26
> I have just written an article about my personal acquaintance with the Czar and Czarina of Russia—I think you would find it interesting,

and it seems to be particularly timely now. I can give you with it some reproductions of signed photographs of the Czar and Czarina which they presented at the time. I was painting their miniatures. Would you like me to submit the article to you—& could you give me a decision soon.[44]

She quickly followed up on her initial query:

53 West 48th Street—Sunday

Dear Mr. Gilder,

Four days ago I wrote asking if the Century would care to see an article which I have written describing my personal acquaintance with the Czar. I received an answer asking me to submit the article—It is now ready—however I do not wish to submit the article in the general way—I would prefer to bring it personally & give it to yourself—asking an especially early decision. Will you be kind enough to tell me when I may call feeling sure of seeing you—

Yours sincerely
Amalia Kussner Coudert[45]

The next letter she sent, dated May 10, indicated that the publisher had accepted her article, but there was some discussion regarding what she would be paid.

In answer to a recent letter from the [illegible] regarding our understanding about the price of my article & illustrations of the Czar— you will recall my saying that I had expected $500—but would take $250—& later I telephoned this to Mr. Drake.

Hope to see it soon in print.

Someone at *Century Magazine* wrote at the top of the letter in pencil that "$250 in all" was to be paid, which implied including the illustrations.[46]

Amalia's final letter to Mr. Gilder, which is undated but possibly from the summer of 1906, inquired whether he had seen another article about the czar published in the *New York Evening Sun*. Amalia noted that the content aligned with her own opinion of Nicholas.[47] The overall theme of the *Sun* article was that no matter how much the public disagreed with the czar's "failure to realize the changes that have taken place in his own people," Nicholas still showed courage. The article quoted the czar's reference to the "terrorist" revolutionaries who were striking all around him and who had "forfeited all claims to our clemency and are unworthy to be citizens of our Empire." It ended by saying:

> This is not the talk of a weak man. Peter the Great or Catherine II could not have shown more grim determination in defense of Autocracy. At any rate, if it comes to dying for his opinions, it will be possible to say of Nicholas that he died like a Romanov.

In an abrupt change of subject, her letter to Mr. Gilder then mentioned the drawing of Amalia done by Violet, the marchioness of Granby, emphasizing that this titled woman would now be known as "the Duchess of Rutland" and "one of the highest duchesses."[48]

It was initially confusing as to why that portrait was mentioned, since the drawing did not accompany Amalia's article on her visit to Russia. But further research revealed that *Century Magazine* placed advertisements in various greater New York newspapers, including New Jersey and Connecticut,[49] for the upcoming October issue featuring Amalia's article and used Violet's sketch of Amalia. Furthermore, it was clearly important to Amalia that the titled lady from England was *now* a duchess, a point she felt worth relaying to the editor.[50]

The theme throughout these letters is that Amalia wanted things done her way, from demanding a prompt response to her initial query to insisting she deliver the article in person. And the assumption could be made that her original request for a payment of five hundred dollars was excessively high, and that she very reluctantly accepted a lower commission.

As to why this article was published six years after her initial query, the delay may have had to do with the very public lawsuit and negative press from 1901. However, *Century Magazine* went to great lengths to advertise the article when it ultimately did appear, both providing newspapers with early release copies for review in September and placing the advertisements for the article.

Though her coverage in newspapers and magazines was less in the new decade than it had been in the 1890s, her portraits of royalty remained worthy news items, and the popularity of the miniature art form was still strong. She was referenced in *Success* magazine in 1907, in a piece about the paintings of beautiful women. The article showed an image of a miniature done by Amalia of Mrs. Gerald Lowther, previously Miss Alice Blight. This was the same miniature that was part of the 1898 Great Beauties collection nine years in the past.

More and more, Amalia would be referenced as one of the most accomplished miniature portrait artists and as someone whom other aspiring women with similar talent should be compared against. Often her name was listed along with a summary of accomplishments in newspaper columns covering women of importance in society. Of course, her accomplishments always included the standard list of her most famous miniatures of Edward VII, Czar Nicholas, and Cecil Rhodes.

In a South Carolina newspaper, under the column titled "Feminine Fancies," she was listed as "One of the most widely known of American miniature painters." This column included the mention of Amalia alongside those of other prominent women such as Mrs. Theodore Roosevelt, who had just been appointed to an honorary position in the State Mothers' Assembly of New York.[51]

In late 1907, as reported by a Terre Haute newspaper, Amalia was still receiving a few commissions from New York. She was referred to as the "world-known American miniaturist," and her work apparently had delayed the couple's return to Europe. Soon after completing the additional miniatures, she and du Pont would cross the Atlantic once more, with their first destination the Riviera, and then on to England, where they were spending more and more of their time and "where they hope to spend the summer."[52] The couple's return to Europe was even mentioned in a London newspaper, indicating their prominence in British society.[53]

However, the news coverage became more about her past accomplishments, as opposed to her current artistic activities. Some further articles appeared in early 1907 newspapers, but these were mostly later reviews of her October 1906 article in *Century Magazine*. Between 1908 and the end of that decade, there was very little news coverage of either Amalia or her husband. Amalia's work was also seen less and less at art shows and exhibits, but she did have at least one of her works sent to the 1908 New Orleans Exposition "for the woman's display." Mrs. John M. Judah, a well-to-do art enthusiast from Indianapolis, went to Terre Haute to request artwork for the exposition from the well-known artists from that city.[54] This would be one of the last public art shows to display Amalia's works. The exposition also included one of her sister Louise's pieces.

Given the frequent trips between New York and London, it's worth mentioning that Amalia and her husband always traveled on the best luxury liners. These ships included the *Majestic* (White Star Line), the *Lapland* (Red Star Line, comparable to the White Star Line), the *Kronprinzessin Cecilie* (North German Lloyd Line), and the *Campania* (Cunard Line).

The *Campania* and her sister ship, *Lucania*, had quite luxurious interiors (see color insert). Reviews of the *Campania* were published by Cunard and described the comforts onboard to potential travelers: "The ladies salon is a charming retreat, the carpets are of a very pretty pattern, the lounges are wide . . . geraniums are blooming and the mignonette is exhaling its sweetness."[55] A review of the *Lucania*, which had a very similar interior, compared the rooms to that of a palace, rather than "the steel walls of a ship."[56]

Like the many other aspects of Amalia's life, she sailed on the same ships transiting the Atlantic as the high-society families of New York. She and her husband were on another Cunard ship, the ill-fated *Lusitania*, a year before its sinking in May 1915. One of the prized members of the Vanderbilt family, Alfred Vanderbilt, later went down with the ship, sacrificing his life to save others.[57]

Amalia and du Pont sailed on the *Campania* when they returned to New York after the Mrs. Claude Watney trial. The ship's first-class passenger list reveals some interesting details. Amalia's age was listed as twenty-nine and her husband's as thirty. In 1904, Amalia would have been forty-one years old, but her fictitious age would have had to match her passport on which she put a birth year of 1875. Her husband's occupation is listed as "None"; he didn't even note having been a lawyer. After both of their names, a maid was listed, a Marie Lefebre, twenty-seven years old. Other details on the passenger list were that Marie was of French nationality and that it was her first trip to the United States.[58] Possibly, Amalia and du Pont had retained her services while in Europe.

The *Kronprinzessin Cecilie* was yet another luxury ocean liner the couple sailed on, built by the North German Lloyd company and the

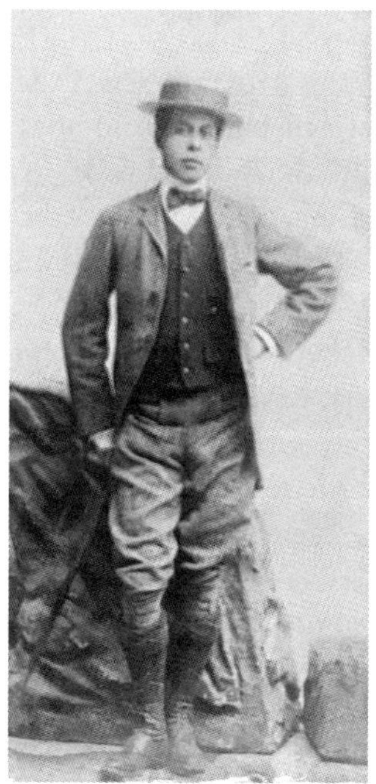

Photo of Charles du Pont Coudert (ca. 1900). *Courtesy of the Coudert family; retouched by Edward Ray*

fourth and last of their super liners, built to honor the German Imperial family. This ship was named after Kaiser Wilhem's daughter, Cecilie. In the salons, passengers would see "rich carvings and art treasures, suites and staterooms fitted with marble bathrooms."[59] Amalia and her husband were passengers en route to England in the spring of 1908, the ship's maiden year. Amalia relayed "they would be very busy in London for a few weeks. Later they will go to Paris and thence to Norway."[60] This trip to Norway was probably her second commission to paint Queen Maud. In a twist of fate, at the beginning of World War I, the German liner was seized by the United States and eventually used as a troop transport ship.

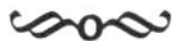

During their extended time in Europe, Amalia and du Pont were to have an unusual introduction to another renowned artist, Auguste Rodin, in France. This encounter was the result of du Pont's sister Claire and her relationship with the famous sculptor.

In 1891, Claire was able to follow the Gilded Age trend of marrying a titled European—in her case, Charles de Choiseul, who at the time of the union was a French marquis. Her title then became the Marquise de Choiseul. Her husband's lineage was "one of the oldest in France, dating back to 1060 when De Choiseul married a daughter of a king of France."[61] Though Charles de Choiseul was titled, their family was not that well-to-do. He and Claire lived an extravagant lifestyle and maintained two residences in France—one in Paris and one in Versailles—but their funds were often exhausted. It is probable that the marquis had expected Claire to have come into more money from the well-known Coudert family.

It was the marquis who reached out to Rodin in 1904 to have him appraise a valuable seventeenth-century sculpture, likely as a potential effort to raise money. History did not record exactly how Claire and Rodin met, but by 1907 the two were involved in an ongoing relationship, when Claire was forty years old and Rodin was sixty-four.[62]

Rodin "became infatuated with the eccentric, impetuous Duchesse de Choiseul." She entered his life certainly as much more than a love interest. She helped with his business and with the promotion of his works in the United States, and even had him dress more fashionably, attiring him in suits fit for high society and dispensing with "his sculptor's smock."[63] By 1908, much of their time was spent at the Hôtel Biron, where he had rented a number of rooms. Claire became a prime influence in his life, both socially and in managing many of his business interests.

Records indicate that both the marquis and Rodin's wife, Rose, were most certainly aware of this relationship. The marquis even wrote to Rodin implying he might leave Claire and stating he wanted a "quiet" life. Ultimately, he did not leave Claire, but they became estranged.[64]

Claire may have thought it would be impressive to have Amalia to do a miniature of Rodin, and of course with Amalia's fondness for painting those of fame, her sister-in-law readily agreed. A note from Rodin was sent to Amalia and du Pont at the end of December 1908, wishing them a happy new year. So, based on the note and various newspaper accounts, it's likely that the portrait was done in the autumn of that year.[65] Rodin also provided to Amalia a signed photo of himself addressed to "Miss Küssner."[66]

In June 1909, another sad passing in the Coudert family occurred with the death of Claire's sister Grace from tuberculosis. At the time of her death, Grace had been living with her sister Claire and the Marquis Choiseul in France; the marquis was designated as the sole beneficiary, not Claire, in part since the laws of France "made it impossible for married women to own property separately." This led to yet another legal battle, primarily waged by two of the sisters, Clarisse and Aimee. They felt that Grace's estate, which included "possessions of the Coudert family" that were "in large part, from her father,"[67] should stay with the family in America. Accusations were made "that undue influence was used in the will's preparations." It is known that the marquis traveled to America to resolve the legalities and his travel expenses were covered by Rodin, upon request of Claire.[68] Records are scarce after that, but it was implied that the marquis won and, with his newly inherited funds, arbitrarily changed his title to duke of Choiseul, making Claire the duchess of Choiseul.

As Rodin and Claire's relationship continued, she acted in many capacities in this life, arranging many social events at the Hôtel Biron and acting as his social secretary, handling all his English correspondences.[69] Through her New York connections, she brought esteemed American families such as the Whitneys and the Vanderbilts to visit him at the Hôtel Biron.[70] She was also active not only in getting him more commissions, but also in ensuring the prices were sufficiently high. Rodin clearly had affection for Claire and completed two sculptures of her during 1910 and 1911. These sculptures of Claire can be found today in the prestigious Victoria and Albert Museum in London and the Musée Rodin in France. (The Hôtel Biron became part of the multiple buildings that now comprise the Musée Rodin.)

It cannot be dismissed that Claire Coudert Choiseul was instrumental in getting Rodin's works introduced into America and aided his career and exposure at an international level during their years together. Eventually, in 1912, their arrangement no longer suited Rodin and there was an extended "break-up." For years, Claire sent a number of desperate letters to the sculptor, as she was estranged from her husband and needed a source of income.[71] Rodin eventually did agree to provide funds to her monthly to support her continuing to live in France.

History has recorded this relationship as either a business arrangement or a true romantic liaison, but ultimately it was both. The *Chicago Sunday Examiner* gave large credit to Claire in 1911 for furthering Rodin's career, when reviewing his large number of works completed in that year: "The extraordinary outburst of marvelous art on the part of the aged sculptor is accounted for by the influence and encouragement of the young and accomplished American Duchess."[72]

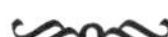

In the early 1900s, Amalia's American friend Nancy Huston Banks left her magazine work and launched into a very successful career, writing three novels in rapid succession. The first two were centered on Kentucky life in the early 1800s, and the third was a more contemporary writing of life in 1900 Kentucky. All of these novels were very positively reviewed. Banks now had attained a prestigious position in the literary world and was actually among those invited to Mark Twain's seventieth birthday party in 1905 at Delmonico's.[73]

Starting around 1905, she was documented as spending every summer abroad, so she may have reconnected with Amalia in Europe starting that year.[74] A ship's passenger log shows that Banks sailed to London in March 1908,[75] and during part of her stay in England she visited with Amalia in the summer. Certainly, the two women had much to share about their lives, and Banks likely told Amalia about one of her last pieces of fiction ever published. This was a short story written for *Cosmopolitan* magazine in 1907: a melodramatic tale titled "The Miniature."[76] The story focuses on a dying woman who, in her last hours, is clutching to a miniature painted of a lost lover, and not her husband. There are even scenes of the relatives trying to take the miniature away from her before her husband's return. These actions are to no avail, and the story does not have a happy ending. One can well imagine this plot could have come from Nancy's knowledge of Amalia's impressive career and the importance of miniatures in many people's lives at the time.

Banks left England that fall. As she was friendly with Amalia's family, she returned to America accompanied by Amalia's mother.[77] Though further documentation is scant, there were later indications that Amalia and Banks stayed in touch throughout the rest of their lives.

Like his sister, Albert's success and fame continued to increase throughout the 1900s. He was a prolific composer and produced numerous romantic and nature-focused piano pieces. An article from his hometown of Terre Haute praised two new works in 1906: "Among his latest compositions is one entitled, 'Dawn,' a tone picture suggestive of the delicacy and beauty of the early morning light. 'Memories' is another which carries with it all that the name reveals."[78] Like his past dedication of *Moon Moths* to Amalia, *Dawn* was dedicated to his sister Louise.

The newspaper also gave credit to Louise for being a composer and a "cultivated interpreter" of piano and song composition. The growing collection of Kussner compositions was becoming popular with piano teachers, possibly since they were very pleasant melodies and not too difficult for the students.

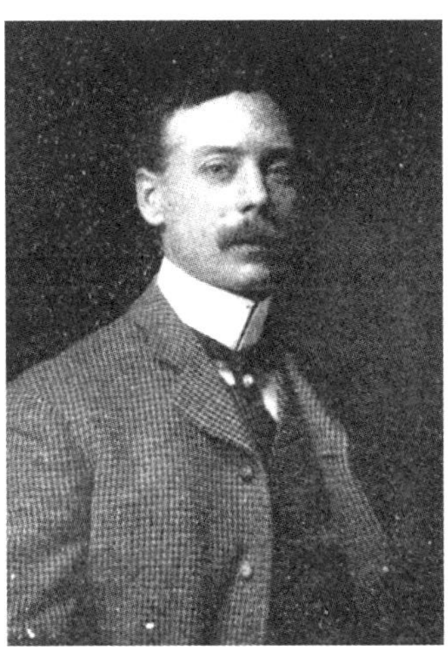

Photo of Albert Kussner, photographer unknown (1903), as seen in "Attracting Attention in the World of Music," *Loretto Rainbow*, Toronto, Ontario, 1903.

Albert's works were owned and published by the L. C. Kussner publishing company, which was started in Chicago primarily to promote his music. Although it is natural to assume that Albert's father Lorenz was the proprietor of this business, the owner was in fact Amalia's sister, Louise Christine Kussner. It was not uncommon in the early 1900s for a woman managing a business to provide only her initials in order to not reveal a woman was in charge. Louise later applied for a trademark in 1908: an image of a moth overlaid on a crescent moon, undoubtedly to represent a moon moth.[79]

By 1910, Albert had enough compositions that one was featured every month in a national music catalog, along with an advertisement declaring that if you enjoyed *Moon Moths*, "you should have his new compositions."[80] His music, which also had orchestral arrangements, was now being performed at many public events, such as graduations, across the country.[81]

With both Albert and Amalia being well-known artists and siblings, they were often compared. "Mr. Kussner's talent comes to him naturally, just as miniature painting does to his gifted sister," wrote one publication.[82]

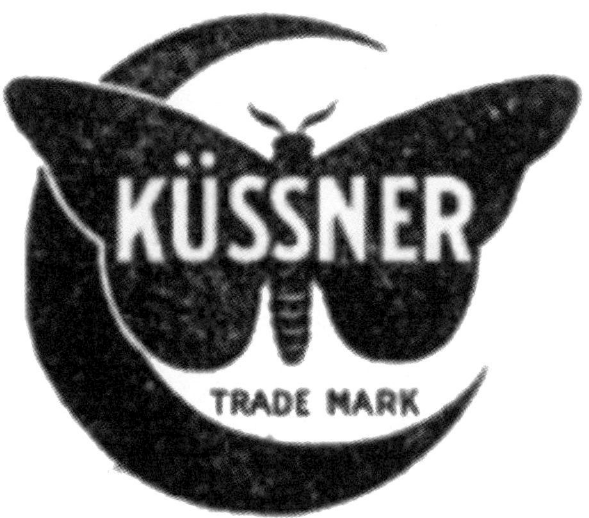

The trademark filed by Louise Kussner for sheet music publications, featuring a lunar moth, a crescent moon, and the Kussner name (1908). Official Gazette of the United States Patent Office, *US Patent Office*

In the first decade of the twentieth century, Amalia had lived in the highest social circles of Europe and was known to most of the royal houses. She had amazingly ensured that two lawsuits did not burnish her reputation. She also managed the dual role of career artist and respected married woman—a combination that was very unusual for her time. But Amalia soon would reflect on her life and begin to realize it was possible she truly had reached the zenith of her career and had finally gotten her desired social acceptance in England.

CHAPTER 8

A Changing World

By 1911, it appears that Amalia had mostly ended her professional career—at least as far as portrait commissions. She may have continued art for her own pleasure, still doing pencil sketches with hints of color. However, she was starting to have more physical limitations with her hands, likely from a previously documented neuritis condition, which was reported by the Terre Haute *Saturday Spectator* in 1908.[1] This, combined with eyesight issues—the result of years of close work with a magnifying glass—would have made continuing to do such trying and exacting artwork difficult.[2] Though of course unknown to her public, Amalia was now forty-seven years old, and it's not surprising her craft would have taken a toll. Furthermore, demand for miniatures was still quite strong, and Amalia would have seen the other up-and-coming miniaturists, such as Eulabee Dix, gaining prominence and getting substantial commissions.

Yet Amalia continued to be mentioned in newspapers, with the usual praise, as still being one of the most accomplished miniature artists and a key figure in the art form's revival. Inevitably, the articles would end with a list of those she had painted from European and Russian royalty, and sometimes with the names of the elite from the Four Hundred who had commissioned her.

The end of Amalia's career coincided with the passing of Edward VII in May 1910. Though he reigned as king for only nine years, his life as the Prince of Wales and his active social circles preceded his reign by

135

many years. Edward the VII seemed to be a "king of the people," and his lifestyle was overall accepted by the British:

> His knowledge of the strength and weakness of the English character; his sympathy as generous as it was profound and outspoken, with all movements tending to improve conditions, assured him the confidence of his subjects from the moment of his accession to the throne and inclined them to judge kindly, if not wholly overlook, the misdeeds of one peculiarly exposed to temptation.[3]

Due to his family relations to numerous European and Russian monarchies, Edward VII was also dubbed "the uncle of Europe."[4] This could have been seen as a uniting and politically stabilizing factor—and one that dissipated with his passing.

A classic photo of European monarchs taken at Windsor Castle in 1907 captured the many different branches of the then royal families, many of whom could trace their relation back to Queen Victoria. Of those in the photograph, multiple figures are known to have been painted by Amalia: King Edward VII, Infanta Isabella of Spain,[5] Grand Duchess Maria of Russia, Queen Maud of Norway, and Queen Victoria of Spain.

The "new" monarchy that began with George V brought some changes, including the temperament of the royal family and the social circles around the monarchy. George V had no defined social circle such as Edward VII's Marlborough Set when he ascended the throne and "had little sympathy or liking for some of his father's more intimate friends."[6]

How did the death of Edward VII—and the loss of the Marlborough Set's influence and those that were loyal to him—affect Amalia's standing in British society? Did Amalia possess a certain cachet and access to royalty and titled nobility that disappeared with Edward VII's passing? She can certainly be seen as one of his favored artists, having painted his family and Alice Keppel, who many considered his last mistress. Potentially, her decision to stop her miniatures had multiple reasons, but the change in Britain's society likely would have been a key factor.

For both Amalia and du Pont, the couple's life in the social and cultural scene of New York was also greatly reduced with their spending

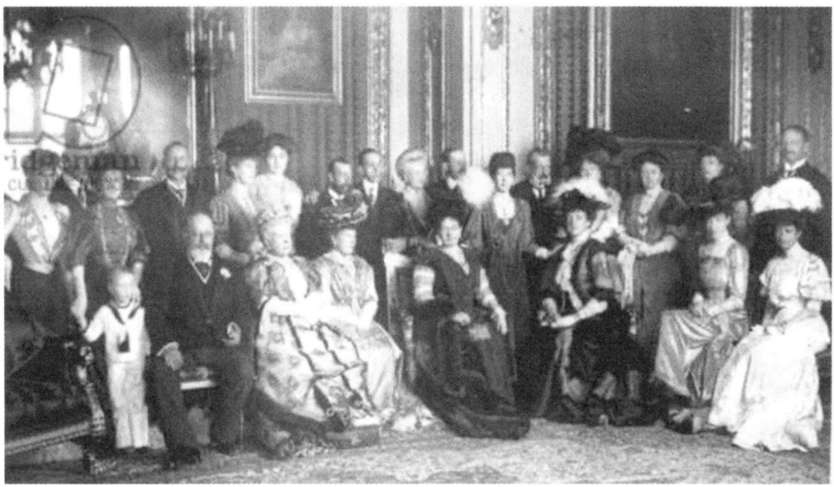

A group picture of the English royal family with international royal guests at Windsor Castle in Wales in 1907. *Suddeutscheh Zeitung Photo/Alamy Stock Photo*

more time in Europe, but they did attain some visibility back in America when they lent two works of art to the Metropolitan Museum of Art in 1911.[7] Both of these paintings were done in the late nineteenth century: *Portrait of a Child* by F. Lenbach and *Child Gathering Apples* by Puvis de Chavannes. These works were on loan to the Met at least through 1922, but ultimately the Lenbach was sent back to the Couderts in England. In a letter dated 1926, a curator from the museum informed Amalia they had decided to also return the work by Chavannes, and instead had selected a pair of his sketches to become part of the permanent collection.[8]

This Coudert family involvement with the Met followed an earlier and quite impressive donation from the Coudert Brothers Law Firm in 1888. One of their clients, Madama D'Olivera from Florence, Italy, expressed "her gratitude to the firm" by giving Frederic René several hundred Byzantine and Renaissance works of art and religious relics.[9] In an effort to appear to not accept this incredible and quite valuable collection, which could have been viewed as inappropriate for the law firm, he divided it between New York's Archbishop Corrigan—with whom the Coudert family had had a long association, dating back to the 1860s—and the nascent Metropolitan Museum of Art, providing them with "tapestries, enamels, and objects d'art as well as eleven paintings."[10] The paintings given to the museum were predominantly religious works from the fourteenth through the sixteenth centuries and mostly by Italian artists. These donations became the start of the museum's Renaissance collection, and a number of the works are still on exhibit today at the Met.

Amalia's attention in the new decade now seemed to focus on her family, and many visits from her immediate relatives from Chicago and Terre Haute started in 1911. Her aunt on her mother's side, Louisa Pence, embarked on a European tour in June of that year. She first arrived in Naples, Italy, where she met up with Amalia and Coudert.[11] The trip was recorded in a Terre Haute newspaper, and the article told of the three of them touring Italy by car. Mrs. Pence was most impressed by Pompeii and enthusiastically referred to how in Italy "Flowers, statues, music and mirrors greet you in the greatest profusion everywhere." The article ended by citing Amalia's closeness to her family: her "devotion to her relatives is a marked characteristic."

It's also evident that Louise's music publishing business in Chicago closed sometime after 1910, although Albert's work continued to be published by a number of other companies offering piano music. He continued to live in Chicago, per his passport application from 1921.[12]

Once again, some negative press about Amalia appeared in a December 1911 *Fort Worth Star-Telegram* article and five other newspapers across the country,[13] although this time the primary person of interest was du Pont's sister Aimee. Amalia and her husband were mentioned at the end. Aimee was just as business-minded as Amalia and through some unfortunate circumstances needed to generate income to support her family. By 1910, she was twice widowed and the mother of six children. Her late second husband, Baron Frederick Brennig, had been a man of Austrian nobility but didn't handle their finances well. He did, however, leave his wife a cigarette tobacco blend that he had created and that was often shared with their friends. Even before her husband passed away, Aimee had brought the tobacco blend to their high society clubs to "test the market" and received great interest; many suggested the Brennigs turn it into a money-making venture. Aimee did just that and started a cigarette business "as A. C. Brennig at 501 Fifth Avenue."[14] She created cigarettes that were "made of the best of materials, and the monogram of the purchaser was printed in each." Her husband passed away shortly after her venture started, but she continued the business for a number of years.[15]

There are two very prescient aspects of this broadly distributed article that bear mentioning. The first is a discussion as to whether smoking is harmful. This is shown through two opposing columns of text, with Aimee's photograph in the center. The left column cites Dr. Charles G. Pease, president of the Non-Smoker's League of America, who goes into great detail on the negative health aspects of smoking, saying in part:

> Smoking is an unclean, unwholesome habit. It poisons the smoker, inflicts unnecessary discomfort on others, and unfits a woman for motherhood.
>
> Smoking is infinitely worse for women than for men.

In the right-hand column, Aimee counters his remarks:

> There is no reason why all women should not smoke cigarettes if they want to. Cigarettes can be made as harmless as sterilized milk!
>
> Cigarette smoking is not injurious to any woman. It aids in digestion, soothes her nerves and keeps her temper.

Even back in the early twentieth century, the medical world declared concerns regarding the negative health aspects of smoking.

Second, in the article Aimee clearly positions herself as someone who supported "the working woman" and would hire women for her business whenever possible. For the production of the cigarettes, such as rolling the papers with the tobacco, she used men who were experts at the process. But she made sure the packaging of the products was done by women, stating firmly, "I employ girls wherever I can."

The Coudert family and some of Aimee's friends were initially disapproving of this venture, and Aimee heard the consistently negative comments: "Make cigarettes!" they cried. "No lady can do such a thing." But eventually they came around to accepting her business. Aimee's other sister, Claire, was quoted in the article as sending her greetings from her home in Paris and requesting "a large order for cigarettes." Cigarette smoking had come into vogue with the society ladies: "For cigarettes must be passed nowadays at every feminine gathering."[16] Also, with the rise of women's independence and the freedom "to do as men do," smoking cigarettes unfortunately became a defiant act of the Suffragettes and part of the image of the "New Woman."[17]

Later in the article, Aimee's only brother du Pont is mentioned, along with his marriage to Amalia, followed by a quite derogatory quote from Aimee: "Miss Kussner was a good deal of a character. She did the most eccentric things to get her name before the public. . . . She married Coudert to spite his sisters, and then some!" There isn't an obvious connection to the "spiting" that Amalia could have done, but this remark could have been a repercussion of the long-term family disagreements between the siblings and du Pont.

Despite the focus on cigarettes and the criticism of Amalia, the article nevertheless ended with the typical listing of Amalia's most famous portraits of the various European royals plus "all the smart women of New York and London. Her social career would be a story in itself."[18] And perhaps not surprisingly, Amalia likely became an avid smoker of her sister-in-law's products. As early as 1898, Amalia had already been seen providing cigarettes at a London party to all her esteemed guests.[19]

The article in its entirety, though initially published in December of 1911, would be reprinted throughout 1912 in many American cities. In reality, Aimee's comments were not the only disparaging remarks made in the press about Amalia. There were occasional newspaper mentions over the years of what certainly would have been seen as eccentric or socially unacceptable behavior. The following was reported in the *Atlanta Constitution* in 1899:

There are many amusing sallies between Latins and Anglo-Saxons and if the fencers happen to be women the fray becomes keener. A French woman of letters here who has made a brilliant marriage was telling me of a funny experience with Amalia Kussner, the American miniature painter. The French woman had very modest means before she married. When Miss Kussner called afterwards and found madame in an elegant apartment the artist looked about her with much surprise and said: "Well, my dear, you seem to have done very well. Your friends must have been proud of you; this place must have cost a great deal."

Madame smiled and changed the subject.

The other day, she met the artist at Doucet's. Miss Kussner raised her eyebrows and said: "Really, do you come to Doucet's?"

"Yes," said Madame simply.

"Oh, but you know," said Miss Kussner, "the department for Americans is much more expensive than that for French people."

"And much less elegant," said madame unruffled.

"And have you the same lovely apartment?" asked the artist.

"No, I have another," answered the countess.

"Dear, but it can't be as nice as that other one," suggested the artist.

"I will tell you a secret," said Madame, shaking with mirth. "To you it would seem far nicer because it cost more money."

And with that shaft, Madame departed.[20]

From this exchange, Amalia seems to have adopted the values of the Gilded Age society, judging the unnamed Parisian woman by the stature of her surroundings. Maison Doucet, like the House of Worth, was another haute couture fashion line that appealed to the younger generation of the Gilded Age, such as Mrs. Orme Wilson (née Carrie Astor) and the Duchess of Marlborough (née Consuelo Vanderbilt), as well as Edith Wharton.[21] Amalia's buying Doucet garments in both Paris and New York is further evidence that she kept up with the latest fashion trends.

The reported encounter at Doucet's was followed just a few months later by an incident at a charity bazaar in London, with Minnie Paget as the hostess, where Amalia treated one of the titled nobles in an arrogant manner. The Duke of Manchester assumed the role of a waiter to assist the charity event, and Amalia "ordered the young man about right and left to do her errands."[22] To add insult to injury, and in view of all in attendance, she then "tossed him a tip of ten pounds and coolly walked off." This incident made it as far as a Chicago newspaper in 1899 and likely became a prominent gossip item in London.

But in parallel, a flourish of positive articles also appeared on Amalia—possibly in response to the negative press. These articles were the now-standard format, recounting her career and most well-known portraits.

Aimee's impressive cigarette business would make headlines again when she married for a third time in September 1912 to William M. D. de Peyster. A *New York Times* article highlighted the interest in this upcoming wedding in part due to "the unique position Mrs. Brennig holds in the business world."[23] Her soon-to-be husband came from a very acceptable lineage, with many family generations dating back to the early Dutch settlers, and he had a successful business in real estate. In terms of her business career, the article stated: "Mrs. Brennig had no present intention of retiring from business after her marriage."

The irony of Aimee's quotes is that her career ambitions and choice to continue working after marriage sound more like Amalia's lifestyle, even though Aimee labeled her sister-in-law as eccentric and "a character." Aimee's dislike of Amalia—and possible issues with her brother—may very well have dated back to the inheritance disputes that started with the passing of their father and their mother Marie's contesting of the will in 1897. These disputes over the administration of their father's estate were still not over.

Around the same time, du Pont also had his share of negative press when George Guion, the brother of Marie Coudert, passed away. Guion had been appointed executor after Frederick René's death in 1903. With Guion dying in May 1912, the role of executor should have passed to du Pont, who had been third on his father's list of executors. But there was a legal challenge from Guion's lawyer, Carl A. Hansmann, over who should be the next executor. The reality is that the original will was quite clear that the son, Charles du Pont Coudert, would be the next in line and this action was a frivolous attempt.[24] The legal challenge was brought before a higher court and the matter resolved, with du Pont legally becoming executor of his father's estate, but the whole incident might have once again inflamed old family resentments in 1912. Interestingly, this legal case and its resolution became a textbook example in some law databases.

The next three years in Amalia's life would bring a mixture of family milestones. Her father, Lorenz Kussner, died in England in May 1912 at the age of seventy-three. He had contracted pneumonia the previous December in Paris, while traveling with Amalia and du Pont, and never quite recovered. At the time of his passing, he was living with his wife and daughter Louise "in a rented villa near London for some months."[25]

His activities in the last twelve years of his life had certainly scaled back. A few US Census records and a city directory list him as a clerk in a music store in 1900, but by 1910 his career is listed as "None." Prior to his final visit to see Amalia in 1911, ship passenger records indicate he made at least a few other trips to England, such as crossing the Atlantic on the *St. Louis* in 1906.

The family in Terre Haute was notified by Albert in a telegram to Amalia's aunt Louisa, and numerous obituaries of course were printed in the local newspapers. Lorenz was cremated and eventually his ashes were interred in the Windlesham Cemetery, the English town in Sussex that just a few years later would become the permanent home of Amalia and du Pont. As a remembrance of Lorenz's being a prominent citizen of Terre Haute, there is a Kussner Street, so named sometime in the first half of the twentieth century, located in the south-central part of the city.[26]

Then two joyous events took place for the Kussner family, with both of Amalia's siblings marrying just a year apart. Albert and Louise finally found suitable spouses, well into middle age.

Amalia's sister, Louise, whose personal life was as equally shrouded in "secrecy" as her sister's, was introduced to John Wells Cloud from Pittsburgh through Amalia and du Pont.[27] This led to her marriage in June 1913 in Paris, at the age of fifty-one, to John, age sixty-two. Cloud had an impressive career, with expertise in mechanical engineering, and at the time of his marriage to Louise he was vice president of Westinghouse

Airbrake.[28] He was divorced with three grown children, but they were never mentioned in newspaper articles about the couple's nuptials or later life. The couple's initial home for the first few years of their marriage was The Grange, Ascot Berkshire, England.[29]

A wedding announcement from a Terre Haute newspaper highlighted Louise's many accomplishments: "She is a thorough musician, playing the piano and singing. She is also a linguist."[30] One gets the sense from this remark and from Louise's earlier involvement in the music publishing business that she could have been equally fascinating as Amalia, had her accomplishments been more public.

Albert married in July 1914 a widow named Mary Petit Dougherty, who was labeled a society leader of Akron, Ohio, where the wedding took place. Mary came from a family active in politics; her father, Judge Upfold Petit, served two terms in Congress during Lincoln's administration and was one of the president's close political advisors.[31] Her brother, Henry, was also active in Indiana politics. Albert would have been fifty-three years old, and Mary was in her forties. They left immediately after the wedding for England and spent their honeymoon with Amalia and their now-married sister, Louise Cloud. Albert and Mary kept his residence in Chicago at 61 Cedar Street, the same address where Albert had lived since his initial move to the city.[32] Albert was also still active in composing music, writing a new piece, *Wild Flowers*, in 1912.[33]

During the years just before World War I, Amalia and du Pont continued to be entertained by English high society. This included being guests of Lord and Lady Alington at their Crichel estate in 1913. Amalia had painted Lady Alington (previously known as Lady Feodorovna Sturt[34]) during her early trips to England, prior to 1900. The Alington residence and grounds were "one of the show places of England, an estate of 1,200 acres."[35] Oddly, the Alingtons owned numerous animals that were all white, which made their estate look like something out of *Alice in Wonderland*. A late 1890s article explained the origin of this unique assortment, which was started by the previous Lady Alington; she wanted to create "a collection of domestic birds and beasts which should all be white, without a coloured hair or feather among them."[36] In late Victorian England, "whiteness"—including the white frocks worn by servants—indicated a sense of wealth, since time and money would be required to keep these possessions clean.[37] This concept was taken to an extreme at Crichel, where "everything was white including the buildings and decorations."

From letters Amalia saved from Minnie Paget, it is evident they also continued their friendship. "Please telephone me the moment you receive this letter," Minnie wrote in a January 1912 note to Amalia. "If you can't manage Friday could you come either Monday or Thursday next week— it will be such a pleasure to see you again. Till then, Yours affectionately, Minnie Paget."[38]

⧈

Another family trip occurred in 1913 and involved a visit to the Weinhardt ancestral home in Germany. Amalia, along with her Aunt Louisa, Louise, and her mother, Emilie Weinhardt Kussner, traveled to Schwabach in the Bavarian area of Germany. Upon arriving, they inquired if any Weinhardts still lived there but were informed they all had moved away. However, the Kussner party were able to take photos of the buildings they believed were where their relatives had once lived, based on old records passed down through the family. These photos included the church their family had once belonged to and the original Weinhardt home. The group also found records of the Weinhardt Brewery that was sold by Emilie's father prior to his immigration to Indiana.[39]

In 1914, Amalia and du Pont purchased an extensive estate in Surrey called Windlesham Hall. Built as a grand English manor in the Elizabethan style, it had four bedrooms and three formal reception rooms, plus another four bedrooms for staff. It was nestled in the bucolic rolling hills of the English countryside and had extensive gardens.[40] But to avoid the damp and sometimes cool weather, the two spent their "summers at Dachstein in the Austrian Tyrol."[41]

With both Amalia and Louise permanently living in England, their mother essentially moved there as well after the death of her husband. Albert also visited on occasion but kept his Chicago residence with his new wife. By 1915, Louise and her husband had purchased Thankerton House in Surrey to be nearer to Amalia and du Pont. Emilie Kussner

145

was soon after noted as "dividing her time between the estates of her two daughters, Mrs. John Cloud and Mrs. Charles Dupont Coudert."[42] At the end of that year, Emilie sent her relatives back home in Indiana a Christmas card featuring "a photograph of Mrs. Kussner standing in the beautiful grounds of Mrs. Coudert's place, Windlesham Hall, Windlesham, Surrey, purchased a year ago."[43]

∽o∽

With the onset of the First World War, many updates and letters were sent back to Terre Haute, both to Louisa Pence directly and to the local newspapers. With most of Amalia's family now living in England, they experienced a much more direct impact than their relatives back home, since the United States didn't officially enter the war until April 1917. All of Amalia's immediate family overseas became involved to some degree in supporting the war effort.

In November 1914, the Terre Haute Saturday Spectator reported:

> Mrs. John W. Cloud, and her sister, Mrs. L. Kussner, have been in England for a number of years. They have become very English in their feelings, especially so since the marriage of Louise Kussner to an England gentleman, Mr. Cloud. They have written to Mrs. Pence, asking her to knit abdominal bands for English soldiers in hospitals and on the battlefields. Mrs. Pence's heart goes out to the suffering humanity wherever it may be found and she intends on doing what knitting she can for the Allies, since they are the ones she has been asked to work for, but all the time she thinks of the German soldier with tenderness.[44]

It's important to realize that the Midwest, with its extensive German immigrant population, some of whom had only been in the United States for a short while, had divided attitudes initially about World War I and the fight against Germany. It seems that Louisa shared some of that uncertainty.

The article then detailed Louise's description of the focus on the war efforts:

> Entertaining has almost ceased. No one has the heart to spend lavishly on parties when there is great suffering in their midst. The maids on the estates hurry through their necessary daily tasks and then knit and sew for the hospitals as do their mistresses also.[45]

Although there was hardly any entertaining, Louise supported families whose men had gone to war by having the women and children over for dinner when possible. Amalia arranged a bridge tournament in the fall of 1914 for which participants had to pay an admittance fee. The proceeds were given to both a British War Relief fund and the American Women's War Relief Fund. Amalia might also have been a visitor to wounded American soldiers in King George Hospital, as an undated letter stated she was given a pass to allow her access to the hospital.[46] Also, with Amalia's extensive jewelry collection at this time, she took diamonds from the emerald pendant necklace given to her by Edward VII and donated them to the British War Relief. The necklace was then reset with artificial stones.[47]

A year later, another letter, this time from Emilie, was printed in the Terre Haute newspaper, with a quote included from Amalia: "Oh, we would be so happy if it were not for this cruel war."[48] Mrs. Kussner also reported to the locals that Queen Mary of England had asked the English women to knit three hundred thousand socks for distribution in the fall of 1915.[49]

In another Terre Haute newspaper in July 1915, there was more recording of the feelings Amalia's aunt Louisa had toward the war, as well as memories of her many visits to Europe in the previous four years. Since Louisa had been born in Germany, she still professed love for her homeland, but she had come to America quite young and also loved her new country. Of her final trip to Europe, she recalled, "The last time she went abroad was four years ago with her niece, Mrs. Coudert and her husband. The return trip was made on the *Lusitania*. They had a delightful voyage."[50]

However, she ended this memory with tears in her eyes, having heard the news since of the *Lusitania*'s sinking by a German U-boat. She also acknowledged that her sister, Emilie Kussner, and her nieces were planning to make England their permanent home, and therefore "they naturally sympathize with the British point of view as to the causes of the war."

After the United States joined the conflict in April 1917, du Pont filed paperwork to re-enlist in the Army, as he later indicated on a subsequent passport application:

> As soon as the United States entered the war I applied for a commission at Paris, France, as I held a commission in the United States Volunteers in the Spanish-American war with Philippine insurrection, but I was rejected on account of my health.[51]

He was also still required to provide information for a US draft card, since he had maintained his citizenship with his New York address. His card listed his age as forty-three and his occupation as dealing with "agriculture and personal affairs."[52] Potentially, some of his extensive acreage at Windlesham was allocated to producing crops.

It is unknown what du Pont's health issues might have been, but his desire to serve his country was a sincere effort, and his past military involvement was important to him. Furthermore, as he had done in the United States, he liked having his name be listed publicly as Capt. Charles DuPont Coudert in England, as was seen in the city directory for Windlesham in 1918.

Du Pont's cousin, Fred—whose previous military experience had, in a sense, paralleled du Pont's activity in the Spanish–American War— once again chose to be involved in a military conflict. He also tried to enlist but was rejected in part due to his age. Instead, he found his way to the frontlines of World War I both through international legal issues and as an observer of the war.

Fred Coudert acted as a counsel for the British and French in a complex legal issue in 1915 involving a German merchant ship, the *Dacia*, that had been delivering cotton from the southern United States for sale in the Netherlands.[53] The *Dacia* was seized by the French, then transferred to American registry. Since cotton was designated a contraband product by the British, thus preventing its sale in Europe, Congressmen from the Southern states were threatening legal action against Britain. The legality of the French seizure of the *Dacia* was also being challenged. Fred traveled to Europe that summer to assist in the subsequent legal proceedings, risking the dangers of the German submarines. His role was described by a Coudert historian as "two parts lawyer to one part unofficial diplomat to one part publicist."[54]

Through previous legal cases with France that had positive outcomes, and possibly through his family heritage, "Coudert was already a known quantity—recognized as a friend of France."[55] He was even present at functions with the staff from the French Ministry, where "he and French officials seemed to have discussed at length the prospects for America's entry into the war." At this time, late in 1915, Coudert regrettably advised these officials that such a prospect was doubtful.

In the winter of 1915/1916, through obtaining the unusual permission to be at the frontlines of the conflict, Fred Coudert witnessed firsthand that the war was not going well for the Allies. He felt compelled to do what he could to facilitate receiving America's help. To illustrate to Americans the bitter plight of France and the war in general, he collected letters from French soldiers, translated them, and published them in a book entitled *War Letters from France*.[56] This small, hardcover book was only 110 pages but had powerful messaging, written firsthand by those in battle or lying wounded in hospitals. At the end of the collection, Fred wrote an "open" letter to a French newspaper, highlighting both what he saw as the "barbarism" of the German soldiers and the strong resilience of the French people.

Another family member involved in France was Charles du Pont's sister, Claire Choiseul. Now a few years in the wake of her well-publicized affair with Rodin, she without question redeemed her image by "nursing tubercular French soldiers returned from the German prison camps, work for which she would receive several medals from the French government."[57]

Fred Coudert, again acting as both a legal representative and an unofficial diplomat, continued to travel frequently to France and England. It's unknown if he visited with his cousin at his estate, only twenty-four miles from London, but certainly the couple must have been aware of his activities, along with those of Claire.

Ten months before the end of the war in November 1918, Emilie Weinhardt Kussner passed away at age seventy-four at Windlesham Hall with her eldest daughter. Emilie was buried in the Windlesham cemetery along with her husband's ashes. Her obituaries unfortunately listed more about Amalia than her own life, but one piece did mention that in Lorenz Kussner's Palace of Music, "his wife was a thorough business woman, assisting her husband greatly." This is an intriguing reference, given the fact that their daughter Louise as an adult would initially be in charge of the family-run Chicago music publication business, and of course given Amalia's own business sense.[58] There is no doubt that Emilie Kussner was a steadfast support to Amalia, especially in the early years of her career when she first went to New York.

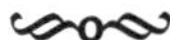

The initial news announcements to the world in July 1918 of the tragic fate of the czar, czarina, and their children only mentioned the execution of the czar, either omitting any details of the fate of the rest of the Romanov family or implying they were safe and in hiding.[59] Regardless, the death of the czar alone would have been a terrible shock to Amalia. She would have known of his being dethroned the previous year, but details since then had been sparse and misleading on the status of his family. After the executions, there continued to be much disinformation, including a supposed eyewitness account, printed in January 1919, by a priest who claimed once again that only the czar was dead—a statement which was completely false.[60]

Though conflicting reports were to last several years, an August 1919 Reuters article, printed in many newspapers, shared a report from a French officer who stated unequivocally that all of the family members had been murdered, as well as a court physician and three servants. His account came in turn from a man who was part of "one of the detachments of soldiers detailed to guard the building at Ekaterinburg in which the Royal Family was detained."[61] This soldier observed the aftermath of the executions and saw the bodies of all members of the royal family.

Confirmed details of the deaths of all the Romanov family members were not reported directly from Russia until an article from the Associated Press that was widely distributed across America in 1922.[62]

Amalia collected newspaper articles that referenced the late czar, including one from a British newspaper that showed photographs of him doing menial tasks during his sixteen months of captivity. The caption reads: "The late Emperor Nicholas II, resigned to his humiliation, shoveling snow."[63] The photo also shows the czarina seated in a wheelchair, doing embroidery work. Clearly, Amalia was keeping track of their fate.

A few years later, fanciful tales of the youngest daughter Anastasia having survived the execution made headlines in 1926.[64] Amalia, on her final trip to Russia in 1901, would have only seen Anastasia as a baby and the third daughter, Maria, as a toddler. (The son, Alexei, was born after her visits.) But she certainly had a close association with the two eldest daughters, Olga and Tatiana, from her visits to the palace in 1899.

Reconciling her memories of the children and Alexandra with the news of their execution had to have been terribly painful. Amalia may very well have lived her final years with the possible hope that one daughter had survived. The rumors and false claims of Anastasia's identity were not permanently disproved through genetic evidence until seventy-six years later.[65]

∽o∾

The end of World War I did not seem to significantly change the lives of Amalia and her husband, except that they engaged once again in travel across Europe and sometimes further afield, including a trip to the Caribbean in 1928. Little was written about the couple during the 1920s, but some of their activities can be ascertained from their passport applications.

One application, dated 1922, has du Pont still claiming US citizenship, with his "legal domicile" of 53 West 48th Street in New York City as a primary residence.[66] Evidently, they still owned that property, but there is no evidence that he or Amalia had been back there since early in 1914.

His application noted that he would be traveling with his wife and thus needed to include her birthday, which per usual had her as younger than her husband by thirteen years, with a birth year of 1876. The document also listed the many countries that they were planning to visit, including Belgium, Switzerland, Spain, Germany, and a number of eastern European countries.

On one such trip, an unusual and dangerous event occurred while Amalia and du Pont were being driven through northern Italy not too far from Venice in September 1930. As recounted in the London *Daily Mirror*, both the travel itinerary and the driver had been arranged by the company Thomas Cook and Son., Ltd. The car was driving along a road that bordered a dike as part of the River Po. The driver somehow went off the road, and the vehicle plunged forty feet down the embankment into the river. The car was soon totally engulfed in water, leaving little breathing space for the couple. The driver easily got out, since his seat had no roof. Du Pont quickly pulled himself free, but had trouble getting Amalia out, and just her head was above water at this point. Luckily, there was a man nearby who hastily provided a rope, which du Pont tied around Amalia and the men then used it to drag her to shore.

All of du Pont's and Amalia's belongings were lost, except for a jewelry case rescued by the driver, with an estimated value of ten thousand dollars.[67] Clearly, du Pont acted quickly and bravely to get Amalia to safety.[68] After the near disaster, du Pont issued a lawsuit against Thomas Cook, and the subsequent legal matters would extend over several years.

Amalia's life in the late 1920s saw continued travel with du Pont, sometimes quite far from Europe, including trips to Barbados in the West Indies in 1925 and to Buenos Aires, Argentina, in 1929.[69]

Albert and his wife left Chicago and moved to St. Petersburg, Florida, in the early 1920s but still visited Amalia and Louise in England from time to time. The last recorded visit of Albert to see his sister was in the fall of 1929.

On one of his visits, Amalia did a pencil portrait of her brother with his hands outstretched, as if suspended over piano keys. This image was used in one of his obituaries. Given that Albert looks older in this sketch, one can assume it was done in the 1920s.

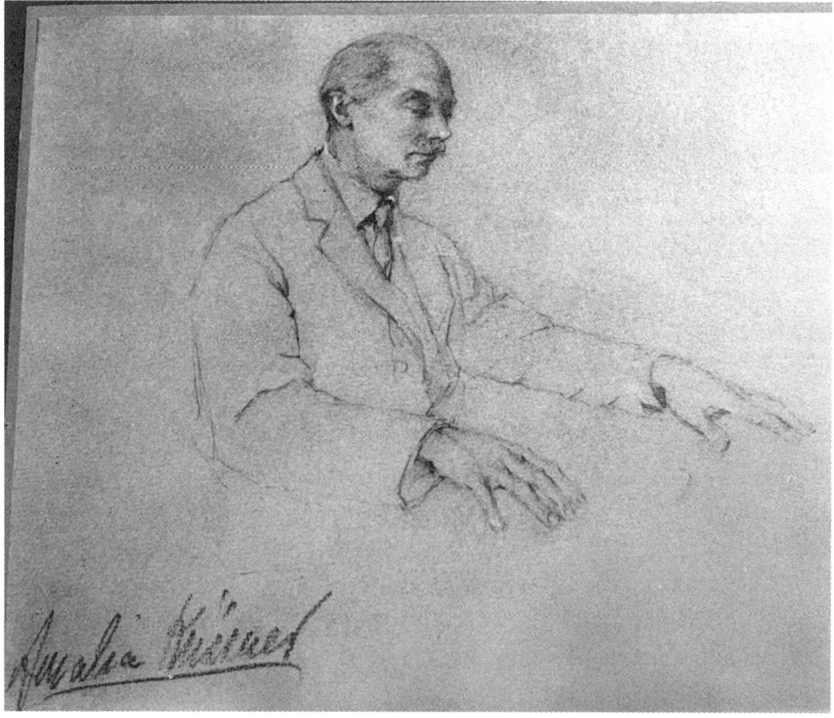

Pencil sketch of Albert Kussner by Amalia Kussner (ca. 1928). *Courtesy of the Amalia Kussner Papers (Private Collection), Sisters of Providence Archives at Saint Mary-of-the-Woods, Indiana*

Albert sent a touching letter to both Amalia and her husband from Florida around their anniversary in 1927, revealing some interesting facts about their marriage.

Dearest Amalia and Du Pont,

Mary joins me in sending you both our heartfelt wishes for your Anniversary. If we could be with you, it would certainly make us most happy to make the toast for many returns of the day.

I recall very distinctly arriving home after a strenuous day at the office about 10 o'clock at night and finding the house all darkened because Mother was away in New York visiting with you, and father and I were alone in Chicago. Upon opening the door father's voice brought me the message—"Amalia is married."

> I had never met you, Du Pont, up to that time and this sudden and startling information so took me by surprise that I did not know whether to be happy or sad over it.
>
> Next morning being a holiday, I was sitting on the front porch and was somewhat in a quandary in trying to answer the many questions of my neighbors who had already read the announcement of your marriage in the morning paper. I remember all this just as vividly as if it happened but a few days ago. I know Du Pont, that you also remember it as well because you have never overlooked to give Amalia some little gift in remembrance of that day.[70]

Not only were most of Amalia's and du Pont's friends not informed of the marriage, but not even her brother and father knew. This further adds to the mystery of the sudden nuptials. But whatever the reason for their quick wedding, du Pont's devotion to her is evident through his tradition of giving Amalia a gift for every anniversary.

Albert passed away in June 1930 at his St. Petersburg home. An article honoring both the deceased composer and Amalia appeared in the *Indianapolis Sunday Star* later that summer:

> Mr. Kussner possessed a most delicate, esthetic appreciation of life. This inherently refined realism and culture found expression in many exquisite musical compositions. Into his artistic soul music sank tenderly and deep, like the melody of a song sounding from out of his childhood days in loving memories.[71]

His many accolades included his composition *By Candlelight*, which had been performed at Buckingham Palace.

Later in the article, Amalia was equally praised as an artist. The writer noted: "This family enjoyed the unusual distinction of having two artists whose accomplishments were known and appreciated both in this country and in Europe."[72]

Her sister Louise was certainly also a part of Amalia's final years, with living so close by. Amalia's infrequent artwork in the last years of her life included a rare watercolor of Thankerton House (see color insert).

The piece was almost Impressionistic in style, showing lush greenery and brilliant purple flowers.

Any public writing about Amalia was now mostly confined to Who's Who directories of artists. Other miniature painters had started to eclipse her singular role as the world's leading artist in the field—but they followed in her footsteps and gained fame by painting wealthy American and European royalty.

Chapter 9

Eulabee Dix, Contemporary of Amalia

In comparing Amalia to her other miniature artist contemporaries, Eulabee Dix comes the closest in similarity. Both women hailed from the Midwest; Eulabee was born fifteen years after Amalia, in Greenfield, Illinois, just north of the Missouri border on the western side of the state. Eulabee grew up in a close-knit family with a conservative, religious background. She exhibited artistic talents at a young age, which her parents supported the best they could. Due to the family's financial difficulties, as a child she was sent to live with relatives of means in St. Louis who provided funds so that she could attend better schools, including the St. Louis School of Fine Arts. She then moved to Michigan, where her family was residing at the time and where the daughter of a local minister showed her the art of miniatures. Eulabee eagerly adopted this style and, just like Amalia, as her talent developed she left the Midwest for greater fortunes in New York City. Eulabee arrived there in 1899, only seven years after Amalia. She studied with several accomplished artists and attended the Art Students League that Amalia had attended in the early 1880s.

There is no doubt that by the time Eulabee arrived in New York, the popularity of miniature portraits was firmly established, in large part brought about by Amalia. Around 1899, Eulabee painted a miniature self-portrait (see color insert) that shows a confident woman looking steadfastly into her future. The miniature revival was starting to become popular in other cities, such as Philadelphia and Los Angeles, which afforded Eulabee far more opportunities than had existed for Amalia

157

at the start of the 1890s. Eulabee was also advised to travel to Saratoga Springs in upstate New York one summer, where the well-to-do clientele would be interested in miniature portraits. She painted at least three miniatures in Saratoga Springs, for one of which she was offered four hundred dollars—an impressive amount for someone just starting out.[1]

Eulabee, like Amalia, also knew the importance of dressing like those in the social class she wanted to paint and of entertaining her potential sitters—two clever methods to help expand her business in New York. To help subsidize her career, Eulabee opened a studio that she used both for her own work and to provide art classes in New York. Well-established by 1903, her studio was part of Carnegie Hall, where she worked mostly alongside those providing music and voice lessons.

In looking at the style of these two artists' miniatures, Eulabee's work can be seen as more traditional. Eulabee's sitters are shown in their own elegant outfits as opposed to Amalia's sitters in her ethereal wraps of tulle and silk flowers. The composition of Eulabee's works also included more of her subject's torso, usually from the waist up and often showing their arms and hands. She often referred to her miniatures as "jewel portraits,"[2] using jewel tones to make her paintings look like stained glass. One other difference is that Eulabee's signature on her miniatures was far less conspicuous, usually seen in fine, red-colored print following the edge of the portrait, in the lower half of the miniature.

Another career parallel between Eulabee and Amalia occurred in 1904, with Minnie Paget assuming the role of patron for Eulabee, in part through the artist's own efforts to seek her out. After Eulabee had established her career as a miniaturist in New York, those close to her often "asked if she had painted someone famous or socially prominent."[3] After that, Eulabee "was on the alert for a famous and beautiful lady," and she subsequently found her via a newspaper article about Minnie Paget, who had just arrived in New York from London.

In a scenario similar to when Amalia called on Mrs. Havemeyer, Eulabee dressed in her finest outfit and went to see Mrs. Paget at the Waldorf Astoria, even without a letter of introduction. There was a very real prospect of being turned away at the door, but Eulabee was welcomed. Minnie agreed to have her portrait done in London, where she would soon be returning, and Eulabee sailed to England to complete the work.

The question must be asked as to why Minnie Paget chose to bestow favor on yet another miniaturist. Certainly, Minnie would have seen in both women their forthrightness in character, which clearly she appreciated. With the popularity of the art form in London and Amalia's doing fewer portraits in the 1900s, Minnie also may have seen a need to bring in another American artist to meet the demand for the sought-after art style in London.

Eulabee provided an almost dreamlike description of when she arrived at Mrs. Paget's home for the first sitting:

> A liveried footman ushered me into the reception room off a wide hall and there I seated myself in the midst of elaborate furnishings, a profusion of beautiful things . . . all reflecting the taste of the new court. . . . Edward VII brought cheer and gladness, a gladness sprung from the long thrifty reign of Victoria, and England was now in full bloom of her tremendous empire.[4]

The task of doing Minnie's miniature lasted several months and was tragically cut short by an accident when Minnie "accidentally stepped into an empty elevator shaft at her home . . . breaking her hip and both legs."[5] Eulabee returned to New York and finished the portrait in her studio. Eventually she traveled back to London to deliver the finished artwork, where she found her dear patron sadly restrained by casts and braces.

Eulabee's portrait of Minnie led to another commission, this time from the Countess of Warwick, whom Amalia had also painted. Eulabee was invited to stay at Warwick Castle and the lady's country estate to finish the portrait, just as Amalia had also been invited to stay at the castle.

These two portraits received very positive reviews and were displayed in a ten-month exhibit lasting from February to December of 1906[6] by the venerable Royal Society of Miniature Painters, an esteemed group of artists that Eulabee joined but Amalia oddly never did. Eulabee's portrait of Minnie Paget was described as giving "a fine impression of style . . .

this work is at once grandiose and modern . . . and is a noteworthy development of art."[7]

Eulabee's fame in America only increased with more gallery and museum showings in New York, St. Louis, and Indianapolis. This is a clear example of where Amalia's and Eulabee's careers varied. Amalia never had showings in galleries and museums outside of New York, whereas these exhibits helped better establish Eulabee in the art history of the early 1900s.

Minnie Paget again provided an impressive connection for Eulabee by introducing her to Mrs. George Gould in New York, who had previously sat for Amalia with her son. This time, however, it was the daughter Marjorie who would be painted.[8]

Whereas some of Amalia's most famous subjects were royalty, one of Eulabee's most famous sitters was Mark Twain (birth name Samuel L. Clemens), who sat for her in 1908. How his portrait transpired is a story in itself. In late 1907, Eulabee knew that the Countess of Warwick was visiting New York and Eulabee wanted to connect with her. Eulabee's elegant studio in Carnegie Tower was a perfect setting to entertain, and she invited the countess to her studio for tea, in part as a thanks for the portrait the countess had commissioned two years earlier. Eulabee then asked the countess if there was anything she could do for her while visiting New York.

The countess boldly replied: "I would like to meet Mark Twain! You know, I missed him at the King's Garden Party."[9]

In an approach very similar to Amalia's, "Eulabee had no difficulty rising to the occasion. After all, it was uncommon boldness that had gained her entrée into English society in the first place. Never mind that she had never met America's most renowned literary icon."[10] Without hesitation, she sent an invitation to Mark Twain to have lunch with her and the Countess of Warwick, and promptly got a reply through his secretary.

The meeting was held at the ever-elegant Delmonico's, where Twain had his seventieth birthday party just two years earlier. Eulabee took care that the meal would be just the three of them in order to make it the best experience for the countess. Undoubtedly, her career as a miniaturist was brought up, as by the end of the meal Twain agreed to a sitting. Though there was some delay in starting the portrait, in the spring of 1908 Twain granted Eulabee "five sittings of an hour's duration each."[11] There may have been an agreed-upon commission, but historical records are unclear as to the amount or even if she was paid for this portrait.[12]

Twain wore his classic white suit but also chose to drape himself in a robe conferred to him from Oxford for a Doctor of Letters. Both Twain and Eulabee liked the robe, since part of it had a bright-red border. During the portrait sessions, the two made easy conversation on a variety of subjects. Though Eulabee found Twain's philosophical and religious attitudes in conflict with her traditional upbringing, she, again like Amalia, had the ability to put her subjects at ease to help them pass the time.

Though Twain had only committed to the five sessions, Eulabee felt there needed to be one more, especially to finish his hands. This extra sitting was not to be, as by 1909 Twain was in ill health and could not sit for another session. The final product of Twain's miniature indeed shows just one exposed hand, which appears hastily painted. Twain never asked for the finished portrait, and Eulabee kept it for many years. The dimensions of the finished product are rather typical for miniatures at that time, 4.5 inches by 3.75 inches, and at the right edge of the portrait in small print is her "stylized" inscription of "E Dix." This work is now at the National Portrait Gallery in Washington, DC.[13]

By 1910, Eulabee's fame was well known on both sides of the Atlantic, as noted in a *Washington Post* review of her exhibit in Chicago: "There's an exhibition of these little paintings on the wall and in cases, all accomplished by a Southern artist, Miss Eulabee Dix. She was made the fashion in the art by Mrs. Arthur Paget, over in London."[14] The article went on to further detail that she had sufficient business to set up a studio in London while still maintaining her studio in New York. Those she painted included the actress Ethel Barrymore and "many other personages of high degree."

Unlike Amalia, Eulabee's personal life was not shrouded in secrecy. She married in the autumn of 1910 after a three-year engagement to Alfred Becker, a lawyer. The couple had an elaborate wedding in New York, as compared to Amalia's unannounced and hasty event. Minnie

Paget even sent the couple a congratulatory note. But as recorded in Eulabee's memoirs, this may not have been a marriage with emotion and passion. She was in her early thirties, having "lived independently for twelve years, most of them in New York City." Her husband wanted them to live in his family home in Buffalo, thinking this would be preferable after her many years of travel and that she would enjoy having the added benefit of servants to assist her. Eulabee entered this marriage with hopes of a compromise on how they could best manage their relationship, but it was not to be.

At the time of the marriage, Eulabee was painted in her wedding gown, standing tall with an arm down by her side, at a slight angle but looking straight ahead. The artist was Robert Henri, a fellow painter in New York City. Eulabee was friendly with Henri and others who were part of the "Ashcan School" of art, so named "because they portrayed the lives of a less privileged turn-of-the century New York City."[15] Henri "preferred to paint people he knew or met on his travels, rather than taking commissions from the wealthy," and had decided he wanted to do a painting of a bride; the timing aligned with Eulabee's wedding. She wanted to purchase the finished painting, "but the asking price of 5,000 dollars in 1910 was too large a sum for her."[16] Henri once again painted Eulabee that autumn in a far starker portrait titled *Lady in Black Velvet*. She stands in a pose very similar to her wedding gown portrait but "wears black velvet against a dark background, as if to suggest the extinguished promise of domestic happiness."[17]

Like Amalia, Eulabee continued to pursue her art after her marriage. But as Amalia's fame faded in the second decade of the twentieth century, Eulabee's star continued to rise. Her works were shown again in 1915, at the prestigious Panama-Pacific International Exposition in San Francisco. Of the three portraits, one was a miniature of her son, Philip Dix Becker, at six months old.[18] It is significant to note that a number of miniatures were on display at this exposition along with Eulabee's, and that many of the artists displayed their credentials as members of art societies such as the American Society of Miniature Painters and the Pennsylvania Society of Miniature Painters.

Her portrait of Mark Twain was also shown publicly on occasion to positive reviews and included in the 1916 volume of *Biographical Sketches of American Artists*:

> The miniature of Mark Twain in a gown of an Oxford doctor of letters shows a prevailing tone of gray, the broad red band of the gown lighting the whole picture. . . . Miss Dix's sense of color values is peculiarly happy.[19]

In 1916, a miniature portrait show was held at the John Herron Art Institute in Indianapolis, where Eulabee's portraits were on exhibit along with those of two contemporaries, Laura Coombs Hills and Lucia Fairchild Fuller.[20] The exhibit was another indication of Amalia's dwindling prominence, as even though the exhibit was held in her home state, none of her works were included.

Although Eulabee's marriage was ultimately not a happy one, she did become the mother of two children, a daughter and a son. In part due to her husband's being a lawyer and his clever legal maneuvers, when their marriage ended in 1925 Eulabee and her children were not left financially secure. Getting income from her artwork was essential now, and she continued her miniatures through the 1920s. She also continued to get positive recognition, such as an award from the Baltimore Water Color Club.[21] However, by the 1930s the market for miniatures had greatly decreased. For the remainder of her career, Eulabee branched into other art styles to support herself, but she never regained a secure income.

Especially during the years that Amalia and Eulabee were both active miniature artists in London, one must wonder what they knew of each other, especially since they now shared the same patron. Given Amalia's established success in the mid-1900s and later, Minnie Paget was more of a society friend to her by this time. To help foster Eulabee's career and establish a good early relationship, Minnie might have chosen not to detail her earlier support of Amalia.

And what did either miniaturist know of each other's careers? In a detailed biography of Eulabee that includes a discussion of her memoirs, Amalia's name is never mentioned.[22] And to date, no documentation has been found to show that the two women ever met. Knowing Amalia's personality and need to be the focus of attention, she likely saw Eulabee as direct competition and never made an effort to reach out.

Though there were many similarities between the two women, Amalia far exceeded Eulabee in her adventurous nature and self-promotion. Amalia was not only known for her artwork, but also for her quite unusual and intimate association with the Romanovs and then for her very publicized travails in Kimberley. And while both artists painted the titled ladies of England, Amalia's number of portraits was more than double Eulabee's. Newspapers and gallery showings recorded Eulabee painting six works while in England, with frequent mentions of the portraits she did of Minnie Paget and the Countess of Warwick, whereas published records for Amalia's portraits of England's titled ladies account for about fifty portraits. Both numbers are likely low, but there's no question that Amalia's portrait volume of titled women and members of the Four Hundred exceeded Eulabee's.

Yet of the American miniaturists and those who were part of the turn-of-the-century revival, it would be Eulabee who ended up the most celebrated and visible in America's museums. Today there is a collection of 106 of her works at the National Museum of Women in the Arts and their miniature gallery is named in her honor.[23] A few of her works are also at the Metropolitan Museum of Art, while the painting of Mark Twain now resides at the National Portrait Gallery.

CHAPTER 10

The Book of Beauty

AMALIA'S CAREER ACCOMPLISHMENTS WERE EXTENSIVE ACROSS MULTI-ple continents for well over twenty years. The extent of her place as an artist in Edwardian society can best be seen in a stunningly produced book that was published in 1902, titled *The Book of Beauty*. Since many of her works did not survive in their original form and few of those that did are on display in museums today, this volume is one of the best historical sources of her works.

In addition to celebrating the coronation of Edward VII, the volume captured many aspects of Edwardian society in the early 1900s. The full title was:

The Book of Beauty
(Era King Edward VII)
A Collection of Beautiful Portraits
with
Literary, Artistic and Musical Contributions
by
Men and Women of the Day

As can be inferred from the title, the content went far beyond images of the beautiful, titled women of England, also including fifty-seven literary and musical works. The written pieces range from historical accounts to dedications to poetry. Among them is an essay discussing the careers

165

of both Amalia and John Singer Sargent, who are the only two American artists selected for the book.

The finely designed volume measures over a foot wide and sixteen inches high. The cover is decorated with a delicate gold floral pattern on the front and a crown design above the title on the spine. At the top of the front cover (see color insert) is a gold-embossed monogram of Edward VII, since the intent of the book was to honor his coronation, which occurred in August of that year.

Some newspaper advertisements referred to *The Book of Beauty* as "A Magnificent Fine-Art Work of Exceptional Interest."[1] It was produced by the London publisher Hutchinson & Co. in two different versions: "an *édition de luxe* of three hundred copies at five guineas, and a limited edition of fifty copies at ten guineas, in which twelve of the portraits will be coloured."[2]

The editor was Mrs. F. Harcourt Williamson (Emma Sara Williamson), who had been a writer for a number of years, including publishing a novel in 1896 with the same publisher as *The Book of Beauty*.[3] She had edited an earlier version of *The Book of Beauty*, with the same dimensions and similar content, in 1896 during the last years of Queen Victoria's reign. However, the list of artists was significantly different for the new 1902 version.

As stated in the *Pall Mall Gazette* in November of that year, *The Book of Beauty* certainly served its purpose:

> This memorable year of the Coronation will have no memorial more artistic in design, more attractive in realizations, or possessing more unfailing sources of pleasure, then the splendid and sumptuous volume.[4]

The stunning and crisp images of the artwork were produced by photographer F. Jenkins, who used the technique of *photogravure*, in which he transferred the negative onto a copper plate, which was then used to print or engrave the image with ink.[5]

Edward VII was personally involved in the selection of the portrait entries, including which of Amalia's works to feature, and in March 1902 he worked directly with one of the other contributing artists,

Mr. Ellis Roberts, in his studio as part of the process. Mr. Roberts was himself an esteemed artist, cited as "a disciple of the Gainsborough style, and [who] excels in full length portraits in a landscape."[6] Roberts was suitably impressed by both the king's interest and artistic discernment during their reviews of the content, relating, "I was much struck . . . with the amount of knowledge the King displayed. Apart from the likeness of a portrait, he discussed its artistic merits and the scheme of colouring."[7]

Another 150 copies of *The Book of Beauty* were released in the United States by the publishing company J. B. Lippincott out of Philadelphia. Each of these copies was hand-signed by Lippincott himself at the time of publication in November 1902. From Amalia's home state, the *Indianapolis News* declared, "The success of the 'coronation book of beauty' seems to be assured."[8] Unfortunately, while the list of artists in this article included John Singer Sargent and the Marchioness of Granby, Amalia's name was omitted because she was not listed in the press release issued from London.

The book was later reviewed in *Vogue* in December, under the column "What they Read":

> The present collection of English beauties is welcome, both as a comparative novelty and because exceptionally well gotten up. A folio, size 16x13 inches . . . with an all-over decorative design in gold on the cover, and printed on very heavy pure white plate paper, with full-page photo-gravure illustrations makes a volume that is all that could be desired as a sumptuous example of bookmaking.[9]

The *Vogue* review ended by providing an extensive list of the portraits and literary contributions, and this time mention of Amalia's name and her portrait of Mrs. Mackay were included.

Of the eighty-four portraits in King Edward VII's edition of *The Book of Beauty*, the artist Ellis Roberts had the largest number of his works included, at a count of fifteen. The second-highest art contributor was Edward Hughes, with thirteen portraits. Amalia and Violet Manners (Marchioness of Granby) both had seven portraits in the book. It's significant that the number of Amalia's works equaled Violet's, although with the small size of the miniatures, they were grouped together on only two pages. Violet's portrait sketches included the one of Amalia, which is placed just prior to Amalia's miniatures, about two-thirds of the way through the book.

Three of the miniatures from Amalia's 1898 *Great Beauties* full-page display in the *New York Journal and Advertiser* appeared again in this book: those of Miss May Goelet (a dollar heiress, soon to marry the 8th Duke of Roxburghe), Minnie Paget, and Louise MacKay. The other four were of the Countess Helena of Stradbroke (wife of the 3rd Earl of Stradbroke, who had distinguished British military appointments), Mrs. Alfred Harmsworth (married to the publisher who started the *Daily Mail*), the Lady Feo Sturt, and Madame von André (neé Mary Alice Palmer from America, married to the wealthy financier Monsieur Adolph von André).[10]

There were three other miniature artists, all British, included in this book. In order of appearance, they were Mrs. Gertrude Massey with one miniature, Miss Winnifred Hope Thomson with four, and Viscountess Maitland with three. The most historically significant is Massey's singular portrait labeled *The Late Queen Victoria and her Great Grandson Prince Edward of Wales—Past and Future*. The queen is depicted looking quite aged and has a protective arm around the young prince, who is shown in a sailor suit and standing in profile, looking away from his grandmother. This child of course would eventually grow up to be King Edward VIII, who had a very short reign since he abdicated to marry Wallis Simpson. Gertrude Massey was a well-established miniaturist whose career coincided with Amalia's in London. Her first exhibit was in 1897, and she later had other displays in the early 1900s in the Royal Academy, as well as a few in the Paris Salon. By 1904, she had painted another eleven miniatures of the British royal family, plus "various dogs belonging to the King and Queen."[11]

Of the other two miniaturists, Thomson appears to have been another career artist, displaying in a few shows in the 1900s, whereas Viscountess Maitland, though talented, enjoyed painting portraits as a pastime.

There were three portraits included by John Singer Sargent, of which the most striking is *The Wyndham Group*, showing three women dressed

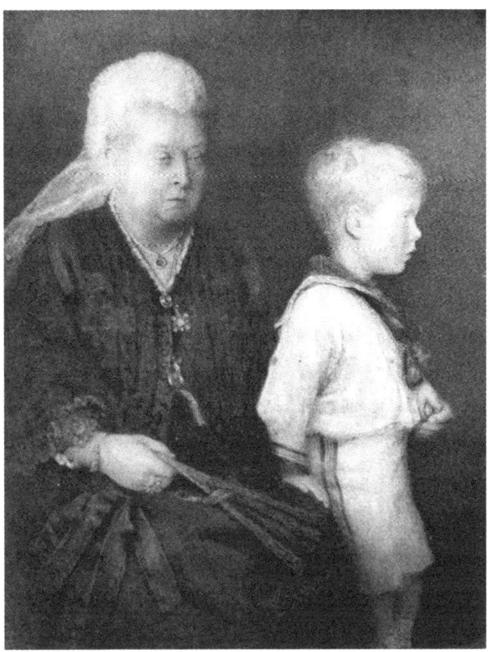

Miniature of Queen Victoria and Prince of Wales by Mrs. Massey (ca. 1901), as seen in *The Book of Beauty*, edited by Mrs. F. Harcourt Williamson (J. B. Lippincott & Co., 1902). *Author's collection; photo by Edward Ray*

in opulent gowns but all seated in natural-looking, relaxed poses. The subjects are the three daughters of a well-to-do Londoner, Percy Wyndham: Madeline Adeane, Pamela Tennant, and Mary Constance (known at the time as Lady Elcho). This painting by Sargent was "hailed by the critics and dubbed 'The Three Graces' by the Prince of Wales."[12] Socially, these three sisters were also part of the Souls; Lady Elcho was "a favourite Souls hostess."[13]

To add a more personal touch to the stunning images of the many women in *The Book of Beauty*, almost each subject included her actual signature below her portrait. These signatures appear very natural; for instance, those of the three sisters from Sargent's *The Wyndham Group* are haphazardly displayed below the painting at all sorts of angles, almost like signatures in a yearbook. For Amalia's miniatures, five have the signatures of the women she painted (Minnie Paget, Countess of Stradbroke, Mary Harmsworth, Louise MacKay, and Lady Feo Sturt).

The writing entries in the book covered a broad style of topics and formats. One of the shortest is labeled as an epigram written by Mrs. Alec Tweedie:

A LOVELESS marriage is entering a hell with one's eyes open. A marriage with love is entering heaven with them shut.[14]

That is a brief but very powerful statement—certainly harkening to the many loveless but purposeful matches among royalty, not to mention the many "dollar heiresses" who married into English society. The name Mrs. Alec Tweedie was a pseudonym of Ethel Brilliana Tweedie, a writer who was active in the first few decades of the twentieth century and who indeed did not have a happy marriage.[15]

Rudyard Kipling submitted a poem that is more of a sentimental verse on love. "Roses Red and Roses White" is about a man who is determined to find roses for his love, but she desires the one color of rose he cannot find. Upon his return to her at last, without the rose she wanted, he discovers she has died, but even beyond the grave she still longs for her lover to bring her the unusual rose.[16] The poem is the second written work in the book, prominently placed only a few pages into the volume and facing a portrait of Princess Louise, daughter of Edward VII, seen holding a bouquet of roses.

Muriel Wilson, one of the hailed beauties of England at this time and who was painted by Amalia, was asked to contribute a brief essay on her thoughts around the concept of beauty. She could have easily submitted a light and coy piece, speaking on the importance of physical beauty for women, but she did not. Instead, she states early in her essay, "I don't think that beauty is so valuable a gift to a woman as she generally supposes."[17] She finishes with:

For is it not the outside world—to whom she is scarcely more than a phantom—that influences her life, but the society or circle by which she is surrounded; and if she has a beautiful nature, great natural gifts, artistic or intellectual, all or any of these will have a far greater influence on her environment than the personal beauty which at first sight is so attractive.[18]

One of the more impressive written entries, covering eight pages, is by Lady Sarah Wilson and titled "The Transvaal War—A Woman's Reminiscence of 1899."[19] Lady Sarah too had been a captive in South Africa during the Boer War, though her risks were far greater than Amalia's. She was there as war correspondent, and her piece tells of the siege of Mafeking, which lasted a number of months. Her account is placed just before the essay about Amalia and Sargent and the display of Amalia's miniatures. The placement was probably intentional by the editor since Amalia had her own harrowing experiences in South Africa during the war.

A second account about the Boer War, found earlier in the book, is titled "A Visit to Ladysmith" and was written by Mrs. George Cornwallis West (Lady Randolph Churchill) while she was assisting on a hospital ship in February 1900. She discusses the freeing of the town of Ladysmith and also tells of her journey there, accompanied by her son, Winston Churchill. Her writing described an arduous trek, including passing by scenes of war's carnage, with details provided by Churchill on recent battles.

Immediately preceding the display of Amalia's portraits is a somewhat satirical essay titled, "Some of Our Conquerors: Being a Recovered Fragment from the Collected Works of an Irresponsible Reader."[20] The writer chose to remain anonymous, with their byline shown only as "Irr. R." The essay discusses the Americans who were seen as conquerors of England's culture or as invaders into the British art scene. It opens with references to America's ironmasters and Wall Street magnates, as well as a mention of how "Chicago's canned goods coldly furnish forth our breakfast tables"—likely referring to products from the Armour family's meatpacking industry.

But the essay is focused primarily on Amalia and John Singer Sargent. At the time the *Book of Beauty* was published, Sargent was an elected member of the Royal Academy, with his works on display at

Burlington House.[21] The tone of the essay is coy, with various references to Greek mythology as well as some contemporary cultural references.

> Here, Frankenstein, look thy Monster in the face. Are the American invaders of our Arts but errant free lances, or the forerunners of an advancing host? Consider the vantage they have already won in the field of Arts and Letters. Sargent writes his name large over the walls of Burlington House as, in daintier letters, Amalia Kussner's name sets it seal on miniatures. A bagatelle, say you? My dear Frankenstein, the worth of Art is not measured by the yard wand. The Kohinoor is none the less precious because it bulks less broadly than Cleopatra's Needle. Amalia Kussner is none the less an artist because her art is miniature. Her career, indeed, is typical of latter-day American conquest. Not for her slow apprenticeship, the halting progress up the slopes of Parnassus. She arrived at the summit in American wise, by cable car, as the greatest miniature painter since the days of Angelica Kaufmann.
>
> Again consider the world of letters. Who with a seeing eye can fail . . .[22]

The brief, unfinished essay is concluded with a tongue-in-cheek editor's note: "*Cetera desunt* [Latin for 'the rest is missing']. Fortunately.—Ed."

Mount Parnassus, in Greek mythology, was the home to the Muses. There are multiple meanings to Kohinoor, but the reference here is probably to the very high-quality Kohinoor pencil, so named after the Koh-i-Noor diamond by Queen Victoria around 1890.[23] Cleopatra's Needle was an obelisk brought from Egypt and installed in the Thames Embankment in 1877. To this anonymous writer, Amalia had been inspired by the Greek Muses themselves, and the fine lines of her miniatures were just as precious as a finely crafted ancient monument.

The comparison of Amalia to Angelica Kauffman was not new; one such instance had already appeared in a British newspaper during the first year of Amalia's arrival in England in 1896:

> Miss Amalia Kussner, whose success has been likened in America to that of Angelica Kauffman, who had only to appear in London for "the sober old town straightaway to run mad with paint;" and, once again in

an incredibly short time, Society has been conquered by the power of
a palette and brush.[24]

Kauffman was a Swiss-born artist but lived for a while in London
at the end of the eighteenth century and was one of the first women to
be admitted to the Royal Academy. Though Kauffman's works included
miniatures, they were not the primary focus of her art. She was broadly
talented and did full-size portraits and decorative ceiling paintings. Like
Amalia, she entered the London art scene with a rapid rise in popularity that was helped by titled women. In a paper written by art historian
Dr. Laurence Shafe, one can clearly see the parallels to Amalia's career:

> She was persuaded to come to London and the rank of Lady Went-
> worth opened society to her, and she was well received everywhere,
> the royal family especially showing her great favor. Her firmest friend,
> however, was Sir Joshua Reynolds who called her "Miss Angelica" or
> "Miss Angel."
>
> She was extremely productive and everything she produced was
> grabbed immediately. One engraver did nothing else but produce
> engravings of the latest Kauffman work. He described the whole
> world as "Angelicamad."[25]

An American magazine, *The Critic*, had already supported this comparison back in 1901:

> Miss Amalia Kussner is considered by some people as the "Miss Angel
> of the present day." In a way she is. She is no better as a draughtsman
> than Angelica Kaufman, but like that lady she pleases.[26]

The fact that Amalia and Sargent were the only two American artists
included in Edward VII's *Book of Beauty* is quite significant. Furthermore,
that the editor decided to include not just their artworks but also the
satirical essay written about them clearly reflects their importance in both
the art and cultural scenes at the turn of the century.

With their prominence in London during the same era, it is easy to wonder if these two artists interacted. It seems they did, per the writing of one Scottish newspaper in 1898 that stated, "she [Amalia] herself has 'sat' to her compatriot, Mr. Sargent."[27] Her hometown of Greencastle, Indiana, also recorded that she had plans to keep the painting for a while, then present it to the Metropolitan Museum of Art.[28]

In a list of Sargent's portraits that he completed around this timeframe, there is record of one simply titled *Portrait of a Lady*. There is no name given along with it, so it can only be speculation to say that this was the portrait the Scottish newspaper reported Sargent doing of Amalia.[29] Ultimately, the whereabouts of this painting are unknown. If it *was* of Amalia, she may very well have brought it back with her to New York. And if that happened, it likely would have been lost in the Windsor Hotel fire.

The Book of Beauty was certainly not widely distributed in either England or America. Those who did purchase it would have primarily been members of the many titled families who had either their portraits or their written works included. But Amalia's prominence in Edwardian England was clearly established by this book. And though there are few works of hers in museums now, *The Book of Beauty* in and of itself can be considered a museum of sorts, displaying a selection of her miniatures for posterity and capturing a glimpse of how she was viewed in London at the time.

Chapter 11

Amalia's Legacy

Amalia's final years were spent primarily in England with du Pont at Windlesham Hall, with her sister Louise and John Cloud close by at Thankerton House. However, in a letter from Amalia to Carrie Weinhardt (wife of her first cousin, William Weinhardt) in December 1929, she indicated that she and du Pont were living in Grosvenor House Hotel in London, having "decided not to open our house this winter . . . the servant question is very difficult in the country during the cold weather."[1] This could be interpreted to mean that their estate was too much effort to heat, given the need for a larger staff to maintain the fireplaces in each room. In the late 1920s, a number of estates in Windlesham had not yet been converted to central heat and were still dependent on fireplaces.[2]

Although Amalia was no longer mentioned in British newspapers, the Kussner name was still seen from time to time as her brother's music was being heard by audiences at concerts internationally. Orchestras played his compositions such as *The Evening Hour* and *Jasmine Waltz* alongside pieces by Schubert and Brahms.[3]

There was one final mention of Amalia and the Kussner family in *The Indianapolis Star* in January 1932, ironically shortly before her death. The article focused on the hundredth anniversary of Memorial Hall in Terre Haute—the same building that had been the location of the Kussner family home and music business; hence, much of the article was about Amalia's family. The writing painted a colorful picture of a creative environment for the children growing up: "In this strong old building they

175

soon had a good business and in the rooms above the store the family life carried on. There the children set up a stage and acted little plays in German, French and English for the pleasure of the family and friends."[4] The article then went on to present the full success story of Amalia's career, describing her efforts upon arriving in New York: "Burning with zeal, knowing that she had talent, she tried again and again to make contacts with persons who could be of service to her and her work." Her connections with Mrs. Havemeyer and later with Minnie Paget certainly were of service to her career. Then the article detailed her portraits in Europe and declared her as a "mid-Western miniaturist of the first rank."

The Memorial Hall still stands today and is noted as "indisputably one of the finest examples of 19th century Greek Revival architecture in this section of Indiana."[5] The structure is the oldest business building in Terre Haute. It is now part of the National Register of Historic Places, and all the accomplishments of the Kussner family and Amalia are documented as a permanent part of its history.

In February 1932, Amalia visited with Louise and her husband when the two couples wintered together in San Remo, Italy. Upon arrival, Amalia was already sick with a bronchial cold, and local specialists were brought in to examine her. Their conclusions were the same as those of other specialists she had seen in London and Paris: a diagnosis of physical exhaustion, and recommendations that she needed rest and a careful diet, after which she would improve.[6]

She remained for a while in San Remo, but her condition worsened. Du Pont decided to take her to a sanatorium in Montreux, Switzerland, called Clinique Florimont.[7] This place specialized in treating lung conditions and in the early 1930s still had a number of tuberculosis patients. The facility was located high atop a hillside and overlooked Lake Geneva. It was also a preferred location for wealthy Europeans and sometimes considered a place of "last resort."

The medical staff at the sanitorium found her condition had become much more serious and performed some sort of operation, the details of which were not specified. Her condition continued to deteriorate, and Amalia passed away on May 21, 1932, at the age of sixty-nine. As with many aspects of Amalia's life, there is some mystery around her

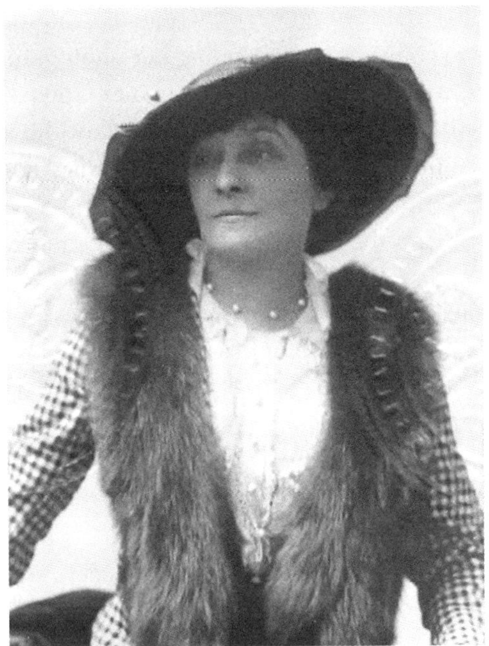

Photo of Amalia Kussner Coudert from her 1915 passport application. *U.S. Passport Applications, 1796–1925, Ancestry.com*

actual cause of death. A report filed by the local American consulate at Lausanne, Switzerland, on June 3, 1932, listed the cause of death as "generalized abdominal carcinoma," which would be some sort of stomach cancer.[8] She might have also had a lung condition at the same time, given the reports of her smoking earlier in life and the fact that she went to an institution known for treating lung ailments. The local consulate's report contrasts with the many historical accounts of her death that state only a "lung condition." And the listing of her fictitious birth date continued on the consulate's report, showing a birth year of 1876 and an age of fifty-six.

Mary Kussner, Albert's widow, drafted an obituary and provided copies to Amalia's cousin Allen Weinhardt in Terre Haute for placement in the local newspapers.[9] She also intended to submit her draft to the *Chicago Tribune* and the *New York Times*. However, even without her efforts, word spread quickly around the world to most major newspapers.

The obituaries would appear over the span of a month and a half, with some covering two columns and including her photograph, such as in the *Indianapolis Star*, with the title "Amalia Kussner Coudert, Indiana-Born Artist of International Fame, Dies."[10] Almost all of the longer write-ups mentioned her painting Edward VII, Czar Nicholas II and the czarina, and Cecil Rhodes. The *Chicago Tribune* also listed esteemed members of American Gilded Age society: Mrs. J. Ogden Armour of Chicago, and Mrs. George Gould and Mrs. John Jacob Astor of New York.[11]

However, outside of the Midwest newspapers, the notices of her death were much briefer, most with only a few short lines printed on a back page of the issue, often included among the other obituaries. The *New York Daily News* printed one such brief notice on page 162:

Mrs. A. K. Coudert Dies

Paris, June 2 (AP)—Mrs. Amalia Kussner Coudert, wife of Charles du Pont Coudert, of Surrey, England, and New York, died today at Montreux.[12]

It was clear her passing was not considered frontpage news at the time. However, the art world paid tribute to her with a brief mention in the periodical *The Art News*:

Mrs. Charles du Pont Coudert (Amalia Kussner Coudert), who for twenty-five years has lived principally in England and was well known, especially during the close of the last century, as a miniaturist of the socially prominent, died recently in Switzerland. She is survived by her husband.[13]

Amalia's funeral was held at the Anglican church of Windlesham Parish on June 11.[14] Du Pont and her brother-in-law, John Cloud, attended but sadly Louise was unable to attend due to illness. Du Pont's family also came, including his niece Miss Natica Nast, daughter of Clarisse and Condé Nast (though they had divorced many years earlier in 1923). There were at least another thirty-two attendees, a mixture of those who lived around Windlesham and some who came from London.

Among them were several titled ladies, such as Lady Ellenborough and Lady Katherine Meade, who lived in or near Windlesham. Mrs. Hutton, the wife of the rector who officiated, was also listed as attending. Many of the local residents were active with the church, and possibly Amalia and du Pont themselves attended on a regular basis. The write-up in the *Surrey Advertiser* indicated that many floral wreaths were seen at the service.

Amalia was buried in Windlesham Cemetery, with an elaborate granite headstone topped by an urn decorated with carved flowers. She was laid to rest about five feet away from her parents' monument. The simple inscription on her stone read:

AMALIA
THE BELOVED WIFE OF
CHARLES DU PONT COUDERT
OF WINDLESHAM HALL
WHO DIED THE 31st MAY 1932[15]

Eventually, the two monuments for Louise and her husband would be added to this gravesite, in 1962 and 1936, respectively.

Amalia had written a detailed will in 1930, in which she surprisingly left two thousand dollars (approximately forty-five thousand dollars today) to Nancy Huston Banks, along with similar sums to relatives in Indiana and West Virginia, and Albert's widow, Mary Kussner, in Florida. It seems that the Windlesham property was jointly owned by her and du Pont, and she explicitly left the land, the house, and all of its contents to him. Her financial holdings still included Terre Haute property on Wabash Avenue, leading to complications in settling the will since it was drafted in England.[16] It took about two years to resolve the legal issues.

In March 1933, both Amalia and du Pont were newspaper headlines again when he finally won his case against Thomas Cook and Son, Ltd. from the 1930 car crash in Italy and was awarded £870. The settlement addressed the loss of some of Amalia's miniatures and other personal belongings in the river.[17] Having this legal case drag on after his wife's death surely must have been difficult for du Pont.

Less than two years after Amalia's passing, du Pont remarried at fifty-eight years old, to a woman seventeen years younger, in February 1934. And this marriage was as mysterious as his first. The only known wedding announcement is found in the *Evening Courier* out of Camden, New Jersey:

> Mrs. Ellen Hilton Young, the former Ellen Hilton, daughter of the late Edward Hilton, of New York, will be married this week. She will marry Capt. duPont Coudert in a quiet ceremony, the witness for the bride being her sister, Lady Cope, wife of Capt. Sir Denzil Cope.[18]

What this announcement failed to mention was that du Pont's new wife was a divorcée and had two children with her first husband, Richard Owen. At the time of her marriage to du Pont, her son and daughter were twenty-one and nineteen, respectively. Her maiden name was Ellen Hilton, and it is not clear where the surname "Young" listed in the article came from. Her earlier life was spent in both America and Europe, with her first marriage taking place in England, but, opposite to Amalia, her residence trended more toward New York from the late 1920s up to 1934. She is listed as divorced by 1929, according to a US naturalization document.[19]

The life of Ellen and du Pont was certainly not publicly documented, and there are essentially no newspaper accounts of their lives. After twenty-four years of marriage, Ellen passed away at age sixty-six in England. Charles du Pont outlived her by six years, passing away at eighty-nine in Switzerland. He is buried in the Calvary Cemetery in Woodside, New York, along with his father and his uncle, Frederic René.[20]

∾o∾

Both of Amalia's siblings provided collections of her personal papers to various Indiana institutions before and after her death. In March 1916, Albert provided a large set of newspaper clippings to the Herron Art Institute in Indianapolis, detailing Amalia's earlier career as well as coverage of her wedding to du Pont. This donation followed only two months after their display of miniatures by Eulabee Dix; possibly this timing was not by chance, but rather because Albert wanted to see recognition from this museum for his sister too.

The collection was saved by Anne E. Turrell, who managed the museum library at that time, and the papers are still there today.[21] From these articles, Ms. Turrell drafted a one-page biography on Amalia that also mentioned her talented brother. Later on, other staff at the museum library added to this collection with retrospective articles written about Amalia in the 1950s and 1960s.

The most significant collection of Amalia's personal papers was donated to the Sisters of Providence in Saint Mary-of-the-Woods, Indiana, by Louise in the 1950s, just before her passing. What is remarkable about this collection is the large volume of newspaper clippings that Amalia had kept covering all aspects of her life—whether positive or negative.

Currently in the United States, there are only three museums and two historical societies that have her miniatures: the Swope Art Museum, the Cincinnati Art Museum, the Worcester Art Museum, the New Orleans Historical Society, and the Newport County Historical Society. With the exception of the Swope Art Museum, which has three of her miniatures, these institutions have just one of Amalia's miniatures each. There is also one work in London at the Victoria and Albert Museum. This is in vast contrast to museums like the National Museum of American Women Artists, which holds a very impressive 106 of Eulabee Dix's works,[22] and the Metropolitan Museum of Art, which has four of Eulabee's pieces.

There are a number of theories as to why Amalia's artwork was never seen as "museum-worthy." Maryann Gunderson, an art historian who has studied three of Amalia's contemporaries—Eulabee Dix, Laura Coombs Hills, and Rosa Hooper—observed that in looking at the miniaturists who were part of the revival of the style, these artists were mostly women and almost all of them joined the societies for portrait miniaturists, which in turn helped promote their business.[23] These societies were most often founded by women and had locations in major metropolitan areas such as New York, Philadelphia, and Los Angeles. For these women to have successful careers, they would have needed a solid body of work and to make earnest attempts to show their art frequently in salons or exhibits. If their businesses were prosperous enough, they could set up their own studios to receive their sitters. The other commonality is that these women typically remained single, especially in the earlier and most active part of their careers.

Laura Coombs Hills, Rosa Hooper, and certainly Eulabee Dix were all active in miniaturist societies, whereas records indicate that Amalia never joined any of them. Timing would not have been an issue for her since the earliest of these societies, the American Society of Miniature Painters, was started in 1899 in New York City. Their first major exhibit took place the year after, at the Knoedler Gallery on Fifth Avenue in New York City in 1900. This would have been at the height of Amalia's career and while she was still primarily living in New York.[24] It is interesting to note, however, that prior to the founding of this society, four of Amalia's works had already been on display six years earlier at the Knoedler Gallery, including her portraits of Mrs. Havemeyer and Lillian Russell.[25]

In another discussion of the history of miniature arts in America, Dale T. Johnson, former curator at the Metropolitan Museum of Art, mentioned Lucia Fairchild Fuller, Lucy M. Stanton, Margaret Foote Hawley, and again Rosa Hooper—four artists who were prominent in the miniature arts revival and were included in a Metropolitan Museum of Art miniatures exhibit held in 1990.[26] Three of these women were active members in major miniature art societies and the fourth, Lucy Stanton, was part of a smaller art organization in Washington, DC, that focused on all sizes of watercolor works.[27] Also important to their careers was their attending art schools and obtaining awards from these institutions. For instance, Hawley was recognized in *The Times* out of Washington, DC, in 1900 for winning a gold medal as a student at the Corcoran Art School.[28] Fuller was documented as being in Cornish, New Hampshire, during the summer of 1903, where she was part of the renowned Cornish Art Colony headed by sculptor Augustus St. Gaudens.[29] One of the most famous artists of the Cornish colony was the illustrator Maxfield Parrish. This association would certainly have established Fuller's credentials as a respected artist. All of these women miniaturists were active during the height of Amalia's career, but their careers also extended well beyond when Amalia retired around 1911.

Amalia's personality, as seen in many instances, was that she needed to be in the spotlight, and she likely felt that attention would have been taken away from her if she were part of these art societies. The one exception was the Royal Academy of London, where Amalia did exhibit in both 1896 and 1905, but these works did not become part of the permanent collections and she did not become a member.[30] Additionally, with her having proclaimed quite early in her career that she received little or no formal art training, she would never have wanted to align herself later on with any established art school. And frankly, Amalia's financial success and huge number of commissions were in no way negatively impacted by not having the academic and society memberships. Except for Eulabee Dix, most of these artists did not have the name recognition that Amalia did, nor did they have her popularity with the high society matrons of the Gilded Age or the titled women of England.

In the last decade of the miniature revival when the art style was still in vogue, there was an extensive exhibit at the Chicago World's Fair in 1933 titled "National Miniature Exhibit," which featured works by Laura Coombs Hills and Rosa Hooper, among others. Sadly, this exhibit focused only on *living* artists or those who were members of miniaturist societies, so Amalia was excluded.

Another difference in terms of Amalia's career is that she basically became an ex-pat, living in England almost exclusively the last twenty years of her life. Aside from a few commissions she had in America during the 1900s, most of her work was done in Europe at the end of her career. While she was not on the membership rosters of the prominent art societies, she was certainly on the invitation lists of the titled families of England. Maybe later in life, this had become more important to her than her artistic legacy.

In looking at Amalia's career and legacy compared to a few other Midwestern women artists of her time, brief mention should be given to Janet Scudder, who was also from Terre Haute. Though her artistic ability was quite different, as she was a sculptor, she too became prominent in Gilded Age New York and in Europe, but more so in France than in

England. A few other Indiana artists—Marie Goth and Julia Graydon Sharpe—were quite popular for doing portrait work at this time.[31] In looking at these women from the Midwest, plus Eulabee Dix from Illinois, there is an apt description of the obstacles they encountered:

> Whether trained in the most elite art academy overseas or instructed at the side of a professional living in the farmlands of Indiana, artistically gifted Hoosier women were faced with the same problem. If they wanted to be acknowledged as serious artists at the end of the nineteenth century, it was a daunting—if not sometimes impossible—proposition. For them, having a career was culturally inappropriate and seen as a means of avoiding their rightful responsibilities as females. Only by dint of their single-minded efforts did these women sidestep society's expectations to achieve their goals, often at considerable cost in terms of their personal relationships. Many times on the fringes of popular customs and frequently greeted with charitable condescension, such artists located themselves in places—literally and figuratively—where they were able to follow their muses beyond the censoring sight of society.[32]

All of these women artists faced tremendous challenges to escape geographical and societal boundaries. This certainly applied to Amalia as well, with her move to New York to pursue making a name for herself and her clear intention to continue her career after marriage.

Furthermore, all of these women's careers ran parallel to the suffrage movement and some of them, including Janet Scudder, were actively engaged in the fight for women's rights and vocally supportive of suffragette principles. It is surprising that there is no evidence of Amalia participating in the suffrage movement in any way. The primary reason may simply have been that she wasn't going to wait for society's stringent norms to change to allow her the needed freedoms to conduct her life as she wished. Instead, in what she accomplished, she likely acted, albeit unintentionally, as an inspiration for many who were seeking their freedoms. In fact, she was listed in a 1904 suffrage-themed compendium titled *The New Womanhood*, in the "Women in Trades and Professions" chapter, which listed no fewer than thirty different entries, including doctors, architects, and lawyers. Amalia's entry listed her as "an Indiana girl [who] does the finest miniature painting in the world, and has painted most of the crowned heads of Europe."[33]

Given the many works that Amalia is known to have painted—at least 110—and the many that are still unaccounted for today, they may eventually turn up from private collections or in museum archives that were never processed. There is also one other unique place where her work can still be seen, though only by a select few, that gives her legacy another fascinating connection to British history.

Many years after Amalia's death, when Winston Churchill became prime minister during World War II, he often sought both emotional and physical refuge at the country estate for prime ministers, Chequers. The previous owners of the estate, Lord Lee of Fareham and his wife Ruth, a former American dollar heiress, gave the estate to Britain in 1917 as part of a trust, in the "hope that the future Prime Ministers would thereby be enabled to maintain the dignity of the office without sacrificing their independence."[34] When Lord Lee and Ruth moved out in 1921,[35] they willingly left behind some of their prized artworks for décor, with one of those pieces being the miniature Amalia had painted of Ruth for her engagement in 1899 (see color insert). The painting is very much in Amalia's classic style, with a diaphanous wrap of fabric and tendrils of hair framing her face.

The miniature, stored in a jewel case, was known to be situated near other quite valuable miniatures of the Cromwell family, the previous owners of the estate many centuries earlier, and close by a ring that once belonged to Queen Elizabeth I. Amalia no doubt would have been delighted to know the good company in which her miniature of Ruth was displayed. The portrait is still listed as part of the Chequers Trust collection today.

Churchill "wrote some of his most famous radio speeches"[36] at Chequers, which became one of his favorite retreats during the war. With his avid interest in history, he likely walked by the jewel case on occasion and very well may have gazed upon the lovely miniature done by Amalia.

Amalia and Winston Churchill, though not direct friends, were part of similar social circles, and their paths may have crossed at several earlier times in history—it is almost certain they would have known *about* each other. Their first potential introduction would have been a connection through Consuelo Vanderbilt, the Duchess of Marlborough. Her husband, the 9th Duke of Marlborough, was a first cousin to Churchill, and the two men had a close friendship. Upon Consuelo's arrival in London at the end of their honeymoon in early March 1896, she met the young Churchill, along with his mother Lady Randolph Churchill, and described the young man "as ardent and vital and seemed to have every intention of getting the most out of life, whether in sport, in love, in adventure or politics."[37] Consuelo was clearly impressed by his personality and they did in fact develop a genuine friendship, with Churchill often visiting Blenheim.[38] Amalia herself made several trips to Blenheim during Consuelo's first year there, spending at least two weeks as a guest later that March to create the first portrait. She returned shortly thereafter to complete more miniatures, as ordered by Consuelo's husband. So, she and Churchill may very well have met in person, or Churchill may have at least seen the finished miniatures and heard mention of her name.

Their second intersection in history was that Amalia and Churchill both were in South Africa at the start of the Boer War, though geographically separated. Churchill was sent there as a war correspondent, arriving at the end of October, and attempted to reach Ladysmith, which was significantly east of the diamond mining camps of Kimberley. By early November, reports were already being sent to newspapers about Amalia and Nancy Huston Banks being "cooped in Kimberley"—a situation which Churchill may have heard of."

Later that month, "while helping to defend an armoured train, Churchill was captured and imprisoned. His arguments to be released as a non-combatant were rejected by the Boers, so he escaped and became the object of a man-hunt. Once he found safety, he opted to continue covering the war and to fight in it too."[39] Not surprisingly, when he returned to Britain in 1900, he was hailed a hero and his travails were well publicized. Amalia was a frequent reader of newspapers, since she was always on the lookout for mentions of her art or activities in society and would have seen the headlines about his adventures.

Given the overlap in their social circles, did Amalia ever paint miniatures of any of Churchill's relatives? We do know that at the party she gave at the Willis's rooms in July 1898, her guests included two of his aunts, Lady Tweedmouth and Lady Sarah Wilson, sisters to his father. So, it's probable, but records are inconclusive. A listing of all known portraits done by Amalia can be found in the appendix, "List of Those Amalia Painted."

Amalia Kussner Coudert had many dimensions and became who she needed to be to pursue her career ambitions. She certainly possessed a genuine talent as an artist, but her personality and the way she deftly navigated the society elite of both New York and London were clearly some of her strengths.

The art historian Lewis Hoyer Rabbage, one of the most renowned collectors of miniatures of the twentieth century, compared Amalia to other miniaturists and highlighted her unique characteristics:

> Though many were more formally trained and perhaps more talented, they were "too genteel to move their careers along in any dynamic senses," lacking Kussner's skill at self-promotion. "The artist," says Rabbage, "sensed, early on, that a little saucy and sassy behavior might rile a few social or art world conservatives, but it would also serve to keep her name the subject of many conversations among the ladies affluent, and paintable."[40]

In one of Amalia's last interviews in 1913, the writer of the article recorded a future desire of the miniature painter's:

> She contemplates writing her reminiscences some day, however, and will have the book illustrated with her most interesting and noted miniatures, reproduced in color by the very best process possible. Such a volume would be of literary interest, I am sure, as Mrs. Coudert possesses the rare gift of narrative and remembers many interesting

incidents in connection with her work in the homes of royal and famous people.[41]

Amalia's compiling her miniatures and her many stories into a volume never seems to have happened. Thankfully, a myriad of resources—magazines, newspapers, and biographies of her friends and contemporaries—did survive to provide a fairly complete account of the many "interesting incidents" in her life that she likely would have wanted to record for posterity and share with the world.

Amalia would undoubtedly be pleased to know that her name is being brought back into conversation and her legacy revived within the pages of this book. Historical accounts showed her as many things: a talented artist, a social climber, a dedicated friend, a devoted family member, and more. But her true motivations will never be fully understood. Amalia Kussner Coudert will remain an enigma—and maybe that's just what she wanted.

Acknowledgments

Many thanks go to those who have helped provide materials for this book and who also helped me better understand Amalia Kussner, both as an artist and the times she lived in.

For those in Indiana—my thanks go to Sean Eisele, special collections librarian, and Janet Hatcher, special collections assistant, at Vigo County Library; Suzy Quick, curator at Vigo County History Center; Karen Zach, Indiana historian; Anastasia Karel, archivist and interim library director at Indianapolis Museum of Art at Newfields; Larry Paarlberg, executive director at General Lew Wallace Study and Museum; Meredith McGovern, arts and culture collections manager, and Paula Katz, curator of art, at Indiana State Museum. A special thanks to Sister Janet Gilligan at Sisters of Providence Archives for helping me research the superb collection of papers donated by Amalia's sister, Louise.

For those in other parts of the country—my thanks go to Kate Seno Bradshaw, digital researcher, Dani Brogdon, reference and technical services librarian, and Dominique Manuel, digital asset manager, at the National Museum of Women in the Arts; Eve Loftus, curatorial research assistant, Dr. Nicole Williams, curator of collections, and Victoria McKenna-Ratjen, digitization specialist, at Newport County History Society; Taína Caragol, curator at Smithsonian National Portrait Gallery; Jeff Fontana, associate professor of art history at Austin College; Mallory Howard, assistant curator at the Mark Twain House & Museum; and Kerstin Burlingame, park ranger at the Saint-Gaudens National Historical Park.

From my own town of Middleton, Massachusetts—my thanks go to the library staff at the Flint Public Library for providing me access to unusual history books through the extended network of lending libraries in Massachusetts.

A thanks for those "over the pond" in England: Adam Waterton, librarian at the Royal Academy of Art; Sally Clark and Moira Nairn, both historians in Windlesham, England; and Vicky Perry, archivist at Belvoir Castle.

Special thanks go to Maryann Gunderson, assistant professor at Ohio University, who has a unique academic background in the miniature revival and helped me understand this art form and its part in history.

The sharing of images of Charles du Pont Coudert from his great-nieces, Maria Stanton and Catherine Del Guercio, was greatly appreciated and added much to the visual history of Amalia's husband.

If I missed anyone who may have helped me from the numerous historical societies and museums I contacted, my apologies. Your efforts are always invaluable for those of us who do in-depth research.

Thanks to my cousins and more distant relatives from the Weinhardt family for images, letters, and stories on our shared relative, Amalia Kussner. First, thanks to my cousin Seth Weinhardt and his father Carl J. Weinhardt Jr. (1927–1986) for sharing tales of her incredible life. The content from my distant cousin, John Weinhardt, and his providing materials from his uncle John V. Weinhardt (1900–1960) was quite helpful in shining light on the last years of Amalia's life.

To both sides of my family—the Weinhardts and Langones—who were all incredible storytellers and kept my attention as a small child, which then inspired me as an adult to write about our family history.

I was truly fortunate to have Brittany Stoner as my editor, for having an appreciation for women who were "hidden in history" and recognizing the interesting life of Amalia Kussner. Her superb guidance on my writing was especially helpful for someone new to the publishing process. And many thanks to Lyons Press, an imprint of Globe Pequot, for ultimately making this book a reality.

And finally—a heartfelt thanks to my husband, Edward Ray, for his support and tolerating my spending long hours writing and researching over almost a year. Without him, this endeavor would not have been possible.

Appendix

List of Those Amalia Painted

Miniature Portraits Done Primarily in America

Mrs. H. B. Gilbert
Charles du Pont Coudert
Lillian Russell
Marie Tempest
Mrs. Phillip D. Armour (two portraits)
Mrs. Ogden Armour (three portraits)
Hon. Charles Kern
Mrs. Charles Kern
Mrs. M. A. Tyler
Mrs. William L. Scott
Mrs. Caroline Astor
Mrs. Orme Wilson (née Carrie Astor)
Mrs. John Jacob Astor (née Ava Willing)
Mrs. Stuyvesant Fish (Mamie)
Mrs. Gould and son
Charles Hamot Strong
Annie Wainwright Scott Strong
Matilda Thora Wainwright Strong (two portraits)
Mrs. Perry Belmont (née Jessie Ann Robbins)
Mrs. Alva Vanderbilt Belmont
Miss May Goelet
Mrs. Herbert Leslie Terrell
Mrs. McLane Van Ingen
Matilda Townsend
Mrs. E. Reeve Merritt
Mrs. W. S. Walker
Mrs. John Gerow Dutcher
Dr. Allen Pence
Crawford Fairbanks
Charles Minshall
Stephen Reynolds and family (estimated four portraits)
Mrs. Paran Stevens
Dolly Radnor
Mrs. Frank Tilford
Mrs. Van Rensselaer Cruger
Ruth Moore (later Lady Lee)

Mrs. John Mayer
Mrs. Richard H. Townsend
Miss Atherton Blight
Mrs. Eleanor Le Roy
Miss Sophie Scott
Minnie Paget (first portrait)
Mrs. John Gerome Dutcher
Miss Jennie Chamberlain

Mrs. Theodore Havemeyer
Mrs. Ogden Mills
Mrs. Cyrus Hall McCormick
Horace G. Chase
Mrs. Lorillard Spencer
Mrs. G. P. Morosini
Mrs. Harold McCormick
Mrs. George Laflin

MINIATURE PORTRAITS DONE PRIMARILY IN EUROPE

Madame von André
Minnie Paget (second portrait)
Lady Dudley
Lady Feodorovna (later Lady
Alington) (three portraits)
Lady Sutherland
Lady Portland
Lady Devonshire
Lady Chelsea
Lady Colebrook
Lady Sophie Scott
Lady Naylor Leyland
Lady Henry Vincent (Helen)
Countess of Warwick (two portraits)
Lily, Duchess of Marlborough
Prince of Wales (later
Edward VII)
Mrs. George Keppel (Alice)
Princess Alexandra (later Queen
Alexandra)
Consuelo, Duchess of Marlbor-
ough (four portraits)
Countess of Dudley
Lady Werner
Countess of Stradbroke

Mrs. Edward Balfour
Dame Nellie Melba (opera singer)
Czar Nicholas II
Czarina Alexandra
Romanov daughters—likely
Olga, Tatiana, and Maria (three
portraits)
Grand Duchess Maria
Grand Duchess Ellen
King Alfonso XIII of Spain
Queen Victoria Eugenia of Spain
Spanish royal children (estimated
three portraits)
Queen Maud of Norway (two
portraits)
Cecil Rhodes
Mrs. Alfred Harmsworth
Mrs. Willie James
Miss Muriel Wilson
Mrs. Gerald Lowther (née Alice
Blight)
Mrs. Claude Watney (Ada)
Lady de Grey
Princess of Pless
Auguste Rodin

Notes

Introduction

1. Maude Andrews, "The First from the Klondike," *The Atlanta Constitution*, September 26, 1898, 11.

Chapter 1

1. Mike McCormick, "Artist's Talent Was Miniatures," *Terre Haute Tribute Star*, March 23, 1997, 7.

2. Entry for Lorence [Lorenz] Kissner [Kussner], Indiana, United States, Marriages, 1810–2001, Ancestry.com.

3. Carl A. Zenor, "Putnam County in the Civil War: Local History of a Critical Period," thesis (DePauw University, June 1956).

4. McCormick, "Artist's Talent Was Miniatures."

5. McCormick, "Artist's Talent Was Miniatures."

6. Dorothy J. Clark, "National Register of Historic Place Inventory—Nomination Form, Memorial Hall," 1973.

7. Tim Crumrin, *Hidden History of Terre Haute* (The History Press, 2020), 57.

8. Beck and Pauli, panoramic map of Terre Haute, 1880, Library of Congress.

9. Lorenz Kussner, *Woodland Home, Music for the Nation: American Sheet Music, Ca. 1870 to 1885*, Library of Congress, https://www.loc.gov/resource/music.mussm-sm1875 -02384/?st=gallery.

10. McCormick, "Artist's Talent Was Miniatures."

11. Dr. Dipa Sarkar, "Historical Treasure: Historic Tile Done by Famous Miniature Artist," *Tribune-Star* (Terre Haute, IN), November 19, 2006.

12. Frances Hughes, "Local Woman Was World-Famous as Miniatures Painter in Her Day," *The Terre Haute Star*, August 31, 1961.

13. St. Mary of the Woods College, "Our History," https://www.smwc.edu/about/ history/.

14. Brylynn Ellis, "Historical Treasure: Miniature Portrait Artist Was Sought Out," *Tribune-Star* (Terre Haute, IN), March 18, 2023.

15. Staff, "The Raffling of the Parlor Organ," *The Daily Wabash Express* (Terre Haute, IN), June 30, 1889, 4.

16. William H. Wiley, "Fifty-Four Specimens of Drawing from Flat Copy—Free Hand," Vigo County Library Special Collections, Terre Haute, Indiana, February 25, 1876.

17. Staff, "Fifteenth Annual Commencement of the High School," *Saturday Evening Mail* (Terre Haute, IN), vol. 11, no. 52, June 25, 1881.

18. Anderson Cooper and Katherine Howe, *Vanderbilt: The Rise and Fall of an American Dynasty* (Harper Collins, 2021), 87.

19. Crumrin, *Hidden History of Terre Haute*, 58.

20. Flatiron Nomad, "The Art Students League of New York," September 27, 2019, https://flatironnomad.nyc/history/the-art-students-league-of-new-york/.

21. Staff, "Decorative Art Society," *Terre Haute Daily Wabash Express*, June 18, 1882.

22. Staff, "Square Pianos at Kussner's Palace of Music," *Saturday Evening Mail* (Terre Haute, IN), vol. 16, no. 17, October 17, 1885.

23. Staff, "Did Fairbanks Lie?" *Indianapolis Journal*, January 1, 1894, 2; staff, "Personal, Local and General News," *Indianapolis Journal*, May 24, 1892, 6; Mike McCormick, *Terre Haute: Queen City of the Wabash* (Arcadia Publishing, 2005), 97.

24. Staff, "The Amusement World: Ben Hur to Be Put on at Naylor's Monday Night," *Terre Haute Daily News*, October 11, 1890.

25. Staff, "The Play and the Players, Opening Performance of Ben Hur," *Terre Haute Daily News*, October 14, 1890.

26. Staff, "New Suits—Circuit Court," *Terre Haute Weekly Gazette*, June 24, 1880; staff, "The Courts," *Daily Wabash Express*, October 26, 1882; staff, "Circuit Court," *Terre Haute Weekly Gazette*, December 30, 1886.

27. Amalia was not alone as a Terre Haute resident rising to national fame. Included in her timeframe were author Theodore Dreiser (1871–1945) and Eugene V. Debbs (1855–1926), a political activist and major supporter of the "new" workers unions.

Chapter 2

1. Staff, "A Quaint Theatrical Organization," *The New York Times*, January 20, 1907, 21.

2. Alyn Williams, "The History and Revival of Miniature Portrait Painting," *The American Magazine of Art*, vol. 15, no. 9, 1924, 462.

3. Williams, "History and Revival of Miniature Portrait Painting," 462.

4. Maryann Sudnick Gunderson, "Dismissed Yet Disarming: The Portrait Miniature Revival, 1890–1930" (thesis, Ohio University, 2012), 28.

5. Gunderson, "Dismissed Yet Disarming," 11.

6. Gunderson, "Dismissed Yet Disarming," 28.

7. Gunderson, "Dismissed Yet Disarming," 28.

8. Frances E. Hughes, "Local Woman Was World-Famous as Miniature Painter in Her Day," *Terre Haute Star*, August 31, 1961.

9. Elaine Louie, "Overlooked No More: Clara Driscoll, Designer of Visions in Glass for Tiffany," *New York Times*, February 23, 2023, https://www.nytimes.com/2023/02/23/obituaries/clara-driscoll-overlooked.html.

10. Staff, "A Painter of Miniatures," *Greencastle Banner and Times*, October 4, 1895.

11. Lena Weisman, "Beyond Fancy, Beyond Taste: Gender, Art, and Culture in America's Gilded Age" (history honors thesis, Lehigh University, 2022), 22.

12. Elinor Evans, "Mrs Astor and the Four Hundred," *History Extra*, February 21, 2022, https://www.historyextra.com/period/victorian/mrs-astor-who-four-hundred-new-york-society-list-ward-mcallister-gilded-age/.

13. Staff, "Maids and Matrons," *St. Joseph News-Press*, March 5, 1897, 5.

14. Rhoda Nathan, "Ward McAllister: Beau Nash of 'The Age of Innocence,'" *College Literature*, vol. 14, no. 3, 1987.

15. Mei-En Lai, "Social Status, the Patriarch and Assembly Balls, and the Transformation in Elite Identity in Gilded Age New York" (thesis, Simon Fraser University, 2013), 19, www.lib.sfu.ca.

16. Anne de Courcy, "Mrs. Astor Invites," *St. Regis Magazine*, https://magazine.stregis.com/mrs-astor-invites-2/.

17. Frances E. Hughes, "Amalia Kussner: High Priestess of the Daintiest of Arts," *Traces of Indiana and Midwestern History*, Indiana Historical Society, vol. 2, no. 4, Fall 1990, 39.

18. Tom Miller, "The Lost H.O. Havemeyer Mansion—No. 1 E. 66th Street," *Daytonian in Manhattan*, January 12, 2015, http://daytoninmanhattan.blogspot.com/2015/01/the-lost-h-o-havemeyer-mansion-no-1-e.html/.

19. Miller, "Lost H.O. Havemeyer Mansion."

20. Chas. Fdc. Nirdlinger, "Of a Certain Painter-In-Little," *The Illustrated American*, April 29, 1893, 505.

21. Nirdlinger, "Of a Certain Painter-in-Little," 509.

22. Staff, "Society Notes," *Elite* (Chicago), vol. XIV, no. 28, October 10, 1896.

23. Nancy Huston Banks, "A Painter of Miniatures," *Ladies Home Journal*, vol. 12, no. 11, October 1895, 7.

24. Nancy Huston Banks, "Success in Her Art," *Altoona Mirror* (PA), June 7, 1895, 3.

25. Banks, "Success," 3.

26. Velma Lou Hines, "Nancy Huston Banks: Her Life & Works" (master's thesis and special projects, Western Kentucky University, 1933), 1.

27. Hines, "Nancy Huston Banks," 3.

28. Staff, *A Souvenir of World's Fair Women and Wives of Prominent Officials Connected with the World's Columbian Exposition* (The Blocker Company, 1892), 31.

29. Nancy Huston Banks, *The Bookman* (Open Court Publishing, 1895), 224.

30. Hines, "Nancy Huston Banks," 4.

31. Staff, *Portraits of Women—Loan Exhibition* (National Academy of Design, The Knickerbocker Press, 1894), 71–72.

32. Hughes, "Amalia Kussner: High Priestess," 42.

33. Caroline Astor, letter to Amalia, July 1902, Amalia Kussner Papers (Private Collection), Sisters of Providence Archives at Saint Mary-of-the-Woods, Indiana. An interesting anecdote is that there was a fascination in the late Victorian period with miniature objects of all sorts, not just portraits, as was demonstrated at one of Mrs. Astor's parties. She was known to provide her guests "with tiny gifts—trinkets of papier mâché, Dutch tiles, little fans, and other such miniature items" (see Gunderson, "Dismissed Yet Disarming," 29).

34. Staff, "A Miniature Painter," *The Queen* (London), November 25, 1905, 95. Mamie Fish is a featured character in HBO's series *The Gilded Age* and is portrayed by Ashlie Atkinson.

35. Hogan Associates, "Newport Stories: Mamie Fish, the Grand Dame of Newport's Gilded Age," Hogan Associates Blog, August 18, 2023, https://hoganblog.com/2023/08/18/newport-stories-mamie-fish-the-grand-dame-of-newports-gilded-age.

36. Staff, *The Journal* (New York), March 17, 1896.

37. Mary Carter, "A Royal Conquest: The Life of Minnie Stevens," *Eagle Times* (Claremont, NH), September 6, 2023.

38. Stephanie Barron, "Minnie Paget. Because with Friends Like These . . . ," November 4, 2018, https://francinemathews.blogspot.com/2018/11/day-79-with-friends-like-these.html.

39. Staff, "Editorial," *Elite* (Chicago), vol. XIV, no. 27, October 3, 1896, 2.

40. Staff, "Society Notes," *Elite* (Chicago), vol. XIV, no. 27, October 3, 1896, 12.

41. Staff, "Miniatures by Amalia Kussner and Her Triumphs in London," *The Journal* (New York), March 17, 1896, 11.

42. Staff, "Miniatures by Amalia Kussner," 11.

43. Staff, "Miniatures by Amalia Kussner," 11.

44. Staff, "Society Notes," *Elite* (Chicago), April 18, 1896.

45. Staff, "A Native of Greencastle at Blenheim Castle," *Greencastle Star Press*, May 30, 1896, 8.

46. Staff, "A Native of Greencastle," 8.

47. Anderson Cooper and Katherine Howe, *Vanderbilt: The Rise and Fall of an American Dynasty* (Harper Collins, 2021), 117.

48. Frank S. Arnett, "Amalia Kussner Coudert," *Ainslee's Magazine* (NY), vol. 9, no. 4, May 1902, 294. An equerry was an attendant for male royalty and could sometimes be someone who served in the military.

49. Arnett, "Amalia Kussner Coudert," 294.

50. Staff, "Gifts Shock Englishers," *The Evening Journal* (Wilmington, DE), December 8, 1903.

51. Author, personal family history, recounted from Indianapolis, Indiana.

52. Staff, miscellaneous entry, *Livestock Journal*, Vinton and Company, London, June 23, 1897.

53. Jane Ridley, "Marlborough House Set," May 27, 2010, https://doi.org/10.1093/ref:odnb/53154.

54. Ridley, "Marlborough House Set."

55. Ridley, "Marlborough House Set."

56. Staff, "Debutantes of the Season," *London West End*, May 17, 1899, 10.

57. Staff, music composition reviews, *Musical Courier*, Summy-Birchard Publishing Company, New York, vol. 25, no. 926, December 1, 1897, 29.

58. Staff, "Goddess of the Moon: The Life History of the Luna Moth," Finger Lakes Land Trust, July 31, 2018, https://www.fllt.org/goddess-of-the-moon-the-life-history-of-the-luna-moth/.

59. Karen Zach, the INGenWeb project, Putnam County Biographies (Amalia Kussner), http://ingenweb.org/inputnam/Putnam%20Biographies%20H_M/k---bios.html.

60. Maude Andrews, "The First from the Klondike," *The Atlanta Constitution*, vol. 30, September 26, 1898.

61. Staff, "Society Notes," *Elite* (Chicago), July 11, 1896.

62. Staff, "Society Notes," *Elite* (Chicago), February 27, 1897; staff, "Portrait of Alva Belmont," The Preservation Society of Newport County, https://newportalri.org/items/show/24583.

63. C. W. de Lyon Nichols, *The Décadents: A Story of Blackwell's Island and Newport* (J.S. Ogilvie Publishing Company, 1899), 134.

64. Staff, "People Talked About," *The New Peterson Magazine*, vol. 12, no. 6, December 1896, 1271.

65. Lillie Hamilton French, "The Portrait Show," *Harper's Bazaar*, December 31, 1898, 1132.

66. Staff, "What Is Doing in Society," *New York Times*, vol. 48, no. 15269, December 18, 1898, 15.

67. Staff, "Miss Kussner's Miniatures Gone," possibly *New York Journal*, 1898, Amalia Kussner Papers (Private Collection), Sisters of Providence Archives at Saint Mary-of-the-Woods, Indiana.

68. Staff, "Collection: New York Journal and Related Titles, 1896 to 1899," Library of Congress, https://www.loc.gov/collections/new-york-journal/about-this-collection/.

69. Staff, "Five Members of England's Swellest Set," *The New York Journal*, December 12, 1897, 10, https://www.loc.gov/resource/sn83030180/1897-12-12/ed-1/?sp=10.

70. Carol Wallace Hamlin, author, email correspondence with author, December 23, 2023.

Chapter 3

1. Staff, "A Maker of Pretty Women," *The Buffalo Times*, January 15, 1899, 16.

2. Nancy Huston Banks, "Success in Her Art," *Altoona Mirror* (PA), June 7, 1895, 3.

3. Staff, "Miss Kussner's Experience," *Indianapolis Journal*, vol. l, no. 12, January 12, 1900, 4.

4. Staff, "Miss Kussner's Experience," 4.

5. Staff, "Society Notes," *Elite* (Chicago), vol. xiv, no. 27, October 3, 1896, 5.

6. George Keyes, "Portraiture—Mirror or Mask," *Bulletin of the Detroit Institute of Arts*, vol. 83, no. 1/4, 2009, 6.

7. Staff, "George Romney, British Art's Forgotten Genius," exhibition, Walker Gallery of Art, 2001, https://www.liverpoolmuseums.org.uk/.

8. Staff, "Society Notes," *Elite* (Chicago), vol. XIV, no. 27, October 3, 1896, 5.

9. Staff, "People Talked About," *The Peterson Magazine* (New York), vol. VI, January–June 1896, 1271.

10. Staff, "Types of Fair Women," *Munsey's Magazine* (London), vol. XVII, no. 3, June 1897, 366.

11. Martha Gandy Fales, *Jewelry in America, 1600–1900* (Antique Collectors Club, 1995), 328.

12. Maud Richards Turlay, "Amalia Kussner Coudert, Highest Priced Miniaturist, Has Won Fame and Fortune," *Chicago Inter Ocean* (Chicago), October 26, 1913, 34.

13. Staff, "Girls' Interests and Occupations," *The Delineator* (The Butterick Publishing Co., July 1900), 261.

14. Staff, "A Story for the Poor—How John W. Mackay, a Poor Emigrant, Became a Millionaire," *The Virginian-Pilot*, July 30, 1899, 6.

15. Staff, "Not Castles in the Air," *The San Francisco Examiner*, July 14, 1895, 24.

16. Staff, "The Trousseau of Miss Catherine Duer," *The Sunday Spy* (Worcester, MA), April 8, 1898, 13.

17. Perry Belmont, letter to Amalia Kussner, June 30, 1900, Amalia Kussner Papers (Private Collection), Sisters of Providence Archives at Saint Mary-of-the-Woods, Indiana.

18. Staff, "Girls' Interests and Occupations," 260–61.

19. Chas. Fdc. Nirdlinger, "Of a Certain Painter-In-Little," *The Illustrated American* (New York), April 29, 1893, 505.

20. Nancy Huston Banks, "A Modern Miniature Painter," *Harper's Bazaar*, vol. 28, no. 5, February 2, 1896, 88.

21. Staff, "Girls' Interests and Occupations," 260.

22. Staff, "Girls' Interests and Occupations," 260.

23. Staff, "Amalia Kussner's Miniatures of the Astor Family," *The House Beautiful*, Hearst Magazines, vol. 10, no. 4, September 1901, 225.

24. Staff, "He Tells of Amalia," *Logansport Pharos-Tribune* (IN), March 30, 1898, 10.

25. Nancy Huston Banks, "A Painter of Miniatures," *Ladies Home Journal* (Philadelphia, PA), vol. 12, no. 11, October 1895, 7.

26. Bob Gunderson, "Days of Yore: Ivory—The Plastic of the 1800s," *New Haven Register*, June 24, 2018.

27. Staff, "Women the World Over," *The Queen of Fashion* (The McCall Company, March 1894), 107.

28. Becky Wiser, "Long Life and Happiness to All Its Residents," July 2, 2021, https://www.eriehistory.org/blog/long-life-and-happiness-to-all-its-residents-39.

29. Becky Wiser, "Strong Mansion," Erie County's Historic Resources, 2006, http://eriebuildings.info/buildings.php?buildingID=17040004020100.

30. Staff, "The Home Dressmaker," *Ladies Home Journal* (Philadelphia, PA), vol. 12, no. 11, October 1895, 27.

31. Staff, "What She Wears," *Vogue*, vol. 14, no. 16, October 19, 1899, 254.

32. Staff, "Society Notes," *Elite* (Chicago), October 3, 1896, 9.

33. Staff, "Amalia Kussner Home," *Chicago Tribune*, September 24, 1896, 10.

34. Frances Hughes, "High Priestess of the Daintiest of Arts," *Traces of Indiana and Midwestern History*, vol. 2, no. 4, 1990, 38.

35. Lydia Strickling, "Gilded Age Fashion," National Park Service, May 12, 2021, https://www.nps.gov/vama/blogs/gilded-age-fashion.htm.

36. Dr. David S. Shields, "Jacob Schloss," *Broadway Photographs*, https://broadway.library.sc.edu/content/jacob-schloss.html.

37. Staff, "People Talked About," *The New Peterson Magazine* (NY), vol. 12, no. 6, December 1896, 1271.

38. Staff, "Nothing Shocks New York Society—Save Poverty," *The Argus* (Melbourne, Australia), June 10, 1899, 13.

39. Staff, "She Never Took a Lesson," *Progress—The Universion Law of Nature* (Chicago), October 12, 1895.

40. Maryann Sudnick Gunderson, "Dismissed Yet Disarming: The Portrait Miniature Revival, 1890–1930" (thesis, Ohio University, 2012), 28.

41. Staff, "Society Flashes," *Daily Wabash Express* (Terre Haute), June 6, 1886, 7.

42. Gunderson, "Dismissed Yet Disarming," 30.

43. Staff, "Society," *Terre Haute Spectator*, September 22, 1906, 3.

44. Staff, "Girls' Interests and Occupations," *The Delineator*, July 1900, 261.

45. Staff, "Art and Shop," *The Theater*, vol. 9, no. 1, 1893, 8.

46. Staff, *Catalogue of the Eleventh Annual Exhibition of the American Society of Miniature Painters* (M. Knoedler & Co., 1910).

47. Staff, "Artist Lucia Fairchild Fuller," Smithsonian American Art Museum, https://americanart.si.edu/artist/lucia-fairchild-fuller-1700.

Chapter 4

1. Robert K. Massie, *Nicholas and Alexandra* (Random House Trade Paperbacks, 2011), 70.

2. Amalia Kussner Coudert, "The Human Side of the Czar," *Century Magazine*, October 1906, 815.

3. Coudert, "The Human Side of the Czar," 845.

4. Coudert, "The Human Side of the Czar," 846.

5. Coudert, "The Human Side of the Czar," 846.

6. Coudert, "The Human Side of the Czar," 846.

7. Coudert, "The Human Side of the Czar," 846.

8. Frank S. Arnett, "Painting an Empress," *Indianapolis Journal*, May 18, 1902, 24.

9. Coudert, "The Human Side of the Czar," 846.

10. Coudert, "The Human Side of the Czar," 846.

11. Arnett, "Painting an Empress," 24.

12. Coudert, "The Human Side of the Czar," 846.

13. Massie, *Nicholas and Alexandra*, 117; Arnett, "Painting an Empress," 24.

14. Arnett, "Painting an Empress," 24.

15. Coudert, "The Human Side of the Czar," 846.

16. Arnett, "Painting an Empress," 24.

17. Coudert, "The Human Side of the Czar," 847.

18. Coudert, "The Human Side of the Czar," 847.

19. Coudert, "The Human Side of the Czar," 846.

20. Staff, "Fame Came After a Struggle," *Indianapolis Sun*, July 22, 1899.

21. Coudert, "The Human Side of the Czar," 849.

22. Coudert, "The Human Side of the Czar," 855. Properly spelled Preobrazhensky, these guards were the czar's personal elite regiment.

23. Coudert, "The Human Side of the Czar," 855.

24. Princess Nicholas was the grandmother of Queen Elizabeth II's husband, Prince Philip.

25. Coudert, "The Human Side of the Czar," 846.

26. Coudert, "The Human Side of the Czar," 848.

27. Staff, "Fire Destroys Windsor Hotel," *The World* (NY), vol. XXXIX, March 18, 1899, 1.

28. Staff, "Women's Chat," *Millom Gazette* (Cumbria, UK), July 27, 1900, 6.

29. Staff, "At the Hotels," *The New York Times*, March 13, 1900.

30. Staff, "Pretty Barmaids—Mrs. Paget's Bazaar in London," *The Pacific Commercial Advertiser*, August 8, 1899, n.p.

31. Frank S. Arnett, "Amalia Kussner Coudert Miniaturist," *Ainslee's Magazine* (New York), vol. IX, no. 1, May 1902, 295.

32. Staff, "Cooped in Kimberley," *Wichita Eagle*, November 26, 1899, 16.

33. Raymond Sibbald, *The War Correspondents: The Boer War* (Bramley Books, 1997), 10.

34. Christopher Montague Woodhouse, "Cecil Rhodes Prime Minister of Cape Colony," Britannica, https://www.britannica.com/biography/Cecil-Rhodes.

35. Philip Jourdan, letter to Amalia Kussner, September 11, 1899, Amalia Kussner Papers (Private Collection), Sisters of Providence Archives at Saint Mary-of-the-Woods, Indiana.

36. Sibbald, *War Correspondents*, 11.

37. Staff, "Cooped in Kimberley," 16.

38. Staff, "Mr. Rhodes's Portrait Under Difficulties," *Aberdeen Press and Journal* (Scotland), December 20, 1899, 12.

39. Staff, "Cooped in Kimberley," 16.

40. Staff, "Cooped in Kimberley," 16.

41. John P. Wisser, *The Second Boer War, 1899–1900* (Hudson-Kimberly Pub. Co., 1901), 20.

42. Antony Thomas, *Rhodes: The Race for Africa* (St. Martin's Press, 1997), 338.

43. Neil Bates, *Cecil Rhodes* (Wayland Publishers Ltd, 1976), 76.

44. Staff, "Siege of Kimberly," *Fort Wayne Sentinel*, October 31, 1899.

45. Staff, "Cooped in Kimberley," 16.

46. Sibbald, *War Correspondents*, 117.

47. Staff, "Painted Rhodes's Portrait in a Shower of Bursting Shells," *Boston Post*, January 3, 1900, 8.

48. Staff, "Cooped in Kimberley," 16.

49. David Harris, *Pioneer, Soldier and Politician: Summarised Memoirs of Colonel Sir David Harris* (Sampson Low, Marston & Company, Ltd., 1931), 159.

50. Staff, "Cooped in Kimberley," 16.

51. Staff, "Cooped in Kimberley," 16.

52. Staff, "Women Artists," *The Woman's Column* (New York and Boston), vol. XII, no. 25, December 16, 1899, 4.

53. Wisser, *Second Boer War*, 20.

54. Staff, "In Peril," *Hopkinsville Kentuckian*, November 24, 1899, 4.

55. Staff, "Cooped in Kimberley," 16.

56. Bates, *Cecil Rhodes*, 79.

57. Staff, "Cooped in Kimberley," 16.

58. Staff, "Cooped in Kimberley," 16.

59. Sibbald, *War Correspondents*, 114.

60. Philip Jourdan, *Cecil Rhodes: His Private Life* (John Lane Company, 1911), 20.

61. Bates, *Cecil Rhodes*, 56.

62. Staff, "Indomitable Man," *The Evening World* (New York), February 23, 1900, 9.

63. Staff, "In Peril," *Hopkinsville Kentuckian*, November 24, 1899, 4.

64. Staff, "Painted Rhodes's Portrait," 8.

65. Sibbald, *War Correspondents*, 129.

66. Staff, "London Applauds Fete of Mrs. Arthur Paget," *New York World*, February 14, 1900.

67. Staff, "Cecil Rhodes' Portrait," *The Times-Democrat* (Lima, OH), March 1, 1900, 1.

68. Staff, "Cecil Rhodes' Portrait," 1.

69. Staff, "Cecil Rhodes' Portrait," 1.

70. Staff, "Cecil Rhodes' Portrait," 1.

71. Staff, "Cecil Rhodes' Portrait," 1.

Chapter 5

1. Staff, "This Week in Art," *New York Times-Saturday Review*, January 13, 1900, 25.

2. Staff, "Miniature of Lady Colebrook," *New-York Tribune*, March 11, 1900, 26.

3. Staff, "Social and Personal," *Evansville Courier and Press*, March 6, 1900, 4.

4. Greg King, *A Season of Splendor* (John Wiley & Sons, Inc., 2009), 41, 224.

5. George J. Gould, letter to Amalia Kussner, June 18, 1900, Amalia Kussner Papers (Private Collection), Sisters of Providence Archives at Saint Mary-of-the-Woods, Indiana.

6. Hoosier (origin unknown but commonly used) is a term used for those native to Indiana.

7. Staff, "A Hoosier Club," *Indianapolis Journal*, vol. 50, no. 157, June 6, 1900.

8. Amalia Kussner, letter to editor Mr. Johnson, *The New York Public Library Digital Collections*, Spring 1900, https://digitalcollections.nypl.org/items/296a03f0-7e87-0134 -b9c0-00505686a51c.

9. Worman and Worman, "Outing," The Outing Publishing Company, New York, vol. XXXIII, Oct. 1898–March 1899; Carol Wallace Hamlin, author, email correspondence with author, February 24, 2024.

10. King, *A Season*, 338.

11. Amalia Kussner Coudert, "The Human Side of the Czar," *Century Magazine*, October 1906, 852.

12. Frances E. Hughes, *Amalia Kussner Painter-In-Little*, unpublished biography, 107, Amalia Kussner Papers (Private Collection), Sisters of Providence Archives at Saint Mary-of-the-Woods, Indiana.

13. Marc J. Seifer, *Wizard: The Life and Times of Nikola Tesla* (Citadel Press, 1998), 208.

14. Seifer, *Wizard*, 211.

15. Seifer, *Wizard*, 159.

16. Seifer, *Wizard*, 207.

17. Seifer, *Wizard*, 263.

18. Staff, "He Tells of Amalia," *Logansport Pharos-Tribune* (IN), March 20, 1898, 10.

19. Staff, "In the Social World," *The Standard Union* (Brooklyn), July 5, 1900, 7.

20. Staff, "In the Social World," 7.

21. Staff, "New York Society Surprised," *The St. Louis Republic*, July 4, 1900, 14.

22. Staff, "Some Happenings in Good Society," *The New York Times*, July 8, 1900, 14.

23. Staff, "New York Society Surprised," 14.

24. Hughes, Frances, "High Priestess of the Daintiest of Arts," *Traces of Indiana and Midwestern History*, Indiana Historical Society, Indianapolis, Indiana, vol. 2, no. 4, 1990, 43.

25. Staff, "Amalia Kussner as a Bride," *The St. Louis Republic*, July 8, 1900, 5.

26. Hughes, *Amalia Kussner Painter-In-Little*, 162.

27. Abbie Mac Flynn, "Woman's Page," *The Evening Gazette* (Burlington, IA), July 7, 1900, 6.

28. Staff, "Stole a March Upon Their Friends," *The Philadelphia Inquirer*, July 4, 1900, 14.

29. Staff, "Wedded in Haste," *Buffalo Times*, July 5, 1900, 3.

30. Staff, "Wedded in Haste," 3.

31. Virginia Kays Veenswijk, *Coudert Brothers: A Legacy in Law* (Truman Talley/Dutton, 1994), 7.

32. Veenswijk, *Coudert Brothers*, 12.

33. Veenswijk, *Coudert Brothers*, 12.

34. Veenswijk, *Coudert Brothers*, 26.

35. Veenswijk, *Coudert Brothers*, 96.

36. U.S., School Yearbooks, 1900–2016, for Dupont Coudert, Columbia College, 1896, Ancestry.com.

37. Richard Jay Hutto, author and historian, phone conversation with author, January 2, 2024.

38. Veenswijk, *Coudert Brothers*, 111.

39. Staff, "Fear Mrs. Coudert May Marry Again," *New York Journal and Advertiser*, August 29, 1897, 2.

40. Veenswijk, *Coudert Brothers*, 114.

41. Veenswijk, *Coudert Brothers*, 116.

42. Staff, "In The Social World," *The Standard Union* (Brooklyn), July 5, 1900, 7.

43. Staff, "Amalia Kussner as a Bride," *The St. Louis Republic*, July 8, 1900, 15.

44. Staff, "In the Social World," *The Standard Union* (Brooklyn), July 10, 1900, 7.

45. Will Roulett, "Minuteman Minute—Lt. Frederick Coudert Spanish-American War Uniform," National Guard Association of the United States, March 15, 2023. https://www.ngaus.org/video-library/minuteman-minute-lt-frederic-coudert-spanish-american-war-uniform.

46. Grace Courneau, "Social Gossip of Paris," *Chicago Tribune*, January 17, 1900, 2.

47. Staff, "London Applauds Mrs. Arthur Paget," *New York World*, February 14, 1900.

48. Staff, "Amalia Kussner on the Liner Teutonic," *The Evening World*, New York, NY, February 14, 1900.

49. Staff, "Wedded in Haste," *Buffalo Times*, July 5, 1900, 3.

50. Staff, "Wedding Event," *Star Tribune* (Minneapolis), July 15, 1900, 14.

51. Staff, "Literary Notes," *York Semi-Weekly Democratic Press* (PA), August 31, 1900, 4.

52. Staff, "Clubs," *Vogue*, February 22, 1900, iii.

53. Staff, "USA Badminton History," USA Badminton, https://usabadminton.org/about/history/.

54. Staff, "Incidents in Society," *New York Daily Tribune*, July 5, 1900, 10.

55. Staff, "Some Happenings in Good Society," *The New York Times*, October 7, 1900, 15.

56. Kussner, letter to Mr. Johnson.

CHAPTER 6

1. Staff, "The Coudert Estate," *Star-Gazette* (Elmira, NY), April 20, 1901, 1.

2. Staff, "Coudert Estate," 1.

3. Staff, "Coudert Estate," 1.

4. Staff, "Mysterious Suit," *Defiance Crescent News* (Ohio), June 28, 1901, 6.

5. Staff, "The Greencastle Banner—Harry M. Smith" (IN), July 26, 1901, 2.

6. Staff, "Amalia Kussner Sued," *The Indianapolis Journal*, July 24, 1901, 3.

7. Frank Kintrea, "Larcenous Mrs. Cody Vs. Pious Miss Gould," *American Heritage*, vol. 26, no. 4, June 1975.

8. Staff, "Morse Tells of Hummel's Graft," *The Chicago Daily Tribune*, December 19, 1905, 9.

9. Staff, "Bissert's Case in Federal Court," *The New York Times*, October 8, 1901, 5; staff, "Petitions in Bankruptcy," *The New York Times*, August 11, 1900, 10.

10. Staff, *Variety*, The Variety Publishing Company, March 1907, 26.

11. Staff, "Amalia Coudert in Mysterious Suit," *New York World*, vol. XLI, June 27, 1901, 1.

12. Staff, "Free from Wiliam, Mrs. Alva E. Vanderbilt Secures an Absolute Divorce," *The San Francisco Call*, March 6, 1895, 2.

13. Staff, "Mysterious Suit Settled," *Boston Post*, June 28, 1901, 2.

14. Staff, "Departures for Europe," *Brooklyn Life*, July 27, 1901, 16.

15. Staff, "Amalia Kussner Lionized in London," *New York Times*, July 28, 1901, 3.

16. Grace Corneau, "Foretells Striking Colors," *Chicago Tribune*, September 29, 1901, 67.

17. Staff, "May Paint Loubet's Portrait," *St. Louis Post-Dispatch*, September 15, 1901, 10.

18. Staff, "The Lounger," *The Critic* (New York), vol. 39, no. 5, November 1901, 398.

19. Staff, "The Superstitious Sex," *The New York Times*, October 6, 1901, 5.

CHAPTER 7

1. Staff, "Love and a Famous Beauty," *The San Francisco Examiner*, January 4, 1903, 43.

2. Staff, "Furs for a Favorite," *St. Louis Post-Dispatch*, November 11, 1903, 10.

3. Staff, untitled entry, Minnesota Historical Society, St. Paul, Minnesota, February 18, 1904, 8.

4. Staff, "At Exeter—Arrival of Amalia Kussner, Famous Artist," *Boston Sunday Post*, May 22, 1904, 3.

5. Edward Legge, *King George and the Royal Family*, volume 2 (Digital Library of India Item 2015.526557, 1918), 141.

6. Prince Carl took the name Haakon VII, implying he was a successor of King Haakon VI, the last Norwegian king centuries prior to the twentieth century. (See Dag Thorklidson, "Norwegian National Myths and Nation Building," *Kirchliche Zeistgeschichte*, vol. 27, no. 2, 2014.)

7. Staff, "Lady Mary's Gossip," *Minneapolis Journal*, September 26, 1906, 18.

8. Staff, "Americans in London Hotels," *Boston Sunday Post*, April 26, 1908, 17.

9. Staff, "Queen Maud—150 Years," National Museum of Norway, https://www .nasjonalmuseet.no/en/stories/explore-the-collection/queen-maud--150-years/.

10. Frank S. Arnett, "Amalia Kussner Coudert—Miniaturist," *Ainslee's Magazine* (NY), vol. IX, no. 4, May 1902, 300.

11. Letter from Francis Lascelles to Amalia, Amalia Kussner Papers (Private Collection), Sisters of Providence Archives at Saint Mary-of-the-Woods, Indiana, September 14, 1901.

12. Staff, "Chicago Painter of Kings and Queens," *The Chicago Inter Ocean* (Chicago), October 26, 1913, 5.

13. Henry Manners became marquess of Granby in 1888.

14. Susan Elizabeth Slattery, "Performing Portraiture: Picturing the Upper-Class English Woman in an Age of Change, 1890–1914" (thesis, University of Toronto, 2019), 59. Violet, however, was not in a happy marriage and began an affair with Harry Cust, a journalist and poet. He was seen as a dilettante and certainly "a lover of women," with many known affairs. See Angela Lambert, *Unquiet Souls: A Social History of the Illustrious, Irreverent, Intimate Group of British Aristocrats Known as "the Souls"* (Harper & Row, 1984), xvi.

15. Lambert, *Unquiet Souls*, 21.

16. Lambert, *Unquiet Souls*, 7.

17. Lambert, *Unquiet Souls*, 8.

18. Staff, "Violet Manners, Duchess of Rutland," National Portrait Gallery, https:// www.npg.org.uk/collections/search/person/mp03927.

19. Slattery, "Performing Portraiture," 112.

20. Staff, society column, *The World* (London), July 13, 1898.

21. Staff, newspaper clipping ca. July 1898, publisher unknown, Amalia Kussner Papers (Private Collection), Sisters of Providence Archives at Saint Mary-of-the-Woods, Indiana.

22. Frank S. Arnett, "Amalia Kussner Coudert—Miniaturist," *Ainslee's Magazine* (NY), vol. IX, no. 4, May 1902, 299.

23. Violet, Marchioness of Granby, letter to Amalia Kussner, August 22, 1899, transcribed by Victoria Perry, Amalia Kussner Papers (Private Collection), Sisters of Providence Archives at Saint Mary-of-the-Woods, Indiana.

24. Catherine Bailey, *The Secret Rooms: A True Story of a Haunted Castle, a Plotting Duchess, & a Family Secret* (Penguin Books, 2013), 119.

25. Bailey, *Secret Rooms*, 119.

26. Victoria Perry, archivist, Belvoir Castle, email correspondence with author, May 2, 2024.

27. Slattery, "Performing Portraiture," 61.

28. Staff, "Society Miniature—What They Cost," *Broken Hill Barrier Miner* (New South Wales, Australia), June 10, 1904, 3.

29. Staff, "Society Miniature—What They Cost," 3.

30. Staff, "Society Miniature—What They Cost," 3.

31. Staff, "Artist Refuses to Accept Defeat," *Philadelphia Inquirer*, May 1, 1904.

32. Staff, "Give Up in Her Suit Against Mrs. Claude Watney," *Buffalo Courier*, May 1, 1904, 17.

33. Staff, "Amalia Kussner Wins Her Suit," *New York World*, March 5, 1905.

34. Staff, "Mrs. Chas., Not Mrs. F. R. Coudert, Ill," *The New York Times*, August 12, 1902, 7.

35. Staff, "Mary Marie Guion Coudert (obituary)," *The New York Times*, September 14, 1903, 7.

36. Staff, "Social Season Is Later Every Year," *The Chicago Inter Ocean* (Chicago), September 20, 1903, 42.

37. Amalia Kussner, "The Human Side of the Czar," *Century Magazine*, vol. LXXII, October 1906, 845.

38. Kussner, "The Human Side of the Czar," 845.

39. Kussner, "The Human Side of the Czar," 845.

40. Staff, unnamed news column, *San Antonio Daily Light*, October 28, 1906.

41. Staff, "The Magazines," *Journal of Education* (Boston), October 4, 1906, 377.

42. Staff, "The Czar's Predicament," *The New York Times*, October 2, 1906.

43. Staff, "Women: Their Fads," *New Oxford Item* (PA), January 10, 1907, 2; staff, "The Czarina's Charm," *The Atlanta Constitution*, September 29, 1906, 1.

44. Amalia Kussner, letter to editor Mr. Gilder, December 1900, The New York Public Library Digital Collections, https://digitalcollections.nypl.org/items/296a03f0-7e87-0134-b9c0-00505686a51c.

45. Amalia Kussner, letter to editor Mr. Gilder, December 1900, The New York Public Library Digital Collections, https://digitalcollections.nypl.org/items/296a03f0-7e87-0134-b9c0-00505686a51c.

46. Amalia Kussner, letter to editor Mr. Gilder, 1906, The New York Public Library Digital Collections, https://digitalcollections.nypl.org/items/296a03f0-7e87-0134-b9c0-00505686a51c.

47. Amalia Kussner, letter to Mr. Gilder, 1906.

48. Amalia Kussner, letter to Mr. Gilder, 1906.

49. Staff, unlabeled column, *The Newtown Bee* (CT), September 28, 1906, 6; staff, photo with caption, *Passaic Daily News* (NJ), October 26, 1906, 6.

50. The marchioness of Granby became a duchess in August of 1906 with the death of her father-in-law and her husband's becoming the duke of Rutland.

51. Staff, "Feminine Fancies," *Abbeville Press and Banner* (SC), January 31, 1906, 2.

52. Staff, "Personals and Society," *Terre Haute Saturday Spectator*, May 4, 1907, 12.

53. Staff, "London Gossip," *The American Register* (London), January 12, 1907, 5.

54. Susan Ball, "Woman's World," *Terre Haute Saturday Spectator*, February 29, 1908, 2.

55. Elspeth Wills, *Cunardia: A Steam Trunk of Titbits, Trivia and Trifles* (Open Agency, 2005), 16.

56. Wills, *Cunardia*, 16.

57. Anderson Cooper and Katherine Howe, *The Vanderbilts: The Rise and Fall of an American Dynasty* (Harper, 2021), 178.

58. S.S. *Campania*, List or Manifest of Alien Passengers for the U.S. Immigration Officer at Port of Arrival, May 7, 1904, Ancestry.com.

59. William H. Miller, *The Great Liners Story* (The History Press, 2012), 21.

60. Staff, "More Americans," *Boston Sunday Post*, April 26, 1908, 17.

61. Staff, "Duchess De Choiseul, Claire Coudert, Dead," *Omaha World-Herald*, March 15, 1919, 4.

62. Ruth Butler, *Rodin: The Shape of Genius* (Yale University Press, 1993), 456.

63. Raphaël Masson and Véronique Mattiussi, *Rodin* (Rizzoli International Publications, 2004), 166.

64. Butler, *Rodin*, 458.

65. Auguste Rodin, note to Amalia and du Pont, December 1908, Amalia Kussner Papers (Private Collection), Sisters of Providence Archives at Saint Mary-of-the-Woods, Indiana.

66. Seth Weinhardt, signed photo of Auguste Rodin, 1909, Seth Weinhardt family papers.

67. Staff, "Passing of Treasured Heirlooms to the Duke of Choiseul Starts Hostilities," *Evening Star* (Washington, DC), December 8, 1910, 15.

68. Butler, *Rodin*, 459.

69. Butler, *Rodin*, 463.

70. Butler, *Rodin*, 464.

71. Butler, *Rodin*, 474.

72. Paul Pierre Rignaux, "Rodin Finds New Art Inspiration in U.S. Woman," *Chicago Sunday Examiner*, October 29, 1911, 32.

73. Staff, "Record of a Dinner Given in Celebration thereof at Delmonico's on the Evening of December 5, 1905," *Harpers Weekly* (NY), December 23, 1905.

74. Flora Mai Holly, "Some Prominent Southerners in New York," *The Taylor-Trotwood Magazine* (Nashville), December 1905, 292.

75. Ship *Minneapolis*, Names and Descriptions of Alien Passengers, March 24, 1908, Ancestry.com.

76. Nancy Huston Banks, "The Miniature," *Cosmopolitan*, vol. 43, May 1907, 23.

77. Staff, "Personal and Society," *Terre Haute Saturday Spectator*, October 31, 1908, 14.

78. Staff, "Personal and Society," *Terre Haute Saturday Spectator*, November 24, 1906, 14.

79. *Official Gazette of the United States Patent Office*, Government Printing Office, July 1908, 882.

80. Staff, advertisement, "The Etude," *The Etude*, Theodore Presser Company, vol. 28, no. 4, April 1910, 221.

81. Staff, "School Graduation," *The Glendale Evening News* (Los Angeles), January 25, 1917, 1.

82. Staff, "Attracting Attention in the World of Music," *Loretto Rainbow*, Loretto College, Toronto, Ontario, 1903.

Chapter 8

1. Staff, "Society," *Terre Haute Saturday Spectator*, August 18, 1906, 3.

2. Frances E. Hughes, *Amalia Kussner Painter-In-Little*, unpublished biography, Amalia Kussner Papers (Private Collection) Sisters of Providence Archives at Saint Mary-of-the-Woods, Indiana, 178.

3. James Brown Scott, "Edward VII," *The American Journal of International Law*, vol. 4, no. 3, July 1910, 663.

4. Tracy Borman, *Crown & Sceptre: A New History of the British Monarchy, from William the Conqueror to Charles III* (Hodder and Stoughton, 2021), 403.

5. Staff, title unknown, *Herald* (Calgary, Alberta), May 31, 1913, 15.

6. Anonymous, "King Edward VII," *North American Review* (Boston), no. DCLV, June 1910, 728.

7. Bryson Burroughs, *Metropolitan Museum of Art—Catalogue of Paintings*, third edition (Metropolitan Museum of Art, 1917).

8. Bryson Burroughs, two letters from the Metropolitan Museum of Art to Mrs. Coudert, 1922 and 1926, Amalia Kussner Papers (Private Collection), Sisters of Providence Archives at Saint Mary-of-the-Woods, Indiana.

9. Virginia Kays Veenswijk, *Coudert Brothers: A Legacy in Law* (Truman Talley/Dutton, 1994), 121.

10. Veenswijk, *Coudert Brothers*, 42.

11. Susan W. Ball, "Woman's World," *Terre Haute Saturday Spectator*, June 10, 1911, 6.

12. "Department Passport Application," U.S. Passport Applications, 1795–1925, for Albert H. Kussner, September 29, 1921, Ancestry.com.

13. Staff, "A Society Woman Who Makes and Sells Cigarettes for Society Women," *Fort Worth Star-Telegram*, December 31, 1911, 9.

14. Staff, "Mrs. Brennig to Wed W. M. D. De Peyster," *The New York Times*, December 8, 1912, 7.

15. Staff, "Mrs. Brennig to Wed," 7.

16. Staff, "Society Woman," 9.

17. Michelle Elizabeth Tusan, "Inventing the New Woman: Print Culture and the Identity Politics During the Fin-de-Siecle," *Victorian Periodicals Review*, vol. 31, no. 2, Summer 1998, 175.

18. Staff, "Society Woman," 9.

19. Staff, "The Cigarette in London," *New York Morning Telegraph*, July 21, 1898.

20. Maude Andrews, "Shopping in Gay Paris; How the Women Buy Hats," *The Atlanta Constitution*, vol. 31, May 1, 1899, 2.

21. *The Courtauld* (blog), "Maison Doucet," December 2, 2016, https://sites.courtauld .ac.uk/documentingfashion/2016/12/02/maison-doucet/.

22. Staff, "Miss Kussner Tips the Duke," *The Chicago Daily Tribune*, vol. LVIII, no. 177, June 26, 1899.

23. Staff, "Mrs. Brennig to Wed," 8.

24. Miranda R. Patton, Esq., phone conversation with author, May 31, 2024.

25. Staff, "Lorenz Kussner Dead," *Terre Haute Saturday Spectator*, June 8, 1912, 5.

26. Frances E. Hughes, "Founding Fathers Name Street in City," Vigo County Public Library Collection, October 14, 1978.

27. Hughes, *Amalia Kussner Painter-In-Little*, 192.

28. Westinghouse Airbrakes were an innovative braking system for trains that allowed safer and faster train travel.

29. Staff, "Former Chicago Girl Becomes a Paris Bride," *Chicago Daily Tribune*, July 11, 1913, 9.

30. Staff, "Personal and Society," *Terre Haute Evening Spectator*, July 12, 1913, 13.

31. Staff, "Personal and Society," *Terre Haute Saturday Spectator*, July 11, 1914, 18.

32. Staff, "Personal and Society," *Terre Haute Saturday Spectator*, August 1, 1914, 14.

33. Staff, "Personal and Society," *Terre Haute Saturday Spectator*, April 20, 1912, 15.

34. Lady Feodorovna Sturt became Lady Alington when her husband, Humphrey Sturt, became Lord Alington in 1904.

35. Staff, "Personals and Society," *Terre Haute Saturday Spectator*, September 27, 1913, 5.

36. Staff, "Lord Allington's White Farm," *The Bacchus Marsh Express* (Victoria, Australia), September 19, 1896, 1.

37. Staff, "The White Farm," Smock Shock: Deception and Disguise, Smock Frock Histories, May 29, 2015, http://www.smockfrock.co.uk/tag/home-farm-crichel-estate/.

38. Minnie Paget, letter to Amalia Kussner Coudert, 1912, Amalia Kussner Papers (Private Collection), Sisters of Providence Archives at Saint Mary-of-the-Woods, Indiana.

39. John V. Weinhardt, Weinhardt genealogy and photos of Schwabach, 1913, John Weinhardt family papers.

40. Staff, "Windlesham Hall," *Country Life* supplement (Britain), October 8, 1970, 18.

41. Frances E. Hughes, "A World-Famous Miniature Painter," *The Indianapolis Star*, March 12, 1961.

42. Staff, "Christmas Cards from England," *Terre Haute Saturday Spectator*, January 8, 1916, 3.

43. Staff, "Christmas Cards," 3.

44. Staff, "Knitting for European Soldiers," *Terre Haute Saturday Spectator*, November 21, 1914, 21.

45. Staff, "Knitting," 21.

46. Two acknowledgments of Amalia Kussner Coudert donating her time and money during World War I, ca. 1914, Amalia Kussner Papers (Private Collection), Sisters of Providence Archives at Saint Mary-of-the-Woods, Indiana.

47. Carl Weinhardt Jr., "Amalia Coudert 'Unique' Artist," *The Indianapolis News*, January 31, 1976, 4.

48. Staff, "Personal and Society," *Terre Haute Saturday Spectator*, July 31, 1915, 8.

49. Staff, "Personal and Society," *Terre Haute Saturday Spectator*, July 31, 1915, 8.

50. Staff, "Feels Keenly War in Europe," *Terre Haute Saturday Spectator*, July 31, 1915, 5.

51. U.S., Passport Applications, 1795–1925, for Charles Du Pont Coudert, 1917, Ancestry.com.

52. U.S., World War I Draft Registration Cards, 1917–1918, for Charles Dupont Coudert, October 7, 1918, Ancestry.com.

53. Staff, "The *Dacia*—Validity Confirmed," *The Scotsman* (Edinburgh), August 5, 1915, 5.

54. Veenswijk, *Coudert Brothers*, 179.

55. Veenswijk, *Coudert Brothers*, 180.

56. A. De Lapradelle and Frederic R. Coudert, *War Letters from France* (D. Appleton and Company, 1916).

57. Veenswijk, *Coudert Brothers*, 187.

58. Staff, "Mrs. Emilie Kussner Dead," *Terre Haute Saturday Spectator*, January 26, 1918, 25.

59. Staff, "The Ex-Czarina," *Yorkshire Evening Post*, October 5, 1918, 6.

60. Staff, "How Nicholas Died," *Perth Daily News* (Western Australia), January 6, 1919.

61. Staff, "Fate of the Romanovs," *Yorkshire Evening Post*, August 25, 1919, 5.

62. Staff, "Bolshevist Book Describes Death of Russ Rulers," *Wisconsin Rapids Daily Tribune* (from Associated Press), February 21, 1922, 3.

63. Staff, "The Closing Scenes of a Great Imperial Family," *Sunday Pictorial* (London), January 23, 1921, 8.

64. Staff, "Newest Twists in the Mystery of the Saved Romanoffs," *The Salt Lake Tribune*, February 7, 1926, 62.

65. Rebecca J. Fowler, "Anastasia—The Mystery Resolved," *Washington Post*, October 6, 1994, https://www.washingtonpost.com/archive/lifestyle/1994/10/06/anastasia-the-mystery-resolved/f208f264-a141-4f54-8354-934a3005f091/.

66. U.S., Passport Applications, 1795–1925, for Charles Du Pont Coudert, July 31, 1921, Ancestry.com.

67. Staff, "Couderts Escape Drowning in Car," *Paris Herald*, September 18, 1930.

68. Staff, "Car That Dived into River," *Daily Mirror* (London), March 22, 1933.

69. UK and Ireland, Outward Passenger Lists, 1890–1960, Charles De P Coudert (Dupont Coudert), Destination Barbados, December 27, 1925, Ancestry.com.

70. Albert Kussner, letter to Amalia and du Pont, 1927, Amalia Kussner Papers (Private Collection), Sisters of Providence Archives at Saint Mary-of-the-Woods, Indiana.

71. Anita Joenisch, "Two Renowned Artists in Generation is Distinction of Old Indiana Family," *The Indianapolis Star*, August 10, 1930, 19.

72. Joenisch, "Two Renowned Artists," 19.

Chapter 9

1. Jo Ann Ridley, *Looking for Eulabee Dix* (The National Museum of Women in Art, 1997), 58.

2. Staff, "Artist Eulabee Dix," Smithsonian American Art Museum, https://americanart.si.edu/artist/eulabee-dix-5766.

3. Ridley, *Looking for Eulabee Dix*, 68.

4. Ridley, *Looking for Eulabee Dix*, 73.

5. Ridley, *Looking for Eulabee Dix*, 77.

6. Staff, "The Fine Art Society's Exhibitions," *Morning Post* (London), December 5, 1906, 1.

7. Staff, "Art and Artists," *The Gentlewoman* (London), February 3, 1906, 18.

8. Staff, "Among the Artists," *American Art News* (NY), vol. 4, no. 5, 1905, 3, http://www.jstor.org/stable/25590144.

9. Ridley, *Looking for Eulabee Dix*, 105.

10. Ridley, *Looking for Eulabee Dix*, 105.

11. Ridley, *Looking for Eulabee Dix*, 106.

12. Taína Caragol, curator of painting, sculpture, and Latino art and history, Smithsonian National Portrait Gallery, email correspondence with the author, May 15, 2024.

13. Taína Caragol, email correspondence with author.

14. Staff, "Snapshots at Social Leaders," *Washington Post*, October 9, 1910, 86.

15. Jean Jacobson, collections coordinator, Nebraska Museum of Art, phone conversation with author, May 15, 2024.

16. Staff, transcription of audio about *Portrait of Eulabee Dix (Becker) in her Wedding Gown*, Museum of Nebraska Art, Kearney, NE, https://mona.unk.edu/mona/robert-henri-mona-collection/.

17. Staff, *Lady in Black Velvet (Portrait of Eulabee Dix Becker)*, High Museum of Art, Atlanta, GA, https://high.org/collection/lady-in-black-velvet-portrait-of-eulabee-dix-becker/.

18. John E. D. Trask, *Catalogue de Luxe of the Department of Fine Arts, Panama-Pacific International Exposition* (P. Elder and Company, 1915), 288.

19. Julian Alden Weir, *Biographical Sketches of American Artists*, fourth edition (Michigan State Library, 1916), 87.

20. Rena Tucker Kohlman, "Miniature Paintings in Art Institute Exhibition," *Indianapolis News*, January 27, 1916, 5.

21. Staff, "Baltimore," *The Art News*, Brant Publications (New York, NY), vol. 22, no. 24, March 22, 1924, 9.

22. Ridley, *Looking for Eulabee Dix*, 72.

23. Kate Seno Bradshaw, digital researcher, National Museum of Women Artists, email correspondence with author, May 14, 2024.

Chapter 10

1. Staff, advertisement, *The Athenaeum*, New Statesman, Ltd., no. 3888, May 3, 1902, 573.

2. Staff, "The Literary Lounger," *The Sketch*, Illustrated London News Company, November 5, 1902, 22.

3. Staff, "Publisher's Column," *Manchester Courier* (England), February 12, 1896, 2.

4. Staff, advertisement, *Pall Mall Gazette*, The Illustrated London News, November 7, 1902, 3.

5. Dennis Gaffney, "Explainer: What is Photogravure," PBS, February 14, 2005, https://www.pbs.org/wgbh/roadshow/articles/explainer-what-is-photogravure/.

6. Staff, "The King and Art—His Majesty Inspects Sketches for a Book of Beauty," *Evening News* (London), March 29, 1902, 2.

7. Staff, "King and Art," 2.

8. Staff, "Coronation Book of Beauty," *Indianapolis News*, April 18, 1902, 5.

9. Staff, "What They Read," *Vogue*, vol. 20, no. 24, December 11, 1902.

10. Staff, "George Rous, 3rd Earl of Stradbroke," Alchetron website, January 30, 2024, https://alchetron.com/George-Rous,-3rd-Earl-of-Stradbroke; staff, "Mrs. Alfred Harmsworth," *Penny Illustrated Paper* (London), June 19, 1897, 11; staff, "Monsieur Adolf von André (1844–1911), as Benvenuto Cellini," http://www.rvondeh.dircon.co.uk/incalmprose/andre1.html.

11. Staff, "The Role of Honour for Women," *The Gentlewoman* (London), September 3, 1904, 58.

12. Staff, "The Wyndham Sisters: Lady Elcho, Mrs. Adeane, and Mrs. Tennant," The Metropolitan Museum of Art, https://www.metmuseum.org/art/collection/search/12477.

13. Angela Lambert, *Unquiet Souls: A Social History of the Illustrious, Irreverent, Intimate Group of British Aristocrats Known as "the Souls"* (Harper and Row, 1984), 71.

14. Mrs. F. Harcourt Williamson (ed.), *The Book of Beauty* (J. B. Lippincott Company, 1902), 107.

15. Kathryn, "Adventure and Tragedy: The Life of Mrs. Alec-Tweedie," January 24, 2021, http://www.kathrynshistoryblog.com/2021/01/adventure-and-tragedy-life-of-mrs-alec.html.

16. Williamson, *Book of Beauty*, 4.

17. Williamson, *Book of Beauty*, 60.

18. Williamson, *Book of Beauty*, 60.

19. Williamson, *Book of Beauty*, 117.

20. Williamson, *Book of Beauty*, 133.

21. Staff, "John Singer Sargent RA (1865–1925)," Royal Academy, https://www.royalacademy.org.uk/art-artists/name/john-singer-sargent-ra.

22. Williamson, *Book of Beauty*, 133.

23. Staff, "About Koh-I-Noor," Website of dickblick.com.[AQ1]

24. Staff, "A Successful Painter," *Chichester Observer* (Sussex), September 23, 1896, 6.

25. Dr. Laurence Shafe, "The World Is Angelicamad," November 11, 2021, https://www.shafe.co.uk/wp-content/uploads/17-Angelica-Kaufmann.pdf.

26. Staff, "The Lounger," *The Critic* (NY), vol. XXIX, no. 5, November 1901, 398.

27. Staff, "Ladies Column," *Dundee Evening Telegraph* (Edinburgh), October 17, 1898, 6.

28. Staff, "Miss Amalia Kussner," *Greencastle Star Press*, March 18, 1899, 1.

29. Adam Waterton, librarian, Royal Academy of Art, email communication with author, April 25, 2024.

Chapter 11

1. Amalia Kussner, letter to Carrie Weinhardt, December 18, 1929, John Weinhardt Family papers (private collection).

2. Sally Clark, Windlesham historian, email correspondence with author, May 16, 2024.

3. Staff, "Concert," *Flintshire County Herald* (Wales), December 6, 1929, 5; staff, "Orchestral Concert," *Buckinghamshire Examiner*, April 4, 1930, 8.

4. Agnes McCulloch Hanna, "Terre Haute Building Has Been Home of Finance, Art, Patriotism 98 Years," *The Indianapolis Star*, January 24, 1932, 32.

5. National Register of Historic Places Inventory—Nomination Form (Memorial Hall), September 2, 1973, https://npgallery.nps.gov/GetAsset/6cdb40ed-6958-4797 -b809-30b9f596b086.

6. Mary Kussner, letter to William Weinhardt, May 31, 1932, John Weinhardt Family papers (private collection).

7. Kussner, letter to Weinhardt, 1932.

8. "Report of the Death of an American Citizen—American Consular Service," U.S., Reports of Deaths of American Citizens Abroad, 1835–1974, June 3, 1932, Ancestry.com.

9. Allen Weinhardt was the author's godfather; his father was first cousin to Amalia.

10. Staff, "Amalia Kussner Coudert, Indiana-Born Artist of International Fame, Dies," *The Indianapolis Star*, June 8, 1932, 5.

11. Staff, "Amalia Kussner Coudert, Artist of the '90s, Dies," *Chicago Tribune*, June 1, 1932, 10.

12. Staff, "Mrs. A. K. Coudert Dies," *Daily News* (NY), June 3, 1932, 28.

13. Staff, obituaries, *The Art News*, Brant Publications, vol. 30, no. 36, June 4, 1932, 12.

14. Staff, "Funeral at Windlesham," *Surrey Advertiser*, June 11, 1932, 12.

15. Find a Grave, Amalia Kussner Coudert, memorial content from Baby Stegosaurus, January 8, 2021, and images from whispyblink, August 19, 2022, https://www.findagrave .com/memorial/220812100/amalia-coudert.

16. William Weinhardt, letter of the filing of Amalia's will and financial holdings, April 13, 1933, John Weinhardt Family papers (private collection).

17. Staff, "Car-In-River Sequel," *Gloucester Citizen* (Gloucestershire), March 24, 1933, 11.

18. Staff, social announcements, *Evening Courier* (Camden), February 17, 1934, 10.

19. "New York, U.S. Naturalization Records, 1882–1944, for Ellen Dorothy Hilton," filed 1929, Ancestry.com.

20. Find a Grave, memorial page for Charles DuPont Coudert, https://www.findagrave .com/memorial/214535045/charles_dupont_coudert.

21. Anastasia Karel, librarian, Newfields Museum, email correspondence with author, April 10, 2024.

22. Kate Seno Bradshaw, digital researcher, National Museum of Women in the Arts, email correspondence with author, May 14, 2024.

23. Maryann Sudnick Gunderson, assistant professor, Ohio University, email correspondence with author, March 29, 2024.

24. Multiple Miniature Art Societies, *Catalogue of an Exhibitions of Miniature Paintings by Living Artists*, for Chicago World's Fair (Graphic Arts Pavilion), Spring 1933, 8.

25. Staff, "Art Notes," *The Brooklyn Daily Eagle*, April 2, 1894, 5.

26. Dale T. Johnson, "An Introduction to the History of American Portrait Miniatures," *American Portrait Miniatures in the Manney Collection*, The Metropolitan Museum of Art, 1990, 26.

27. Staff, "A Catalog of the Twenty-Fourth Annual Exhibition of the Washington Water Color Club," Washington Water Color Club, Washington, DC, 1919, 13.

28. Staff, "Two Great Art Schools," *The Times* (Washington, DC), June 3, 1900, 8.

29. Staff, miscellaneous art updates, *Boston Sunday Globe*, October 25, 1903, 42; Virginia Reed Colby and James B. Atkinson, *Footprints of the Past: Images of Cornish, New Hampshire & the Cornish Colony* (New Hampshire Historical Society, 1996), 203.

30. Adam Waterton, librarian, Royal Academy of London, email communication with author, April 25, 2024.

31. Meredith McGovern, arts and collections manager, Indiana State Museum and Historic Sites, email correspondence with author, May 21, 2024.

32. Judith Vale Newton, *Skirting the Issue: Stories of Indiana's Historical Women Artists* (Historical Society Press, 2004), 13.

33. Winnifred Harper Cooley, *The New Womanhood* (Broadway Publishing Company, 1904), 113. Another of the accomplished women listed in this book was British designer Charlotte Robinson, who had been the decorator for the rooms on the *Campania*, the ocean liner on which Amalia and du Pont sailed.

34. Norma Majors, *Chequers: The Prime Minister's Country House and Its History* (Little & Brown, 2001), 11.

35. Majors, *Chequers*, 8.

36. Mike Dewey, "Chequers—History of Prime Minister's Country Mansion that Winston Churchill Initially Refused to Use," *Bucks Free Press*, January 17, 2021, https://www.bucksfreepress.co.uk/news/19015672.chequers---history-prime-ministers-country-mansion-winston-churchill-initially-refused-use/.

37. Consuelo Vanderbilt Balsan, *The Glitter and the Gold: The American Duchess—in Her Own Words* (St. Martin's Press, 2011), 59.

38. Mary Cummings, "High-Style in the Gilded Age: Consuelo Vanderbilt," Southampton History Museum, August 26, 2022, https://www.southamptonhistory.org/post/high-style-in-the-gilded-age-consuelo-vanderbilt.

39. Jane Dismore, *Tangled Souls: Love and Scandal Among the Victorian Aristocracy* (The History Press, 2022), 193.

40. Frances E. Hughes, "Amalia Kussner: High Priestess of the Daintiest of Arts," *Traces of Indiana and Midwestern History*, Indiana Historical Society, Indianapolis, Indiana, vol. 2, no. 4, Fall 1990, 38.

41. Staff, "Chicago Painter of Kings and Queens," *The Chicago Inter Ocean* (Chicago), October 26, 1913, 5.

BIBLIOGRAPHY

ARCHIVE COLLECTIONS

LOC Digital Collection, Images and Articles, Library of Congress, Washington, DC

NYPL Manuscripts and Archives Division, The New York Public Library, "Kussner, Amalia," *The* New York Public Library Digital Collections. 1900 and 1906.

SMWA Amalia Kussner Papers (Private Collection), Sisters of Providence Archives at Saint Mary-of-the-Woods, Indiana

VCL Vigo County Library Special Collections, Terre Haute, Indiana

JWFP John Weinhardt family papers (private collection)

SWFP Seth Weinhardt family papers (private collection)

BOOKS AND CATALOGUES

American Society of Miniature Painters. *Catalogue of an Exhibition of Miniature Paintings by Living Artists.* New York, 1933.

Bailey, Catherine. *The Secret Rooms.* New York: Penguin Books, 2013.

Balsan, Consuelo Vanderbilt. *The Glitter and the Gold: The American Duchess—in Her Own Words.* New York: St. Martin's Press, 2011.

Bates, Neil. *Cecil Rhodes.* East Sussex, England: Wayland Publishers Ltd., 1976.

Borman, Tracy. *Crown & Sceptre: A New History of the British Monarchy, from William the Conqueror to Elizabeth II.* London: Hodder and Stoughton, 2021.

Burroughs, Bryson. *Metropolitan Museum of Art—Catalogue of Paintings.* New York Metropolitan Museum of Art, 1917.

Butler, Ruth. *Rodin: The Shape of Genius.* New Haven, CT: Yale University Press, 1993.

Colby, Virginia Reed, and Atkinson, James B. *Footprints of the Past: Images of Cornish, New Hampshire & the Cornish Colony.* Concord: New Hampshire Historical Society, 1996.

Cooley, Winnifred Harper. *The New Womanhood.* New York: Broadway Publishing Company, 1904.

Cooper, Anderson, and Howe, Katherine. *Vanderbilt: The Rise And Fall of an American Dynasty.* New York: Harper Collins, 2021.

Crumrin, Tim. *Hidden Terre Haute*. Mount Pleasant, SC: Arcadia Publishing/The History Press, 2020.

Dismore, Jane. *Tangled Souls*. Gloucestershire, England: The History Press, 2022.

Harris, David. *Pioneer, Soldier and Politician: Summarised Memoirs of Colonel Sir David Harris*. London: Sampson Low, Marston & Company, Limited, 1931.

Hughes, Frances E. *Amalia Kussner Painter-in-Little* (unpublished biography). Amalia Kussner Papers (Private Collection), Sisters of Providence Archives at Saint Mary-of-the-Woods, Indiana, 1998.

Jourdan, Philip. *Cecil Rhodes: His Private Life*. London: John Lane Company, 1911.

King, Greg. *A Season of Splendor*. Hoboken, NJ: John Wiley & Sons, Inc., 2009.

Lambert, Angela. *Unquiet Souls: A Social History of the Illustrious, Irreverent, Intimate Group of British Aristocrats Known as "the Souls."* New York: Harper & Row, 1984.

Lapradelle, A. De, and Frederic R. Coudert. *War Letters from France*. New York: D. Appleton and Company, 1916.

Legge, Edward. *King George and the Royal Family*, volume 2. Digital Library of India, 1918. https://archive.org/details/digitallibraryindia.

Masson, Raphaël, and Mattiussi, Véronique. *Rodin*. New York: Rizzoli International Publications, 2004.

McCormick, Mike. *Terre Haute: Queen City of the Wabash*. Mount Pleasant, SC: Arcadia Publishing, 2005.

Fales, Martha Gandy. *Jewelry in America, 1600–1900*. Woodbridge, Suffolk, UK: Antique Collector' Club, 1995.

Majors, Norma. *Chequers: The Prime Minister's Country House and Its History*. London: Little & Brown, 2001.

Massie, Robert K. *Nicholas and Alexandra*. New York: Random House Trade Paperbacks, 2011.

Miller, William H. *The Great Liners Story*. United Kingdom: The History Press, 2012.

National Academy of Design. *Portraits of Women—Loan Exhibition*. New York: The Knickerbocker Press, 1894.

Newton, Judith Vale. *Skirting the Issue: Stories of Indiana's Historical Women Artists*. Indianapolis: Indiana Historical Society Press, 2004.

Nichols, C. W. de Lyon. *The Décadents: A Story of Blackwell's Island and Newport*. New York: J. S. Ogilvie Publishing Company, 1899.

Ridley, Jo Ann. *Looking for Eulabee Dix*. Washington, DC: The National Museum of Women in Art, 1997.

Seifer, Marc J. *Wizard: The Life and Times of Nikola Tesla*. New York: Kensington Publishing, 1998.

Sibbald, Raymond. *The War Correspondents: The Boer War*. England: Bramley Books, 1997.

Thomas, Antony. *Rhodes: The Race for Africa*. New York: St. Martin's Press, 1997.

Trask, John E. D. *Catalogue de Luxe of the Department of Fine Arts, Panama-Pacific International Exposition*. San Francisco: P. Edler and Company, 1915.

Veenswijk, Virginia Kays. *Coudert Brothers: A Legacy in Law*. New York: Truman Talley/Dutton, 1994.

Washington Water Color Club. *A Catalog of the Twenty-fourth Annual Exhibition of the Washington Water Color Club*. Washington, DC: Washington Water Color Club, 1919.

Weir, Julian Alden. *Biographical Sketches of American Artists*. Lansing: Michigan State Library. 1916.

Williamson, Mrs. F. Harcourt. *The Book of Beauty*. Philadelphia: J. B. Lippincott Company, 1902.

Wills, Elspeth. *Cunardia: A Steam Trunk of Titbits, Trivia and Trifles*. London: Open Agency, 2005.

Wisser, John P. *The Second Boer War, 1899–1900*. Kansas City, MO: Hudson-Kimberly Pub. Co., 1901.

Worman and Worman. "Outing." (Listing of Horses and Race) The Outing Publishing Company, vol. XXXIII, Oct. 1898–Mar. 1899.

ARTICLES

Andrews, Maude. "The First from the Klondike." *The Atlanta Constitution*, September 26, 1898.

Andrews, Maude. "Shopping in Gay Paris; How the Woman Buy Hats." *The Atlanta Constitution*, May 1, 1899.

Anonymous. "King Edward VII." *North American Review* (June 1910): 728.

Arnett, Frank S. "Amalia Kussner Coudert—Miniaturist." *Ainslee's Magazine*, vol. IX, no. 1 (May 1902): 294–95, 299–300.

Arnett, Frank S. "Painting an Empress." *Indianapolis Journal*, May 18, 1902, 24.

Ball, Susan. "Woman's World." *The Saturday Spectator*, February 29, 1908, 2.

Ball, Susan. "Woman's World." *Terre Haute Saturday Spectator*, June 10, 1911.

Britanica. https://www.britannica.com/biography/Cecil-Rhodes.

Banks, Nancy Huston. "A Painter of Miniatures." *Ladies Home Journal*, vol. 12, no. 11 (1895): 7.

Banks, Nancy Huston. "Success in Her Art." *Altoona Mirror*, June 7, 1895, 3.

Banks, Nancy Huston. "A Modern Miniature Painter." *Harper's Bazaar*, vol. 28, no. 5 (1896): 88.

Banks, Nancy Huston. Listing as book reviewer, *The Bookman*. (November 1895): 224.

Banks, Nancy Huston. "The Miniature." *Cosmopolitan*, vol. 43 (1907): 23.

Barron, Stephanie. "Minnie Paget. Because with Friends Like These . . ." https://francinemathews.blogspot.com/2018/11/day-79-with-friends-like-these.html.

Carter, Mary. "A Royal Conquest: The Life of Minnie Stevens." *Eagle Times*, September 6, 2023. https://www.eagletimes.com/news/a-royal-conquest-the-life-of-minnie-stevens/article_41c05d66-5395-5a9f-8fed-7851ed35baab.html.

Clark, Dorothy J. "National Register of Historic Place Inventory – Nomination Form, Memorial Hall." October 25, 1973. https://npgallery.nps.gov/GetAsset/6cdb40ed-6958-4797-b809-30b9f596b086.

Corneau, Grace. "Foretells Striking Colors." *Chicago Tribune*, September 29, 1901, 67.

Corneau, Grace. "Social Gossip of Paris." *Chicago Tribune*, January 17, 1900, 2.

de Courcy, Anne. "Mrs. Astor Invites." *St. Regis Magazine.* https://magazine.stregis.com/mrs-astor-invites-2/.

The Courtauld (blog). "Maison Doucet." December 2, 2016. https://sites.courtauld.ac.uk/documentingfashion/2016/12/02/maison-doucet.

Cummings, Mary. "High-Style in the Gilded Age: Consuelo Vanderbilt." Southampton History Museum. August 26, 2022. https://www.southamptonhistory.org/post/high-style-in-the-gilded-age-consuelo-vanderbilt.

Dewey, Mike. "Chequers—History of Prime Minister's Country Mansion that Winston Churchill Initially Refused to Use." *Bucks Free Press.* https://www.bucksfreepress.co.uk/news/19015672.chequers---history-prime-ministers-country-mansion-winston-churchill-initially-refused-use/.

Ellis, Brylynn. "Historical Treasure: Miniature Portrait Artist Was Sought Out." *Tribune-Star,* March 18, 2023. https://www.tribstar.com/features/history/historical-treasure-miniature-portrait-artist-was-sought-out/article_0d28fbbe-c1a0-11ed-b37b-d798950ad92e.html.

Emery, Tom. "Artist Took Her Craft from Greenfield to the World's Galleries." *The Journal-Courier,* June 3, 2019.

Evans, Elinor. "Mrs. Astor and the Four Hundred." February 21, 2022. https://www.historyextra.com/period/victorian/mrs-astor-who-four-hundred-new-york-society-list-ward-mcallister-gilded-age/.

Finger Lakes Land Trust. "Goddess of the Moon: The Life History of the Luna Moth." July 31, 2018. https://www.fllt.org/goddess-of-the-moon-the-life-history-of-the-luna-moth/.

Flatiron Nomad. "The Art Students League of New York." https://flatironnomad.nyc/history/the-art-students-league-of-new-york/.

Fowler, Rebecca J. "Anastasia—The Mystery Resolved." *Washington Post,* October 6, 1994. https://www.washingtonpost.com/archive/lifestyle/1994/10/06/anastasia-the-mystery-resolved/f208f264-a141-4f54-8354-934a3005f091/.

French, Lillie Hamilton. "The Portrait Show." *Harper's Bazaar* (December 31, 1898): 1132.

Gaffney, Dennis, "Explainer: What is Photogravure." *Antiques Roadshow,* February 14, 2005. https://www.pbs.org/wgbh/roadshow/stories/articles/2005/2/14/explainer-what-is-photogravure.

Gunderson, Bob. "Days of Yore: Ivory—The Plastic of the 1800s." *New Haven Register,* June 24, 2018.

Hanna, Agnes McCulloch. "Terre Haute Building Has Been Home of Finance, Art, Patriotism 98 Years." *The Indianapolis Star,* January 24, 1932.

Harris, Russel. Biography of Monsieur Adolf von André, 2011. http://www.rvondeh.dircon.co.uk/incalmprose/andre1.html.

High Museum of Art. Write-up of Portrait by Robert Henri, *Lady in Black Velvet* (Portrait of Eulabee Dix Becker). https://high.org/collection/lady-in-black-velvet-portrait-of-eulabee-dix-becker/.

Hogan Associates. "Newport Stories: Mamie Fish, the Grand Dame of Newport's Gilded Age." Hogan Associates Blog. August 18, 2023. https://hoganblog.com/2023/08/18/newport-stories-mamie-fish-the-grand-dame-of-newports-gilded-age.

Holly, Flora Mai. "Some Prominent Southerners in New York." *The Taylor-Trotwood Magazine* (December 1905): 292.

Hughes, Frances E. "A World-Famous Miniature Painter." *The Indianapolis Star*, March 12, 1961.

Hughes, Frances E. "Local Woman Was World-Famous as Miniatures Painter in Her Day." *The Terre Haute Star*, August 31, 1961.

Hughes, Frances E. "Founding Fathers Name Street in City." Vigo County Public Library Collection, October 14, 1978.

Hughes, Frances E. "Amalia Kussner: High Priestess of the Daintiest of Arts." *Traces of Indiana and Midwestern History*, vol. 2, no. 4 (1990): 38–39, 43.

Joenisch, Anita. "Two Renowned Artists in Generation Is Distinction of Old Indiana Family." *The Indianapolis Star*, August 10, 1930, 19.

Johnson, Dale T. "An Introduction to the History of American Portrait Miniatures." *American Portrait Miniatures in the Manney Collection.* New York: The Metropolitan Museum of Art, 1990.

Kathryn's History Blog. "Adventure and Tragedy: The Life of Mrs. Alec-Tweedie." http://www.kathrynshistoryblog.com/2021/01/adventure-and-tragedy-life-of-mrs-alec.html.

Keyes, George. "Portraiture—Mirror or Mask." *Bulletin of the Detroit Institute of Arts*, vol. 83, no. 1 (2009): 6.

Kintrea, Frank. "Larcenous Mrs. Cody Vs. Pious Miss Gould." *American Heritage*, vol. 26, no. 4 (June 1975).

Kohlman, Rena Tucker. "Miniature Paintings in Art Institute Exhibition." *Indianapolis News*, January 27, 1916.

Kussner, Amalia. "The Human Side of the Czar." *Century Magazine* (October 1906): 815, 842, 845–46, 848, 855.

Louie, Elaine. "Overlooked No More: Clara Driscoll, Designer of Visions in Glass for Tiffany." *The New York Times*, February 23, 2023. https://www.nytimes.com/2023/02/23/obituaries/clara-driscoll-overlooked.html.

Mac Flynn, Abbie. "Women's Page." *The Evening Gazette*, July 7, 1900, 6.

McCormick, Mike. "Artist's Talent Was Miniatures." *Terre Haute Tribute Star*, March 23, 1997.

Metropolitan Museum of Art. Details of painting: *The Wyndham Sisters*: Lady Elcho, Mrs. Adeane, and Mrs. Tennant. https://www.metmuseum.org/art/collection/search/12477.

Miller, Tom. "The Lost H.O. Havemeyer Mansion—No. 1 E. 66th Street." Daytonian in Manhattan (blog), January 12, 2015. https://daytoninmanhattan.blogspot.com/2015/01/the-lost-h-o-havemeyer-mansion-no-1-e.html.

Museum of Nebraska Art. Audio file transcription of work by Robert Henri, *Portrait of Eulabee Dix in her Wedding Gown.* Kearney, Nebraska.

Nathan, Rhoda. "Ward McAllister: Beau Nash of 'The Age of Innocence.'" *College Literature*, vol. 14, no. 3 (1987).

National Academy of Design. "Portraits of Women—Loan Exhibition." 1894.

National Museum of Norway. "Queen Maud—150 Years." https://www.nasjonalmuseet. no/en/stories/explore-the-collection/queen-maud--150-years.

National Portrait Gallery. "Violet Manners, Duchess of Rutland." https://www.npg.org. uk/collections/search/person/mp03927.

Nirdlinger, Chas. Fdc. "Of a Certain Painter-in-Little." *The Illustrated American*, April 29, 1893.

The Preservation Society of Newport County. "Portrait Miniature of Alva Belmont." https://newportalri.org/items/show/24583.

Ridley, Jane. "Marlborough House Set." May 27, 2010. https://doi.org/10.1093/ ref:odnb/53154.

Rignaux, Paul Pierre. "Rodin Finds New Art Inspiration in U. S. Woman." *Chicago Sunday Examiner*, October 29, 1911.

Roulett, Will. "Minuteman Minute – Lt. Frederick Coudert Spanish-American War Uniform." March 15, 2023. https://www.ngaus.org/video-library/ minuteman-minute-lt-frederic-coudert-spanish-american-war-uniform.

Rous, George. "Biography—Earl of Stradbroke." January 30, 2024. https://alchetron. com/George-Rous,-3rd-Earl-of-Stradbroke.

Royal Academy. "John Singer Sargent RA (1865–1925)." https://www.royalacademy.org. uk/art-artists/name/john-singer-sargent-ra.

St. Mary-of-the-Woods College. "Our History." https://www.smwc.edu/about/history/.

Sarkar, Dr. Dipa. "Historical Treasure: Historic Tile Done by Famous Miniature Artist." *Tribune-Star*, November 19, 2006.

Scott, James Brown. "Edward VII." *The American Journal of International Law*, vol. 4, no. 3 (1910): 663.

Shafe, Dr. Laurence. "The World Is Angelicamad." November 11, 2021. https://www. shafe.co.uk/wp-content/uploads/17-Angelica-Kaufmann.pdf.

Shields, Dr. David S. "Jacob Schloss." Broadway Photographs. https://broadway.library. sc.edu/content/jacob-schloss.html.

Smithsonian American Art Museum. Webpage for Eulabee Dix. https://americanart. si.edu/artist/eulabee-dix-5766.

Strickling, Lydia. "Gilded Age Fashion." May 12, 2021. https://www.nps.gov/vama/ blogs/gilded-age-fashion.htm.

Thorklidson, Dag. "Norwegian National Myths and Nation Building." *Kirchliche Zeistgeschichte*, vol. 27, no. 2 (2014).

Turlay, Maud Richards. "Amalia Kussner Coudert, Highest Priced Miniaturist, Has Won Fame and Fortune." *The Chicago Inter Ocean*, October 26, 1913, 34.

Tusan, Michelle Elizabeth. "Inventing the New Woman: Print Culture and the Identity Politics During the Fin-de-Siecle." *Victorian Periodicals Review*, vol. 31, no. 2 (Summer 1998): 175.

US Patent Office. *Official Gazette of the United States Patent Office*. Government Printing Office, July 1908, 882.

USA Badminton. "USA Badminton History." https://usabadminton.org/about/history/.

Walker Gallery of Art. "George Romney, British Art's Forgotten Genius." Exhibition, 2001. https://www.liverpoolmuseums.org.uk/whatson/walker-art-gallery/exhibition/george-romney-british-arts-forgotten-genius.

Weinhardt, Carl Jr. "Amalia Coudert 'Unique' Artist." *The Indianapolis News*, January 31, 1976, 4.

Williams, Alyn. "The History and Revival of Miniature Portrait Painting." *The American Magazine of Art*, vol. 15, no. 9 (1924): 462.

Wiser, Becky. "Long Life and Happiness to All Its Residents." July 6, 2021. https://www.eriehistory.org/blog/long-life-and-happiness-to-all-its-residents-39.

Wiser, Becky. "Strong Mansion." 2006. http://eriebuildings.info/buildings.php?buildingID=17040004020100.

Woodhouse, Christopher Montague. "Cecil Rhodes: Prime Minister of Cape Colony." Britannica. https://www.britannica.com/biography/Cecil-Rhodes.

Zach, Karen. Putnam County Biographies (Amalia Kussner). http://ingenweb.org/inputnam/Putnam%20Biographies%20H_M/k---bios.html.

THESES AND DISSERTATIONS

Gunderson, Maryann Sudnick. "Dismissed Yet Disarming: The Portrait Miniature Revival, 1890–1930." Thesis, College of Fine Arts of Ohio University, 2003. http://rave.ohiolink.edu/etdc/view?acc_num=ohiou1080666457.

Hines, Velma Lou. "Nancy Huston Banks: Her Life & Works." Masters Theses & Special Projects. Paper 2479. 1933. https://digitalcommons.wku.edu/theses/2479.

Lai, Mei-En. "Social Status, the Patriarch and Assembly Balls, and the Transformation in Elite Identity in Gilded Age New York." Thesis, Simon Fraser University, 2013.

Slattery, Susan Elizabeth. "Performing Portraiture: Picturing the Upper-Class English Woman in an Age of Change, 1890–1914." Thesis for Graduate Department of Art History, University of Toronto, 2019.

Weisman, Lena. "Beyond Fancy, Beyond Taste: Gender, Art, and Culture in America's Gilded Age." History Honors Thesis, Lehigh University, 2022.

Zenor, Carl A. "Putnam County in the Civil War: Local History of a Critical Period." Thesis, DePauw University, 1956.

PERIODICALS

Abbeville Press and Banner (SC). January 31, 1906.

Aberdeen Press and Journal (Scotland). December 20, 1800.

American Art News (New York, NY). November 11, 1905.

The American Register (London). January 12, 1907.

The Argus (Melbourne, Australia). June 10, 1899.

The Art News (New York, NY). March 22, 1924; and June 4, 1932.

The Athenaeum (London). May 3, 1902.

The Atlanta Constitution. September 29, 1906.

The Bacchus Marsh Express (Victoria, Australia). September 19, 1896.

Boston Post. January 3, 1900; and June 28, 1901.

Boston Sunday Globe. October 25, 1903.

Boston Sunday Post. May 22, 1904; and April 26, 1908.

Broken Hill Barrier Miner (New South Wales, Australia). June 10, 1904.

The Brooklyn Daily Eagle. April 2, 1894.

Brooklyn Life. July 27, 1901.

Buckinghamshire Examiner. April 4, 1930.

Buffalo Courier. May 1, 1904.

The Buffalo Times. January 15, 1899; and July 5, 1900.

The Chicago Daily Tribune. June 26, 1899; and December 19, 1905.

Chicago Tribune. September 24, 1896; July 11, 1912; and June 1, 1932.

Chichester Observer (West Sussex, England). September 23, 1896.

Country Life (Britain). October 8, 1970.

The Critic (New York, NY). November 1901.

Daily Mirror (London). March 22, 1933.

Daily News (New York, NY). June 3, 1932.

The Daily Wabash Express (Terre Haute, IN). October 26, 1882; June 6, 1886; and June 30, 1889.

Defiance Crescent News (OH). June 28, 1901.

The Delineator (Philadelphia). January–March 1900 and July 1900.

Dundee Evening Telegraph (Edinburgh). October 17, 1898.

Elite (Chicago). April 18, 1896; July 11, 1896; October 3, 1896; October 10, 1896; and February 27, 1897.

The Etude (Philadelphia). April 1910.

Evening Courier (Camden). February 17, 1934.

The Evening Journal (Wilmington). December 8, 1903.

Evening News (London). March 29, 1902.

Evening Star (Washington, DC). December 8, 1910.

The Evening World (New York, NY). February 14, 1900; and February 23, 1900.

Evansville Courier and Press (IN). March 6, 1900.

Flintshire County Herald (Holywell, Flintshire, Wales). December 6, 1929.

Fort Wayne Sentinel (IN). October 31, 1899.

Fort Worth Star-Telegram. December 31, 1911.

The Gentlewoman (London). September 3, 1904; and February 3, 1906.

The Glendale Evening News (Los Angeles). January 25, 1917.

Gloucester Citizen (England). March 24, 1933.

The Greencastle Banner (IN). July 26, 1901.

Greencastle Banner and Times (IN). October 4, 1895.

Greencastle Star Press (IN). May 30, 1896; and March 18, 1899.

Harpers Weekly (New York, NY). December 23, 1905.

Hopkinsville Kentuckian. November 24, 1899.

The House Beautiful (Chicago). September 1901.

Indianapolis Journal. May 24, 1892; January 1, 1894; January 12, 1900; June 6, 1900; and July 24, 1901.

Indianapolis News. April 18, 1902.

The Indianapolis Star. June 8, 1932.

Indianapolis Sun. July 22, 1899.

The Inter Ocean (Chicago). September 20, 1903.

The Journal (New York, NY). March 17, 1896.

Journal of Education (Boston). October 4, 1906.

Ladies Home Journal (Philadelphia). October 1895.

Livestock Journal (London). June 23, 1897.

Logansport Pharos-Tribute (IN). March 30, 1898.

London West End. May 17, 1899.

Loretto Rainbow (Toronto, Ontario). 1903.

Manchester Courier (England). February 12, 1896.

Millom Gazette (Cumbria, UK). July 27, 1900.

Minneapolis Journal. September 26, 1906.

Morning Post (London). December 5, 1906.

Munsey's Magazine (London). June 1897.

Musical Courier (New York, NY). December 1, 1897.

New Oxford Item (PA). January 10, 1907.

The New Peterson Magazine (Philadelphia). December 1896.

New-York Daily Tribune. July 5, 1900.

New York Journal. 1898.

New York Journal and Advertiser. August 29, 1897.

New York Morning Telegraph. July 21, 1898.

The New York Times. December 18, 1898; March 13, 1900; July 9, 1900; August 11, 1900; October 7, 1900; July 28, 1901; October 6, 1901; October 8, 1901; August 12, 1902; September 14, 1903; December 21, 1903; October 2, 1906; January 20, 1907; and December 8, 1912.

The New York Time-Saturday Review. January 13, 1900.

New-York Tribune. May 11, 1900.

New York World. February 14, 1900; and June 27, 1901.

North American Review (Boston). June 1910.

Omaha World-Herald. March 15, 1919.

The Pacific Commercial Advertiser (Honolulu, territory of Hawaii). August 8, 1899.

Pall Mall Gazette (London). November 7, 1902.

Paris Herald. September 18, 1930.

Passaic Daily News (NJ). October 26, 1906.

Penny Illustrated Paper (London). June 19, 1897.

Perth Daily News (Western Australia). January 6, 1919.

The Philadelphia Inquirer. July 4, 1900; and May 1, 1904.

Progress—The Universion Law of Nature (Chicago). October 12, 1895.

The Queen (London). November 25, 1905.

The Queen of Fashion (New York, NY). March 1894.

The Salt Lake Tribune. February 7, 1926.

San Antonio Daily Light. October 28, 1906.

The San Francisco Call. March 6, 1895.

The San Francisco Examiner. July 14, 1895.
Saturday Evening Mail (Terre Haute, IN). June 1881; and October 17, 1885.
The Scotsman (Edinburgh). August 5, 1915.
The Sketch (London). November 5, 1902.
St. Joseph News-Press (St. Joseph, Missouri). March 5, 1897.
St. Louis Post-Dispatch. September 15, 1901; and November 11, 1903.
The St. Louis Republic. July 4, 1900; and July 8, 1900.
The Standard Union (Brooklyn). July 5, 1900; and July 10, 1900.
Star-Gazette (Elmira, NY). April 20, 1901.
Star Tribune (Minneapolis). July 15, 1900.
Sunday Pictorial (London). January 23, 1921.
The Sunday Spy (Worcester, MA). April 8, 1898.
Surrey Advertiser (England). June 1, 1932.
Terre Haute Daily News (IN). October 11, 1890; and October 14, 1890.
Terre Haute Daily Wabash Express (IN). June 18, 1882; and July 12, 1913.
Terre Haute Saturday Spectator (Terre Haute, IN). August 18, 1906; November 24, 1906; May 4, 1907; April 20, 1912; June 8, 1912; September 27, 1913; July 11, 1914; August 11, 1914; November 21, 1914; July 31, 1915; January 8, 1916; and January 26, 1918.
Terre Haute Spectator (IN). September 22, 1906.
Terre Haute Weekly Gazette (IN). June 24, 1880; December 30, 1886; and January 4, 1903.
The Theater (New York). Vol. 9, no. 1, 1893.
The Times (Washington, DC). June 3, 1900.
The Times-Democrat (Lima, OH). March 1, 1900.
The Virginian-Pilot (Norfolk). July 30, 1899.
Vogue. October 19, 1899; February 22, 1900; and December 11, 1902.
Washington Post. October 9, 1910.
Wichita Eagle. November 26, 1899.
Wisconsin Rapids Daily Tribune. February 21, 1922.
The Woman's Column (New York, NY). December 16, 1899.
The World (New York, NY). March 18, 1899; and March 5, 1905.
York Semi-Weekly Democratic Press (PA). August 31, 1900.
Yorkshire Evening Post (England). October 5, 1918; and August 25, 1919.

Index